PROBLEMS IN THE FEDERAL INCOME TAXATION

OF

BUSINESS ENTERPRISES

THIRD EDITION

By

NORTON L. STEUBEN
Professor of Law
University of Colorado
School of Law

and

WILLIAM J. TURNIER
Mangum Professor of Law
University of North Carolina
School of Law

$22.35

Westbury, New York
THE FOUNDATION PRESS, INC.
1996

To Judith

N. L. S.

To my parents, William A. and Irene F. Turnier
and to my brother Bob and sister Barbara

W. J. T.

INTRODUCTION

Purposes

The principal innovation in instruction in the history of legal education was the development and use of the case method. In recent years, the clinical method of instruction has been offered as an alternative or supplement to the case method. It can be said that the case method, as originally practiced by Langdell at Harvard, was clinical education for the students of his law school. Many of Langdell's students commenced the practice of law as associates in prestigious law firms, expecting to spend the first few years of apprenticeship working under the guidance of experienced attorneys. In the case-oriented world of the nineteenth century, Langdell's method prepared the graduate for this position relying on the law firm for the continuation of the graduate's legal education and the development of professional skills which were, in many cases, not touched on in the law school. Combining classroom and clinical education in law, medical and dental schools seeks development of professional skills while attempting to give the student a basic mastery of approach and an understanding of underlying policies, principles and analysis. This may be seen merely as an extension of the approach employed by Langdell adapted for a different environment of ultimate application.

The problem method is an attempt to combine the most valuable instructional aspects of both the case and clinical methods. It provides the students with a learning environment which will assist them in developing professional skills while also providing them with challenging insights into the nature of specific areas of the law and the legal system in general. In this context, the problem method satisfies many of the recommendations of the MacCrate Report.

The problem method is sometimes recommended for the reason that its relative novelty often succeeds in stimulating a renewed interest in the study of the law. Although this, standing alone, might be enough to justify its use, the utility of the problem method as a teaching technique is based on a number of more significant considerations.

The case method may not be fully satisfactory in an area such as tax law, where a statute is the primary authority. Students may fail to appreciate the true importance of non-case authority in attempting to resolve a tax dispute. This confusion with respect to the importance of non-case authority is understandable when one considers that much of the first year of law school is dedicated to studying cases. Teachers who are aware of this potential difficulty can use the case method and still develop the students' sense of the relative importance of various types of authority. This same goal can be more easily realized, however, by teaching a course with the assistance of a well developed set of problems.

Normally only those issues about which there is some disagreement are litigated. Cases are excellent devices for exploring such matters, but they do not provide much assistance in developing understanding of those areas in which disputes have not yet arisen or in which the rules are well-defined and agreed upon. The use of a problem set with a casebook or textbook, and statutory materials permits exploration of those areas which are not in dispute as well as those areas where problems were resolved prior to a dispute arising and where disagreement as to the state of the law has not resulted in a reported case.

While the foregoing reasons furnish pedagogical justification for use of the problem method, an equally important reason is that it is an excellent vehicle for developing professional skills and a basic mastery of approach as well as an understanding of the principles, policies and analyses which underlie various areas of the law. Lawyers often employ as well as develop their legal skills to solve a problem presented to them by a client. The problem method places the students in a similar situation. They are called upon to use knowledge and skills which they have already acquired and to add to their knowledge and skills as they explore the full parameters of their fictitious client's problem. In this respect the problem method can be considered "quasi-clinical." The problem method, however, has several advantages over "pure clinical" programs as a device for teaching tax law. First, the tax problems normally encountered in the latter are of limited educational value. Second, the problem method can be structured to provide students with much broader exposure to tax law than that provided by individual, generally low-income, taxpayers who happen to have a problem with the Treasury. Lastly, it is more efficient. A larger group of students can be taught by the problem method and the coverage is known in advance and can be controlled.

To assist students in acquiring a working knowledge of substantive tax law, practice in analysis, and relevant professional skills involved in lawyering, a substantial number of the problems in this book incorporate documents which a lawyer might be called upon to prepare or review. Others require the students to conduct a negotiation or to give tax planning advice. In this regard, this problem set departs substantially from the format used in most problem sets. For example, rather than presenting the students with a set of facts and asking whether a particular series of redemptions will qualify for Section 303 treatment, the students will be asked to review a memorandum which in form is properly drafted, but which contains both legally correct and incorrect responses on the part of the attorney. The students, in preparing the assignment, will thus acquire not only substantive knowledge about Section 303 but also an appreciation of the art of drafting a memorandum and some understanding of its purpose. This technique is employed with a prospectus, a ruling request, a protest letter, a partnership agreement, a Section 534 statement, a tender offer, and a variety of other instruments. When appropriate, such documents are followed by brief commentaries on the importance, function and drafting of the document.[1]

Character of the Materials

This set of problems is intended for use in conjunction with a casebook or textbook as well as statutory materials. Design of a set of problems for use with any casebook or textbook of a teacher's choosing was facilitated by the fact that the Internal Revenue Code virtually mandates that there be a high degree of similarity in income tax instructional material. Students preparing the problem assigned for a given day are expected to study the relevant portions of the casebook or textbook adopted for use by their teacher as well as the Code and possibly Regulations. While solving the assigned problem, the students will be exposed to a variety of authority which they must sift, analyze and select or reject in the process of resolving the various issues presented by the problem. This learning exercise is very similar to the approach of an attorney confronting a tax problem which requires him to sort through and analyze material which relates directly or only tangentially to his client's problem. An alternative pedagogical technique which might be employed is to discuss with the students materials in the casebook or textbook and Code and Regulations and then discuss an

---

[1] The materials depart somewhat from the goal of presenting a realistic environment in order to maintain their value for future years. Where dates are required rather than using specific dates, the convention of using "Year" to designate the current year has been adopted. Pluses and minuses followed by a number have been employed to indicate whether the relevant date is subsequent to, or prior to, the current year. For example, "Year-3" indicates three years ago and "Year+5" indicates five years from the present.

assigned problem or problems in order to focus the students' knowledge and skills in an environment similar to that which the students will face in practice. One of the authors has used the latter technique in the introductory course while using the former in the advanced course.

The materials cover two distinct areas of the tax law: (1) partnership; and (2) corporate. Some problems contain a reference back to other problems in order to aid the students in understanding the interrelation of the concepts they are examining and to provide positive reinforcement of the students' sense of achievement in discovering that newly acquired knowledge can be applied to resolve what previously appeared to be a difficulty in an earlier problem.

Four distinct types of problems are included which involve the students in the following types of situations: (1) review of documents; (2) negotiation and conciliation; (3) tax planning; and (4) analysis of tax consequences of completed or proposed transactions. A number of the problems involve reviewing a document which is to be evaluated on the basis of materials that the students have studied. On some occasions the students are asked to advise a client of the consequences of the document on the client's business affairs. On other occasions the students are asked to evaluate the advice given in a document which might contain both correct and incorrect statements. In all cases, a proper evaluation of the document will require that the students read and understand assigned material which relates to a topic heading under which the problem appears and, at times, material which the students have previously considered. Some of the problems require the students to apply knowledge of tax law in a negotiation or conciliation context. For example, rather than studying a case which deals with sale of the interests in, or assets of, a business, the students are called upon to apply the knowledge derived from the case and possibly from other cases and authorities to the representation of either the purchaser or seller of a business. Other problems are presented in a tax planning context which requires the students to advise a client of the best way to structure a transaction so as to minimize the tax impact on the client's finances while still achieving the client's goals. The balance of the materials involves the students in analyzing the tax consequences of a proposed or completed course of conduct.

A given topic area typically contains several alternative problems. Since different teachers can be expected to emphasize different aspects of a particular issue, these alternative problems are included to permit the teacher to choose the emphasis desired. They also give the teacher the option of varying the content of the course from year to year. When more than one or two problems are included under a topic, the materials generally begin with the "simplest" problem and proceed to the most complex.

Acknowledgments

We owe profound thanks to the students who have passed through our tax classes at the Law Schools of the Universities of Colorado and North Carolina. They constitute the "fire" in which the problems were tested. Their reactions, comments and criticisms greatly contributed to the eventual quality of these materials. The encouragement and help provided by the colleagues on our respective faculties is much appreciated. In this context, the late Henry Brandis, Professor and Dean Emeritus, of the University of North Carolina School of Law, deserves special mention. Henry spent many hours reviewing, editing and commenting on our preliminary drafts of previous editions. For all that is good herein Henry played an important part. For that which may be in error, we should have listened to Henry.

While the secretarial staffs at both schools were of great assistance in producing the final manuscript, special thanks are due to Marjorie Brunner and Gayle Stone who translated our chicken scratching into a readable and well done manuscript, an achievement which cannot be overstated. Lastly, the aid of our research assistants Juliann Dyson and Kyle Boschen of Colorado and Lisa Shepard of North Carolina is much appreciated.

NORTON L. STEUBEN

WILLIAM J. TURNIER

Boulder, Colorado

Chapel Hill, North Carolina

TABLE OF CONTENTS

TABLE OF CONTENTS

TABLE OF CONTENTS

Division I

TAXATION OF ORGANIZATIONS
TREATED AS PARTNERSHIPS

Part A

FORMATION OF A PARTNERSHIP

PROBLEM 1P

Brice Dunesborough (Brice), since quitting his job as Information Officer at the U.S. Consulate in a South Pacific nation, has barely supported his spouse and children through his earnings as a patio contractor. While in the South Pacific, he observed individuals creating electrostatic charges by exposing a mixture of certain plant extracts and water to highly magnified sunlight. Being concerned about the environment and the high cost of fossil fuels, he became intrigued with the idea of using this process to create electric current. Since returning to the United States he has spent every free moment attempting to adapt equipment and to devise a proper formulation of the process in order to create, store and transmit electric current. He finally succeeded in achieving his goal, which he calls the Dunesborough Machine. It has cost him every cent he has in addition to funds derived from a mortgage on his home. He has "written-off," for tax purposes, all of his costs as research and development expenses. He has fully adapted his home to use the electric current generated by the Machine.

Edwina Mannokowsky (Eddie), a friend of Brice's and one whom some would call a financial wizard because of the fortune she has amassed through shrewd investments, has visited Brice's home and observed the Machine in operation. Eddie believes the idea has great commercial possibilities and is prepared to provide the funds necessary to: (1) if possible, secure a mechanical patent on the adaptation of the equipment and a process patent for the formulation of the process; and (2) provide the working capital, production machinery and manufacturing facility necessary to manufacture the Machine. All Eddie wants in return is the repayment of her funds, as soon

1

as the manufacturing operation becomes profitable, and a "piece of the action."

After Eddie and Brice had some discussions with respect to combining Brice's Machine with Eddie's money, they spoke with Ken Crosswaite (Ken), a local lawyer, about setting up a partnership. Ken, who also dabbles in real estate, was enthusiastic about the Machine and offered to do all the legal work required for, and by, the partnership and to convey to it a parcel of real estate he owns near Brice's home, on which the manufacturing facility can be built, in return for a "piece of the action."

All the parties want an equal voice in management of the business and an equal share in its profits and its losses. Ken realizes that the formation of a partnership may have tax implications and, being a general practitioner, he does not feel comfortable in giving tax advice. He has, therefore, delivered to you the draft of the Preformation Agreement among the parties, which he prepared, and asked you to advise him with respect to the tax implications to Brice, Eddie and himself resulting from the formation of the partnership.

PREFORMATION AGREEMENT

The parties hereto, Brice Dunesborough ("Brice"), Edwina Mannokowsky ("Eddie") and Ken Crosswaite ("Ken"), have determined that it is in their mutual interest to form, invest in and operate a partnership to be known as Alternative Energy Company ("the Company") to engage in the business of formulating, designing, manufacturing and selling processes and machinery to produce electrical energy. The parties hereto believe that it is appropriate to set out their intentions and agreements with respect to the contributions to, interests in, and management and conduct of the Company.

In consideration of the promises and agreements of each of the parties hereto, the parties agree as follows:

Article I

Interests in, and Management of, the Company

1.1 Each of the parties hereto shall receive a one-third interest in the following attributes of the Company:

     a. Profits and Losses,

     b. Capital, and

     c. Management.

1.2 No major decision, as further defined in the partnership agreement, with respect to the company shall be made without the concurrence of all the parties hereto.

1.3 Brice shall be designated the Managing Partner of the Company with full authority to make all day-to-day decisions, as further defined in the partnership agreement, affecting the Company.

*   *   *

Article II

Contributions to the Company

2.1 In return for his interest in the Company, Brice agrees to convey to the Company the following assets and the Company agrees to assume the following liabilities: (a) The formula for the process which has an agreed-upon value of $216,000 and in which Brice has an adjusted basis of $0; (b) The know-how required to adapt equipment which has an agreed-upon value of $216,000 and in which Brice has an adjusted basis of $0; (c) The use, which has an agreed-upon value of $52,000, of Brice's home as a demonstration facility at times and days to be defined in the partnership agreement; and (d) The assumption by the partnership of the $84,000 mortgage liability on the home, the proceeds of which were used in developing the formula and know-how.

2.2 In return for her interest in the Company, Eddie agrees to convey to the Company the following assets and liabilities: (a) 1000 shares of Century Motors, Inc. which have a market value of $200 a share and in which Eddie has a basis of $20 a share; (b) 500 shares of Real Estate Equities, Inc. which have a market value of $460 a share and in which Eddie has a basis of $1000 a share; and (c) The assumption by the partnership of a $30,000 debt Eddie owes to First Intrastate Bank which is secured by the stock described in this paragraph.

2.3 In return for his interest in the Company, Ken agrees to provide to the Company all legal services required in the formation and operation of the Company which have an agreed-upon value of $100,000 and certain real estate, to be more particularly defined in the partnership agreement, for use as the location of the Company's manufacturing facility which has an agreed-upon value of $500,000 and in which Ken has an adjusted basis of $250,000.

*   *   *

Article III

Employment by the Company

3.1 Brice agrees that, upon formation of the Company, he will execute an Employment Agreement in the form attached hereto as Exhibit B which, in part, provides for a five-year term of employment as Managing Partner of the Company.

*   *   *

Article VI

Distributions

6.1 One hundred percent of quarterly cash flow, to be more particularly defined in the partnership agreement, but not to include any cash derived from the sale of the shares of stock conveyed to the company by Eddie, shall be distributed to Ken until a total of $200,000 has been distributed by the Company to Ken.

6.2 After the distribution or distributions described in Section 6.1 hereof have been made and completed, then one-third of quarterly cash flow shall be distributed to each of the parties hereto within 30 days after the end of each quarter of the Company's fiscal year.

*   *   *

Note:

Interviewing and Client Counseling

Most of the average attorney's work is done in the office. Perhaps less glamorous than courtroom appearances, it is no less important. Office conferences often have legal effects as crucial and binding as any judicial determination. Frequently at the time of the first interview, the client has not yet decided on a course of action. This presents a chance to practice preventive law and concentrate on analyzing different options. Your primary function is not to control the action but to help your client look at alternatives and make choices which will minimize the risks and maximize the benefits.

Prior to the first interview, you may know little or nothing about the client's problem. Your only information may be a message from your secretary that X called about a particular problem. Of course you would not have agreed to see X if you were not qualified in the problem area, unless you felt you could become qualified or could refer X to a qualified individual. It is not necessary, however, that you be a specialist in the particular area. What is important is that you know about relevant business and social practices as well as applicable law so that you are aware of the right questions to ask. This may require some background reading and research before the interview. The general scope of factual inquiry should be thought through in advance, though not necessarily the precise questions. Consider possible legal issues which may arise and what additional facts you may need to know.

An open-ended question is a good way to begin the interview. Resist the temptation to start by eliciting a number of specific personal and background facts. The client comes to you with something in mind. It is wise from the standpoint of both the continuing relationship with the client and the later elicitation of specific facts to let the client tell you what it is. The client then has a chance to tell you what the client thinks is important and may give you information you would not have thought to seek. Specific factual questions can come later.

Realize that the problem presented by the client is often not the real one. An example is the client who comes to you inquiring about the sale of a home, but the contemplated sale is actually motivated by marital difficulties. The client's best interests may be served by postponing the sale until there is some resolution of the marital difficulties. Be alert to indications that there are underlying causes for the expressed problem of the client. You may want to ask, "How did this problem first arise?" or "What made you decide to do something about it now?" Do not forego a question because you assume you know the answer.

Frequently the client will press you for a solution before you have complete knowledge of the facts. Never ignore this concern. Explain that you can give a better answer when you know all the facts. While control of the interview is not your most important concern, it is not unimportant. The course of the interview should be directed by your choice of questions. Otherwise the client is likely to ramble, dwell on irrelevant facts, or fail to volunteer important ones.

The relationship you develop with the client can be vital to successful representation and advice. An atmosphere of mutual trust may encourage the client to make full disclosure enabling you to determine which aspects of the problem are most significant. Do not take lightly the importance of the client's human, non-legal concerns and frame of mind. If the client is secretive, hostile, or suspicious of attorneys, both the problem and the way you deal with it may be affected. It is important to phrase your questions in a way which demonstrates your understanding and acceptance of the client and the client's concerns. Putting the client on the defensive is almost never desirable.

Ethical considerations may arise. Has the client seen another attorney about this problem? Prior consultation with another attorney may have taught the client what "facts" are desirable. Is someone on retainer? Are you being asked either obliquely or directly to do something unethical or to help the client do something illegal? Does, or will, a conflict of interest exist?

A subtle but real problem is that your questioning may lead the client to take possibly undesirable actions. Asking, "Did you tell that to your spouse?", without more, may lead the client to: (1) tell it to the spouse; (2) not tell it to the spouse; (3) believe that the client should have told the spouse; or (4) believe that the spouse should not have been told. Should you have asked the question? How will the client's interpretation affect the answer given you?

At some point in the interview it will be necessary to get specific personal information about the client and others involved in the matter. Get the names and addresses of people you may wish to interview and your client's feelings as to the appropriateness of such contacts now or in the future.

With a new client you should discuss fees. There is a chance the client will ask you about them and perhaps will not be pleased with your answers. Be prepared to explain how and why you charge what you do.

The client has come to you for advice, and after (or even before) you have elicited the facts, the client is going to want that advice. If you are at all uncertain, say so, and tell the client that sound advice will require legal research and possibly development of further facts from other sources. This is certainly preferable to giving erroneous advice upon which your client may act before you have done your research and corrected the erroneous, off-the-cuff advice. It is advisable from the standpoint of your relationship with the client and the client's peace of mind to set a definite future date on or before which you will render the advice.

At times you will be prepared to give advice or explain the probable consequences of proposed actions. You may want to discuss with the client the possibility of a future dispute, the probable behavior of the parties during it and its legal consequences. Examine possible remedies, but in most cases litigation should not be viewed as the solution to the client's problems. Consider whether your client's goals might be accomplished with informal action or careful planning. Your responsibility to the client includes pointing out all the alternatives. In many cases "non-legal" counseling will be called for. Help the client consider matters such as the "wisdom" of contemplated actions and the possible financial effects.

It is particularly important that the interview be conducted and advice be given in language the client can understand. "Depreciation recapture" and even "torts" often do not qualify. The client's business and professional background and general level of sophistication determine whether legal issues are discussed or technical language is used.

When the client leaves your office after the initial interview the maintenance of a good relationship demands that the client know what will happen next. Make clear what steps you will take. Be certain the client wants such steps taken. If the client is to do something, have you made clear what it is? Have you arranged another appointment or clearly stated when you will get back in touch?

Preformation Agreement

At times, when attorneys deal with a number of parties, all of whom are necessary to carry out a transaction or own and operate an entity, a preformation agreement will be used. The purpose of the preformation agreement is to obtain the agreement of the necessary parties to the major aspects of the course of action to be undertaken before the necessary documents for the transaction or the organic documents for the entity are drafted. Once the agreement of the parties with regard to the major aspects of the transaction or the entity has been obtained, the parties' agreement with respect to the many incidental considerations involved in any transaction or in the formation of any entity is much easier to obtain.

PROBLEM 2P

The chair of the tax department of the firm with which you recently associated has given you the following memorandum from one of the partners in the business department of the firm. The tax partner would like your advice with respect to the steps which should be taken in the formation of the limited liability partnership referred to in the memorandum and the provisions which should be included in the partnership agreement in order to produce the best income tax results for all of the parties.

Gonzales, Street & Jacoby
1410 Courthouse Square
Santa Fe, NM   88201

Memorandum

TO: Andrea Garcia

FROM: Peter DePaulo

RE: Formation of Creative Associates, L.L.P.

DATE: February 15, Year*

Olive Mayer is a 35-year-old sole proprietor of a very successful advertising agency and a good client of this firm. She has spoken to us a number of times about forming a much larger advertising firm by bringing together a number of well-known and successful public relations executives.

---

* See explanatory footnote in Introduction, page vii, note 1.

Recently, she has come to us proposing the formation of such a larger firm. We have advised her that an appropriate entity for such a firm may be a limited liability partnership which was recently authorized by the state legislature. We also have advised her that each of the persons who will be joining with her in this firm should be represented by separate counsel. Olive has informed us that none of the other parties desires separate counsel and all of them are willing to accept our judgment with respect to the many concerns which may arise on formation of the firm. We would like your very careful advice with respect to the formation of the limited liability partnership and the provisions which should be included in the agreement in order to produce the best income tax results for all of the parties. In addition, please advise us of the benefits and detriments which may occur to each party as a result of the formation of the limited liability partnership and the provisions included in the partnership agreement. The members of Creative Associates, L.L.P. and their contributions to the firm are described below.

③   Olive will contribute the assets of her proprietorship which are: land, with a basis of $20,000 and a fair market value of $70,000, and a building, with an adjusted basis of $40,000, an original cost of $130,000 and a fair market value of $110,000, both subject to a mortgage in the amount of $120,000; customer accounts, valued at $80,000 (these are one-to five-year contracts with clients to provide public relations and advertising services); furniture and fixtures, with an adjusted basis of $10,000, an original cost of $70,000 and a fair market value of $35,000; and a newly purchased computer with a cost and an adjusted basis of $5,000 and a fair market value of $5,000. The proprietorship also has $40,000 in receivables which will be contributed and $20,000 in payables which will be assumed.

②   Jefferson Wellknown is a thirty-five-year-old spendthrift who has been associated with one of the leading advertising firms in the city and is known as one of the most creative advertising people in the area. Unfortunately, he has always lived the part of the successful advertising person and therefore has little in the way of assets to contribute to Creative Associates other than his creativity and a large following of satisfied customers whose business will follow him to Creative Associates. If necessary, however, he can scrape together about $60,000 to invest in the partnership.

①   Jackson Wellborn is twenty-six years of age and a recent college graduate with a masters in communication arts. All the participants feel that he has great potential and will be an asset to the firm. He is prepared to contribute securities worth $200,000, in which he has a basis of $140,000. The parties intend to sell most of these securities in the near future to provide working capital for the firm.

1 = easiest to admit

④ = most difficult to admit

Ralph Guidinghand, fifty-three years of age, was a partner in one of the large nation-wide advertising firms. He retired from that firm and set up his own office which is very well-appointed. He will contribute furniture and fixtures with an adjusted basis of $30,000, an original cost of $100,000, a value of $70,000 and subject to liabilities of $20,000. In addition, he will contribute $120,000 in value of customer accounts and $30,000 in cash.

All four individuals use the cash method and the calendar year for income tax purposes. They have agreed that each will have an equal voice in Creative Associates and an equal share in its income. They anticipate that Creative Associates will operate as Mayer's and Guidinghand's sole proprietorships operated, i.e., it will negotiate contracts with clients to provide all the clients' advertising and public relations work for a one- to five-year period. The participants anticipate that Creative Associates will grow and become well-known in future years.

Note:

Representing More Than One Party

A frequent problem which a lawyer faces in forming an entity at the behest of more than one person is that one or more of the participants will not be represented by independent counsel. The facts described in the preceding problem are, more often than not, faced by counsel. One approach to handling the bar against conflicts of interest in Rule 1.7 of the ABA Model Rules of Professional Conduct is to insist that each participant be represented by independent counsel, and at least initially this is an appropriate position for a lawyer to take. Once, however, it is clear that one or more participants are not going to be represented by independent counsel, lawyers usually take one of three alternative approaches. First, the lawyer may take the position that the lawyer represents only the entity and none of the participants. In this case the lawyer will make it clear that the recommendations made will be the best recommendations for the entity. Incidentally, because the participants will be members of the entity, these recommendations may be the best from each one's personal standpoint, although that cannot be guaranteed. The lawyer may agree to provide, to the best of the lawyer's ability, information to each participant about whether certain proposed actions or transactions are in that participant's interest. If this information is provided, the lawyer should not advise the participant with respect to the course of action the participant should choose.

Second, the lawyer may choose to act on behalf of one of the participants. If this course of action is chosen, the lawyer should advise the remaining participants that the lawyer's recommendations will be those in the best interest of the participant for whom the lawyer has chosen to act. Again, the lawyer should assure the other participants that, to the best of the lawyer's ability, the lawyer will inform each participant whether acts and transactions are in that participant's interest.

Third, if the clients come to the attorney in a basically unified posture with no significant fundamental conflicts of interest, the attorney may continue representation as an intermediary under ABA Model Rule 2.2 so long as the clients are made aware of the circumstances and consent, the attorney maintains no confidences in favor of one of the clients and no significant conflict emerges between the clients.

Each of the three alternatives suggested above is ethically possible, provided that the participants each clearly understand the position of the lawyer and are kept advised by the lawyer of acts and transactions which should concern them. Occasionally the lawyer who seeks to act as an intermediary discovers that significant conflicts develop among the clients or one of the parties will object to the attorney's continuing to serve as an intermediary. In such a case, the attorney will find it necessary to withdraw completely from the matter and all parties will have to obtain new independent representation.

Limited Liability Partnerships

A limited liability partnership is a partnership in which the personal liability of the partners is limited. In all other ways the partnership follows the traditional general partnership form. The status of a limited liability partnership is achieved in most states which permit this form of entity by registering the partnership with an appropriate state agency or official. The states differ on the extent of the limited liability provided. A minority of states provide that the liability of the partners is limited to their capital contributions with respect to both contract and tort liabilities. The majority of states do not limit the liability of partners for contract obligations. The personal liability of the partners with respect to tort and similar liabilities, however, is limited to the acts of the partner and those individuals under the partner's supervision. Therefore, in the majority of states a partner in a limited liability partnership is not liable for the acts of the other partners nor for the acts of agents and employees supervised by other partners. You may assume that the limited liability partnerships used and described in the problems in this book are of the latter type. The partners are jointly and severally liable for contract obligations but are not liable for the acts of other partners nor for the acts of agents and employees other than those supervised by the partner under consideration.

PROBLEM 3P

Jackson & Jefferson (J & J), a partnership, is a recently formed law firm which specializes in litigation in the city in which you practice. J & J has always asked for your help in analyzing the income tax problems which the firm has faced. The two equal partners in J & J are Janey Jackson (Janey) and Avram Jefferson (Avram). They are both in their early 30s and have good reputations as litigators. Since J & J has only been in business a couple of years, it has not as yet earned a lot of money. It made about $50,000 last year after the payment of secretarial expenses, rent, interest on loans, miscellaneous office expenses and depreciation on equipment.

Belgium & Liver (B & L), a limited liability partnership, having four equal partners, is an older, well-respected general practice firm in the city in which you practice. B & L made about $400,000 last year after payment of the same type of expenses which J & J paid, but in much larger amounts. Last year, the two litigation partners in B & L retired. The partners in B & L have been searching for some litigators to replace the litigators who retired. The managing partner has approached Janey and Avram to determine their interest in being the replacements for B & L's litigators. Janey and Avram told the managing partner that they were interested in exploring the possibility.

Janey and Avram recently received the following agreement from B & L. They would like you to advise them with respect to the income tax aspects of the agreement. You need not bother with the effects of the liquidation of the J & J and B & L partnerships since the tax partner in B & L is willing to give an opinion that the liquidations are tax-free to both partnerships and their partners. In addition, the opinion will state that the partners of J & J and B & L will have the same adjusted bases in their partnership interests in the new partnership that they had in their partnership interests in their respective partnerships immediately after the conveyances described in the agreement and before the liquidations.

Partnership Merger Agreement

The partners of J & J and B & L have determined that it is in their best interests to combine their practices of law in a new limited liability partnership (new partnership) pursuant to the provisions of this agreement. The new partnership shall be governed by a partnership agreement in the form of Exhibit A. attached hereto.

1. J & J shall convey to the new partnership the following assets subject to the described liabilities which the new partnership will assume.

    (a) Assets to be conveyed, their adjusted bases for income tax purposes and their agreed fair market value:

ASSET			ADJUSTED BASIS	FAIR MARKET VALUE
Matters currently being worked on			---	$ 18,000
Matters completed but not yet billed			---	9,000
Accounts Receivable			---	31,000
Office Equipment:	Cost	$18,000		
	Depreciation	(6,000)	$ 12,000	14,000
Library:	Cost	5,000		
	Depreciation	(2,000)	3,000	3,000
Total Assets			**$ 15,000**	**$ 75,000**

    (b) Recourse liabilities to which the above assets are subject:

Accounts Payable	$ 9,000
Loan for Office Equipment	$14,000
Loan for Library Acquisition	$ 2,000
TOTAL LIABILITIES	$25,000

    (c) J & J uses the cash method of accounting for tax and financial purposes.

2. B & L shall convey to the new partnership the following assets subject to the described liabilities which the new partnership will assume.

(a)   Assets to be conveyed, their adjusted bases for income tax purposes and their agreed fair market value.

ASSET			ADJUSTED BASIS	FAIR MARKET VALUE
Matters currently being worked on			---	$ 30,000
Matters completed but not yet billed			---	10,000
Accounts Receivable			---	70,000
Office Equipment:	Cost	$240,000		
	Depreciation	(120,000)	$120,000	120,000
Library:	Cost	80,000		
	Depreciation	(50,000)	30,000	40,000
Total Assets			$150,000	$270,000

(b)   Recourse liabilities to which the above assets are subject:

Accounts Payable	$ 30,000
Loan for Office Equipment	$ 80,000
Loan for Library Acquisition	$ 10,000
TOTAL LIABILITIES	$120,000

(c)   B & L uses the cash method of accounting for tax and financial purposes.

3.   The parties each warrant and represent that their adjusted bases in their present partnership interests are as follows:

(a)   Each of B & L's four partners has an adjusted basis of $37,500 in her or his partnership interest.

(b)   Each of J & J's two partners has an adjusted basis of $7,500 in her or his partnership interest.

4.   The parties' capital accounts on formation of the new partnership shall be:

       B & L $150,000

       J & J $ 50,000

The parties shall share on liquidation of the new partnership in accord with the amounts then in their respective capital accounts.

* * *

6.   The parties' shares of the net cash flow distributions of the new partnership, as defined in the partnership agreement attached hereto as Exhibit A., shall be:

     (a)   The first $10,000 in each year shall be distributed to B & L until B & L receives $50,000.

     (b)   After the distribution to B & L referred to above, all additional cash flow distributions shall be distributed:

         (i)   Two-thirds to B & L

         (ii)   One-third to J & J

* * *

9.   The profits and losses of the partnership, as defined in the partnership agreement attached hereto as Exhibit A., shall be allocated:

     (a)   Two-thirds to B & L

     (b)   One-third to J & J

* * *

14.   The parties shall have the following votes on matters which, pursuant to the partnership agreement attached hereto as Exhibit A., require the vote of the partners:

     (a)   B & L   Four votes

     (b)   J & J   Two votes

* * *

17.   Immediately after the execution of the new partnership agreement and the conveyances to the new partnership described above, B & L and J & J shall be liquidated and the partnership interests in the new

partnership shall be distributed pro rata by B & L to its four partners and by J & J to its two partners.

* * *

Note:

See the Note on Limited Liability Partnerships following Problem 2P at page 10.

Legal Drafting

A general discussion of legal drafting may include such different instruments as statutes, contracts, leases, trusts and partnership agreements. They have similar objectives. A contract is simply a statute for the specific occasion or matter. A lease is a code governing the use of certain premises. Such instruments also employ common tools of thought and language. The primary difference between statutes and private instruments is that, as a general rule, statutes are devoted to governing conduct or determining status whereas private instruments may include dispositive aspects such as conveyances. In addition, drafting a statute may require the consideration of a greater number of contingencies and a form of drafting which permits an elasticity of construction which need not, and often should not, be present in a private instrument.

The core problems in the drafting of statutes and private instruments, however, are quite similar and permit them to be considered together in a general note. Techniques such as definition sections, cross-references, sectioning and subsectioning are useful in both contexts. A useful way to discuss the concepts involved in good legal drafting is to paraphrase Professor Reed Dickerson's introductory comments in The Fundamentals of Legal Drafting (1986).

The primary goals of legal drafting are precision and internal coherence. The instrument should be free of all color, emotion and rhetoric. A contract or statute does not in general depend on the instrument itself to persuade the parties affected to comply with its terms (other than possibly a penalty clause). The instrument is essentially a source of information.

In order for the instrument to be effective the attorney drafting the instrument must understand that the drafting process operates on two levels, the conceptual and the verbal. One must not only understand the concepts involved, but must select the proper words to express those concepts. Therefore, drafting initially involves precisely ascertaining and perfecting the substantive desires and policies of the parties for whom the drafting is done. Then the proper means for stating and implementing such desires and policies are determined.

In the problem preceding this note several sections of a partnership merger agreement were set out. In considering and discussing the problem you have become aware of the desires and policies which are intended to be effectuated through those sections. Now consider whether the sections of the partnership agreement as set out in the problem properly state such desires and policies. If not, what changes would you make to effect them?

In future problems you will encounter various documents embodying consensual agreements. In considering them, reread this note, and determine whether the document set out in the problem properly expressed the intent of the parties and if not, how it could be improved by redrafting.

Problem 4P

The firm with which you are associated has been asked to provide an opinion letter to Envirotech, L.L.C. (Envirotech), a limited liability company, in connection with the private placement of $300,000 of its membership units. Your firm has been asked to opine on the income tax effects of the formation and private placement of the membership units of Envirotech. Diane Bronstein, one of the other senior associates in the tax department of your firm, has prepared the opinion letter. The chair of the tax department of the firm has asked you to evaluate the opinion letter and inform her of any concerns that you might have.

Woodhouse & Paul
Suite 400
1555 N Street, N.W.
Washington, DC 20005

September 4, Year*

Mr. Jacob Fierstein
Envirotech, L.L.C.
718 Firmont Street
Richwood, WV 26261

Re: The Income Tax Effects of the Formation and Private
Placement of Membership Units in Envirotech, L.L.C.

Dear Mr. Fierstein:

You have asked us to give you our evaluation of the income tax effects of the formation and the private placement of membership units of Envirotech, L.L.C., a limited liability company. This letter presents the facts relative to the formation and private placement of membership units of Envirotech and our opinion of the income tax effects of those acts and transactions. Please be aware that if our understanding of the facts is incorrect or incomplete our opinion may be affected thereby. Therefore, please read the part of this opinion letter entitled Facts very closely and promptly inform us if you find that our understanding of the facts is at all incorrect or incomplete.

FACTS

Jacob Fierstein has taught biological chemistry and done research in this field for the past fifteen years at the University of West Virginia. He specializes in the study of various forms of bacteria. In recent years he has been investigating the effect on organic and inorganic matter of a strain of bacteria called processors. He has found that by making certain molecular changes in the structure of the processors, the processors will attack and consume a wide variety of inorganic materials such as plastic, metals and styrofoam. In addition, the processors will consume various organic materials such as those found in common garbage. It appears that if a sufficient number of processors possessing the changed molecular structure

---

* See explanatory footnote in Introduction, page vii, note 1.

can be manufactured and applied, they can turn a sanitary landfill, even one containing hazardous wastes, into nitrogen-rich soil within two weeks after application.

Mr. Fierstein is quite excited about the potential of these processors and has left his teaching position in order to devote his time to the development and manufacture of the processors. Mr. Fierstein has informed us that the University of West Virginia does not claim any interest in the processors. Mr. Fierstein feels that the concept and development of the processors to this point in time is worth about $300,000. He has not incurred any direct costs in the development of the processors. The changes in the molecular structure of the processors and the technique of achieving the changes may not be patentable. The changes and technique, however, are the products of many hours of research and are not easily copied. Therefore the changes and technique probably can be protected as a trade secret. Mr. Fierstein will receive thirty membership units in Envirotech in return for his conveyance of the trade secret.

Helen Rosen, the president of Interlocking Bankshares, Inc., a commercial bank holding company, is prepared to invest personally in the development of the processors. She will invest $300,000 and receive thirty membership units. She will contribute $150,000 in AT&T stock in which she has a basis of $80,000 and $150,000 of Exxon stock in which she has a basis of $200,000.

Ms. Rosen told Arthur Sampson, a major real estate developer, about the concept. Like Ms. Rosen, Mr. Sampson was fascinated by the concept and is also prepared to invest in Envirotech. Mr. Sampson's investment will be a small, idle manufacturing plant which he presently owns. Mr. Fierstein believes that the plant is well designed and in the perfect location for the development of the processors. The manufacturing plant and the land upon which it is located is valued at about $500,000. It is subject to a recourse mortgage liability of $150,000. Mr. Sampson's adjusted basis in the plant and land is about $50,000. In return for contributing the plant and land subject to the mortgage liability, which Envirotech will assume, Mr. Sampson will receive thirty membership units and an agreement that the first $50,000 of net earned cash flow of Envirotech will be distributed to him.

Messrs. Fierstein and Sampson and Ms. Rosen realized that it was very important to obtain the services of a person capable of supervising the development and the subsequent manufacture of the processors as none of them had the know-how to do so. They approached Bertram Weaver, who was the executive vice-president in charge of new product development and manufacture for Dupont, Inc. Mr. Weaver is very interested in taking on the challenges of a start-up company. He is prepared to invest about $100,000 and will agree to commit at least five years to the task of working on the development and manufacture of the processors. Ms. Rosen and Messrs. Fierstein and Sampson feel that the salary which Mr. Weaver has requested is quite reasonable. Mr. Weaver will receive thirty membership units in return for his investment.

Ms. Rosen has introduced Mr. Fierstein to a commercial loan officer at Arlington National Bank, one of the banks whose stock is owned by Interlocking. After some negotiations, Arlington National Bank has agreed to loan to Envirotech about $300,000 for working capital. The loan will be secured by a first lien on all the assets of Envirotech, except for the manufacturing plant and land. The loan will be secured by a second mortgage on the manufacturing plant and land. The mortgage will be a recourse liability to Envirotech and the bank expects Ms. Rosen and Mr. Sampson to guarantee the loan.

In order to raise the last $300,000 needed for the development and start up of the manufacture of the processors, Ms. Rosen and Messrs. Sampson and Fierstein contacted Grace Milliken, who is a vice-president of Merrill, Lynch & Co., Inc., a securities underwriting firm. Ms. Milliken has been able to place the $300,000 of membership units in Envirotech with five wealthy and sophisticated individuals and the securities firm for which she works. The five individuals will each invest $55,000 and each will receive five membership units. The securities firm will invest $25,000 and receive five membership units.

DISCUSSION

The following opinion is based on our study of the above facts, the sections of the Internal Revenue Code of 1986, as amended, regulations, rulings and judicial and other authorities which we felt appropriate and necessary to enable us to render this opinion. In this opinion we will discuss each contributor to Envirotech, advising you of the income tax effects of the transactions entered into with that contributor.

Since we believe that the trade secret will be classified as property, neither Mr. Fierstein nor Envirotech will recognize any gain or loss on the contribution by Mr. Fierstein of the trade secret. Mr. Fierstein's basis in his membership units will be equal to his basis in the trade secret and Envirotech's basis in the trade secret will be equal to Mr. Fierstein's basis in it. See I.R.C. Sections 722 and 723. Any gain on the sale or exchange of the trade secret by Envirotech up to $300,000 must be allocated to Mr. Fierstein. Unfortunately, if the trade secret should sell for less than $300,000 the economic loss realized by the other members cannot be recognized by them. See I.R.C. Section 704(c)(1). Finally, while the other members of Envirotech have "economically" acquired part of the trade secret and would be entitled to amortize their cost in the trade secret over fifteen years under I.R.C. Section 197 if they had independently acquired the interest, they cannot be allocated any amortization since Envirotech has no basis in the trade secret and therefore there is nothing to amortize.

Ms. Rosen's contribution of AT&T and Exxon stock will certainly be treated as property and therefore neither she nor Envirotech will recognize any gain or loss on her contribution of the stock. Her basis in her membership units in Envirotech will be equal to her basis in the stock contributed and Envirotech's basis in the stock contributed will be equal to Ms. Rosen's basis in that stock. The first $70,000 of gain on the AT&T stock recognized by Envirotech must be allocated to Ms. Rosen. If, however, the AT&T stock is sold for less than $150,000 but more than $80,000 the gain in excess of $80,000 must be allocated to Ms. Rosen but, since Envirotech recognized no loss, the economic loss suffered by the other members cannot be allocated to them. If Envirotech should recognize the $50,000 loss existing in the Exxon stock, this loss can be allocated among the members since I.R.C. Section 704(c)(1) only applies to gains.

The manufacturing plant to be contributed by Mr. Sampson is certainly property and therefore neither Mr. Sampson nor Envirotech will recognize any gain on the contribution of the manufacturing plant. Envirotech will take a basis in the manufacturing plant equal to Mr. Sampson's basis in the plant. Mr. Sampson will have a basis in his membership units equal to his basis in the plant. Under I.R.C. Section 752(b), however, Mr. Sampson will be treated as receiving a cash distribution equal to the amount of the mortgage liability on the plant. Since Mr. Sampson's basis in his membership interest is only $50,000, Mr. Sampson will realize $100,000 of gain under I.R.C. Section 731(e)(1).

While Mr. Weaver is contributing $100,000 for his membership units in Envirotech, it appears from the contributions made by the other members that the value of thirty membership units in Envirotech is $300,000. Although it might be argued that Mr. Weaver is contributing $100,000 of cash and $200,000 of know-how, both of which are property, to Envirotech, we believe that it would be difficult to classify Mr. Weaver's know-how as property for the purposes of I.R.C. Section 721. Therefore, we believe that Mr. Weaver is receiving $200,000 of his membership units in return for his promise of services. Under I.R.C. Section 83, Mr. Weaver must take into income the excess $200,000 value of his membership units. Envirotech will recognize gain on the conveyance to Mr. Weaver of the excess twenty membership units since property held by Envirotech (the trade secret, the manufacturing plant and the AT&T stock) is appreciated and Envirotech is purchasing Mr. Weaver's services using that appreciated property. The gain recognized by Envirotech should be allocated to Mr. Fierstein, Ms. Rosen and Mr. Sampson as appropriate. Finally, Envirotech is entitled to a deduction under I.R.C. Section 162 equal to the $200,000 value of membership units given to Mr. Weaver since this is conceptually a payment for Mr. Weaver's services. The $200,000 deduction should be allocated among the members in the manner in which the members share the profit and loss of Envirotech.

The working capital loan made to Envirotech by Arlington National Bank will have no income tax significance. While Envirotech gains $300,000 it also incurs an obligation to repay that $300,000 and therefore has no gain or loss on the transaction. If Ms. Rosen or Mr. Sampson are forced to make good on their guarantees of the Arlington National Bank loan they may be entitled to claim bad debt deductions if they cannot obtain repayment from Envirotech.

Finally, the five wealthy investors will each have a basis in their membership units of $55,000. Merrill, Lynch & Co., Inc. is going to obtain five membership units for the payment of $25,000. However, since the five investors each paid $55,000 for five membership units, Merrill, Lynch & Co., Inc. is receiving membership units worth $55,000 for a payment of $25,000. The excess $30,000 of membership units received by Merrill, Lynch & Co., Inc. will be treated as compensation to it under I.R.C. Section 83. Merrill, Lynch & Co., Inc. will have a basis in its five membership units of $55,000 and Envirotech will be treated as having paid Merrill, Lynch & Co., Inc. a commission of $30,000. These commissions can be amortized by Envirotech, under I.R.C. Section 709, over the next five years. The amortization should be allocated among the members of Envirotech in accord with the way the members share the profit and loss of Envirotech.

If you have any questions or comments with respect to the above discussion, please do not hesitate to call or write the undersigned. We will be more than willing to discuss with you any of the matters dealt with in this letter.

Sincerely yours,
Woodhouse & Paul
by

Diane Bronstein

Diane Bronstein

Note:

Opinion Letters

When advising a client in writing on the legal consequences of a transaction, attorneys choose between two different types of letters, the letter of advice and the opinion letter. The opinion letter is the more formal document, and the attorney, by using such a letter, indicates that: (1) the matter in question is important; (2) substantial time and effort have been devoted to consideration of the matter; (3) the conclusion reached is reasonably firm; and (4) the client (and perhaps others) are expected to rely extensively on the opinion of the attorney. Opinion letters generally follow the format illustrated in the above problem. The letter sets forth the question which will be answered, the relevant facts provided the attorney by the client and the opinion of the attorney. Opinion letters are frequently signed in the name of the firm, for example, one partner will sign on behalf of a partnership.

There are differing opinions as to the advisability of stating the reasons for reaching a conclusion. Some attorneys feel that reasons should be included since the client is entitled to know why the stated conclusion was reached. It is also felt that, unless the firm is well known and respected, its conclusion will only be respected if the reasons for reaching the conclusion are stated in cogent fashion. Other attorneys feel that it is not necessary to state reasons, since most clients and members of the public will neither understand nor care what the reasons are. One noted member of the New York Bar refused to state reasons because so doing unnecessarily multiplied the opportunities for being wrong. As he coyly put it, "As embarrassing as it is to reach the wrong conclusion, it is equally embarrassing to later be shown to have reached the right conclusion for wholly wrong reasons."

The legal fraternity approaches an opinion letter with more caution than a letter of advice. An opinion letter is viewed as maximizing the exposure of the firm. There does not, however, appear to be any basis for concluding that a letter of advice on firm stationery, in which an attorney gives her views on the law knowing a client will act on the basis of those views, results in any less exposure than a formal opinion letter.

Limited Liability Companies

A limited liability company (LLC) is organized pursuant to the provisions of a state's Limited Liability Company Act (Act). It usually is authorized to engage in any and all business activity permitted by the laws of the state. The management of an LLC may be vested in its members. The Act may permit or allow an LLC operating agreement (LLC agreement) to provide for the management, in whole or in part, of an LLC by a manager or managers chosen by the members. The Act will provide that the debts, obligations, and liabilities of the LLC, whether arising in contract, tort, or otherwise, are solely the debts, obligations, and liabilities of the LLC; no member or manager of the LLC is obligated personally for any debt, obligation, or liability of the LLC solely by reason of being a member or acting as a manager of the LLC.

The Act may provide that an LLC interest is personal property. An LLC interest may be assignable in whole or in part except as provided in the LLC agreement. The assignee of a member's interest, however, may have no right to participate in the management of the business and affairs of an LLC except as provided in the LLC agreement and upon either: (1) the approval of all of the members of the LLC other than the member assigning the member's LLC interest; or (2) compliance with any procedure provided for in the LLC agreement. The Act typically will provide that unless otherwise provided in the LLC agreement an assignment entitles the assignee to share in profits and losses, to receive distributions, and to receive an allocation of income, gain, loss, deduction, or credit or any similar item to which the assignor was entitled, to the extent assigned. The Act will also typically provide that a member ceases to be a member and to have the power to exercise any rights or powers of a member upon assignment of all of the member's LLC interest. An Act may provide that the assignee of a member's LLC interest may become a member as provided in the LLC agreement and upon either: (1) the approval of all of the members of the LLC other than the member assigning the member's LLC interest; or (2) compliance with any procedure provided for in the LLC agreement.

An LLC typically is dissolved upon the first to occur of the following: (1) at the time specified in the LLC agreement; (2) upon the happening of events specified in the LLC agreement; (3) by the written consent of all members; (4) by the death, retirement, resignation, expulsion, bankruptcy, or dissolution of a member or the occurrence of any other event that terminates the continued membership of a member in the LLC unless the business of the LLC is continued either by the consent of all of the remaining members within 90 days following the occurrence of any terminating event or pursuant to a right to continue stated in the LLC agreement; or (5) by the entry of a decree of judicial dissolution under the Act.

Students can assume that the LLC referred to in the immediately preceding problem and those referred to in other problems contained in Division I. Taxation of Organizations Treated as Partnerships of this book will be treated by the Internal Revenue Service and the courts as partnerships for income tax purposes.

Part B

OPERATION OF A PARTNERSHIP

PROBLEM 5P

P.J. Sampson and Company, Inc. ("Sampson") is a developer and manager of residential rental properties such as apartment buildings. A number of years ago it purchased some real estate in Salem, Oregon for $40,000. The real estate is now worth about $400,000 and is an ideal site for an apartment complex. Sampson has examined the possibility of developing an apartment complex on the site. The estimated construction cost of the complex is eleven million dollars. G.E. Pension Trust has agreed to provide nine million dollars of the construction cost by means of a nonrecourse mortgage loan secured by the real estate and improvements and guaranteed by Paul L. Sampson ("Paul") individually to the extent of 50% of the principal balance outstanding from time to time. Paul is the grandson of Paula J. Sampson, now deceased, who was the founder of Sampson. Paul owns 70% of the authorized and outstanding shares of stock of Sampson. The officers of Sampson believe that the other two million dollars needed can be obtained through an investment of $400,000 by five investors, who have invested in other apartment complexes developed by Sampson. The officers have determined that the five investors would require, at the minimum, a 15% cash return on their investment.

The officers have concluded that the best entity to use to construct and operate the apartment complex is a limited partnership. As a result of depreciation and substantial interest deductions, the apartment complex will produce losses, for income tax purposes, during the early years of its operation. Sampson will convey the real estate to the limited partnership, act as general partner, supervise construction and rent-up, and then manage the operation of the apartment complex. Sampson expects to be compensated for its services in managing the complex. Sampson manages residential rental properties for unrelated developers. Sampson's house counsel has prepared a draft of a limited partnership agreement and proposes to use it for the above-described project. Sampson's officers and house counsel would like you to advise them with respect to the income tax effects of the partnership agreement, as drafted, and with regard to any changes or additions which you, as an income tax adviser, would make to the agreement.

Certificate and Agreement
of
Limited Partnership
of
Salem Associates, Ltd.

This Certificate and Agreement of Limited Partnership of Salem Associates, Ltd. ("the Agreement") among P.J. Sampson and Company, Inc. as general partner (the "General Partner") and the five persons listed on the signature pages hereto as limited partners (the "Limited Partners") is effective as of the date of filing the Agreement with the Oregon Secretary of State.

* * *

Article I

Certain Definitions

* * *

1.3 Capital Account shall mean, when used with respect to the General Partner, an initial $400,000 which is the value of the real property contributed by the General Partner to the Partnership and, when used with respect to any Limited Partner, an initial $400,000 which is the amount of money contributed by each of the Limited Partners to the Partnership. In the case of the General Partner and each Limited Partner, the amount of the initial contribution shall be increased by the amount of all net income credited to the account of such Partner and decreased by the amount of all net losses charged to the account of such Partner and the amount of the distributions made to such Partner.

* * *

Article II

Management and Payments to the General Partner and Affiliates

2.4 While the General Partner is not responsible for the management of the operation of the apartment complex owned by the Partnership, as distinguished from the management of the affairs of the Partnership for which it is responsible, the General Partner shall have full power and authority to hire and supervise, on behalf of the Partnership, a manager of the operation of the apartment complex. The annual compensation paid to such a manager shall not exceed 12% of the annual gross income of the Partnership derived from the apartment complex. The General Partner may hire, pursuant to the Real Estate

Management Agreement attached hereto as Exhibit C, itself or an affiliate of it as the manager of the apartment complex if it determines that it or an affiliate is the best qualified applicant for the position.

* * *

2.6 The General Partner is authorized and empowered to pay annually to Paul L. Sampson, in consideration of his continuing partial guaranty of the mortgage loan, 1% of the remaining principal balance of the mortgage loan made to the Partnership by G.E. Pension Trust.

* * *

Article III

Additional Contributions and Accounting

* * *

3.3 The General Partner shall contribute to the Partnership upon its termination any deficit then existing in its capital account.

* * *

3.7 Net income or net loss for any fiscal year shall mean the income or loss of the Partnership, as the case may be, as determined for Federal income tax purposes.

* * *

Article IV

Allocation of Net Income and Net Loss

* * *

4.1 Net loss for any fiscal year or period shall be allocated 98% to the Limited Partners and 2% to the General Partner until the year or period during which the net income of the Partnership would be allocated one-third to the General Partner and two-thirds to the Limited Partners, at which time and thereafter net loss shall be allocated in the same manner as the net income.

4.2 Net income for any fiscal year or period shall be allocated between the General Partner and the Limited Partners:

(a) First, 98% to the Limited Partners and 2% to the General Partner until the Limited Partners have been cumulatively allocated, pursuant to this paragraph, an amount equal to their initial capital accounts plus an amount equal to 15% of their initial capital accounts; and

(b) Second, one-third to the General Partner and two-thirds to the Limited Partners.

* * *

Article V

Distributions

5.1 Distributions of money by the Partnership in any fiscal year shall be made as follows:

(a) First, 98% to the Limited Partners and 2% to the General Partner until the Limited Partners have received distributions, pursuant to this paragraph, in a cumulative amount equal to their initial capital accounts plus an amount equal to 15% of their initial capital accounts; and

(b) Second, one-third to the General Partner and two-thirds to the Limited Partners.

* * *

Article VIII

Dissolution and Termination

* * *

8.3 Upon dissolution and termination, except as otherwise required by law, the assets of the Partnership (including any net proceeds from dispositions of assets) shall be used and distributed in the following order: (i) to pay or provide for the payment of all Partnership liabilities and liquidating expenses and obligations; (ii) to distribute to the Limited Partners the amounts then in their capital accounts; and (iii) to distribute to the General Partner the amount then in its capital account.

Note:

See the Note on Legal Drafting following Problem 3P at page 15.

PROBLEM 6P

One of the attorneys in the federal securities department of the firm with which you are associated has just delivered to you the Description of the Business and Offering of Securities portion of a private placement memorandum which the firm is preparing for a new client, Carnival Airlines, Inc. The attorney would like you to prepare the Federal Income Tax section of the memorandum and to advise her with respect to the income tax concerns raised by the portion of the memorandum that she has given to you.

* * *

3.   Description of the Business and the Offering of Securities

Carnival Airlines, Inc. ("Carnival") is one of the largest nonscheduled airlines in the United States. Its charter business has increased dramatically in the last four years and it has begun to fly a route from New York City to St. Thomas in the Virgin Islands on a once-a-day basis. As a result, Carnival is going to acquire two new aircraft for its fleet. The cost of each of these aircraft is $40,000,000 -- a total expenditure of $80,000,000. About $50,000,000 of the cost can be financed. The purpose of the offering is to raise the remaining $30,000,000 of the cost of the aircraft.

Carnival has caused a limited partnership, Carnival Skies, Ltd. ("Skies"), to be formed. Skies will own the two aircraft. It will lease the aircraft to Carnival at a fair rental. Carnival is the general partner of Skies. It contributed $600,000 (2% of the $30,000,000 contribution to be made by the limited partners) for its general partnership interest. The general partnership interest initially entitles Carnival to 2% of the profits, losses and cash flow distributions of Skies. Morris Abraham ("Abraham"), a vice president of Carnival, has purchased a .01% limited partnership interest for $3000. The remainder of the limited partnership interests will be offered to not more than 30 sophisticated investors pursuant to this private placement memorandum.

The limited partnership interests (other than the Abraham interest) will be divided into 30 units. The price of a limited partnership unit is $980,000. The limited partnership units will be sold only in quantities of one unit or more. The purchaser of a unit can pay for one-half of the unit by delivering to the general partner the purchaser's personal recourse note for $490,000 ("limited partner's note") having a term of fifteen years and bearing a market rate of interest. Carnival anticipates that the cash flow distributions made by Skies to the holder of a limited partnership unit over the 15-year period will be in excess of the amount of cash needed to pay the principal and interest on a limited partner note. Carnival, however, cannot assure a purchaser of this amount of cash flow distributions.

The limited partners (including the Abraham interest) initially will be entitled to 98% of the profits, losses and cash flow distributions of Skies.

Carnival anticipates that, as a result of accelerated depreciation and the payment of interest on the $50,000,000 to be borrowed from Chase Manhattan Bank, Skies will recognize substantial losses for income tax purposes during the four years following the purchase of the aircraft. It is anticipated, but cannot be guaranteed, that the tax losses during this period will exceed the amount of the investments of the limited partners. In addition, it is anticipated, but cannot be guaranteed, that despite the tax losses, Skies will be able to make cash flow distributions to the partners after the second year following the purchase of the aircraft. The allocation of 98% of the profit, loss and cash flow distributions of Skies to the limited partners will continue until the limited partners have recovered their investments in the partnership plus 12% per annum on the unpaid portion of their investments ("payout"). Carnival anticipates, but cannot guarantee, that this will occur in either the seventh or eighth year of the operation of Skies. After payout the limited partners (including the Abraham interest) will be entitled to 70% of the profit, loss and cash flow distributions of Skies and the general partner will be entitled to 30%. The limited partners' liability is limited to the amount of their investments. They are not liable for any deficits in their capital accounts.

As mentioned above, $50,000,000 of the cost of the aircraft will be borrowed from Chase Manhattan Bank for a term of 15 years at an interest rate which will be 4 points in excess of the bank's prime rate ("the loan"). The loan will be secured by a security interest in the two aircraft and any limited partner notes received by Skies. The loan will be recourse to Skies and Carnival. The limited partners will not be liable for the loan, except to the extent of a limited partner note pledged as security for the loan.

Carnival will be entitled to certain payments from Skies for services Carnival performs for Skies. In return for its services in negotiating the purchase of the aircraft, Carnival will receive the first $160,000 of cash flow distributions made by Skies. In addition, Carnival will be allocated the first $160,000 of the income earned by Skies. For its services in the formation of Skies and the sale of the limited partnership units, Carnival will receive an amount equal to .1% of the cash received from the sale of the limited partnership units. The maximum amount Carnival can receive is $147,000 if all the limited partners pay cash for their units. Finally, Carnival will receive annually 4% of the gross income of Skies for Carnival's services in managing the operation of the partnership and the leasing of its aircraft. This payment to Carnival will continue only to payout and will terminate after payout.

* * *

Note:

Private Placement Memoranda

At times, under Regulation D issued by the Securities and Exchange Commission, a substantial amount of dollars can be raised from private investors who are "sophisticated" or "accredited." Usually the securities (in the problem above the limited partnership interests) are sold to a limited number of investors in return for a significant amount invested by each investor. In these instances, while the promoter does not have to file with the Securities and Exchange Commission, it will frequently prepare a Private Placement Memorandum which will contain almost all the information which would have been contained in a filing with the Securities and Exchange Commission. Two important parts of the Private Placement Memorandum are the "Description of the Business and Offering of the Securities" section and the "Income Tax Matters" section. The portion of the Private Placement Memorandum set out in the above problem is quite abbreviated. This section, as contained in a typical Private Placement Memorandum, would be substantially more detailed.

PROBLEM 7P

Nathan Fairplay and Joseph Dealer invested together in real estate for many years. Recently, Nathan died and his daughter Sylvia inherited all his real estate holdings. Nathan and Joseph owned, as tenants-in-common, an apartment house at 641 Lincoln, a supermarket leased to Super Wooper Supermarkets at 1200 Baseline and a medical office building at 231 Broadway. Nathan and Joseph each had provided one-half of the down payments for the properties and had paid one-half of all expenses including amortization of the mortgages. They each had reported one-half of the income and deducted one-half of the expenses, including depreciation computed using the most accelerated rate available, on their personal income tax returns. The fair market value of the investments has remained the same since Nathan's death.

The mortgage liability on, and the fair market value of, each property is as follows: 641 Lincoln, $90,000 liability, $210,000 value; 1200 Baseline, $180,000 liability, $240,000 value; and 231 Broadway, $300,000 liability, $420,000 value. Joseph's adjusted basis in 641 Lincoln is $62,000; in Baseline, it is $90,000; and in 231 Broadway, it is $105,000. The properties were acquired by Nathan and Joseph at various times between two and ten years ago.

Sylvia, being young and aggressive, wants to expand the real estate endeavors using the equity in the present properties as a means of raising capital for new projects. Joseph is willing to expand but does not want to incur any further liabilities nor take an active part in the expanded operation. Sylvia's attorney has suggested the following to accomplish the parties' desires. First, the three present mortgages will be consolidated into a $570,000 mortgage covering all three properties. Joseph and Sylvia will contribute the properties subject to the mortgage to a limited liability company. The limited liability company will assume the mortgage liability and Sylvia and Joseph will be released. Sylvia will receive, for her contribution, a 30% interest in the limited liability company. Pursuant to the limited liability company's operating agreement, Sylvia will be the managing member. Joseph also will receive a 30% interest in the limited liability company. The remaining 40% of the limited liability company will be sold to various investors in order to raise the necessary capital for expansion.

The attorney has suggested to Sylvia that, in order to make the interests in the limited liability company more saleable, it should be organized so that the outside investors have the opportunity to realize income tax losses, substantial tax-free cash distributions and no taxation on the gain inherent in the property contributed by Joseph and Sylvia. He has suggested that the following provisions be included in the limited liability company's operating agreement.

I.　The members shall share in any current distribution of cash or property made by the limited liability company in accord with their membership interests.

II.　The members shall share in a distribution or distributions of cash and/or property in liquidation of the limited liability company in the following order. First, each member shall receive the amount of his or her drawing account. Second, each member shall receive the amount of his or her capital account. Lastly, if the distribution or distributions are in excess of the total of the capital accounts of all members, each member shall share in such excess in accord with his or her interest in the limited liability company.

III.　Contributed Property

　　A.　Depreciation and gain or loss on the sale of contributed property shall be allocated for income tax purposes as follows:

1. To the members other than those who contributed the property, the amount of depreciation or gain or loss on sale computed by using the values at which the properties were contributed; and

2. To the members who contributed the property, the balance of the depreciation or the balance of the gain or loss that is allowed for income tax purposes.

B. The members realize that the income tax regulations impose a ceiling on the amount of depreciation or gain or loss on sale that may be allocated under this provision to the members other than those who contributed the property. If the ceiling applies, it is agreed that it will limit the allocation otherwise required by subsection A. above.

C. Contributed Property shall mean the property located at 641 Lincoln, 1200 Baseline, and 231 Broadway and any property which such described property is exchanged for, or converted into, in a transaction qualifying for treatment under Section 1031 or 1033 of Internal Revenue Code of 1986, as amended, provided that the adjusted basis of the property received in exchange, or into which the described property is converted, immediately after the exchange or conversion is equal to, or less than, the adjusted basis of the described property immediately before the exchange or conversion.

IV. Allocation of Expenses

Any expense, loss, deduction or credit paid or incurred by the limited liability company or to which the limited liability company is entitled, other than any such item relating to the contributed property, shall be allocated to the members who contribute cash to the limited liability company in return for their interests and their transferees, successors and assigns in accord with the percentage that each one's interest bears to 40%, so long as the total amount of such items allocated to such members and their transferees, successors and assigns and to any one thereof does not exceed the total amount of cash contributed by such members or any one thereof. All such allocations shall be subject to the following conditions:

1. When such items are so allocated, the capital account of each member receiving such an allocation shall be reduced by the amount of such items allocated to the member; and

2. When the amount of such items so allocated exceeds the total amount of cash contributed by such members, the excess shall be allocated to all members in accord with their interests.

V. Allocation of Other Income and Expenses

All items of income, gain, loss, deduction or credit, other than those specifically allocated in provisions III and IV above, shall be allocated to the members in accord with their interests.

VI. For her services as managing member and in the management of the limited liability company's investments, Sylvia Fairplay shall receive $36,000 a year or 2% of net annual cash flow from the operation of the limited liability company, whichever is greater, provided that in no event will her compensation exceed $75,000 a year.

Before finalizing the organization of the limited liability company and the transactions described above, Sylvia and Joseph have asked for your advice as a tax expert with respect to the tax effects of the above proposal. Will the proposal result in any adverse income tax effects? Do you have any suggested changes in, modifications of, or additional provisions for, the partnership agreement which will better carry out the desires of the parties?

Note:

See the Note on Limited Liability Companies following Problem 4P at page 22.

PROBLEM 8P

One of the partners in the law firm with which you are associated has given you the following letter. In your capacity as the firm's income tax expert, the partner would like your advice whether there are any income tax problems involved in carrying out the transactions described in the letter and, if there are, how those problems can be handled. She has reminded you that your analysis will form the basis of the firm's income tax opinion letter with respect to this matter.

Van Shock & Company, Inc.
187 17th Street
Denver, Colorado 80203

Emily Calhorn, Esq.
Davis, Holland & Howard, P.C.
1650 17th Street
Denver, Colorado 80203

Dear Emily:

As you know, Van Shock & Company, Inc. (Van Shock) has owned the DeNevar Building (the Building) in downtown Denver for a number of years. The Building has been recently designated a certified historic structure. The Building is in very poor condition at this point in time. In view of the growth of Denver and the demand for office space, however, Van Shock believes that with substantial rehabilitation the Building might become a very valuable rental property. Our original cost for the building was 20 million dollars. We paid 4 million dollars in cash and gave a purchase money mortgage for 16 million dollars. The purchase money mortgage was nonrecourse. The seller agreed to look solely to the Building and not to Van Shock personally for repayment of the loan. We have used the fastest rate of depreciation permitted and our present adjusted basis in the building is 8 million dollars. The present balance of the purchase money mortgage is 12 million dollars. Van Shock has caused the Building to be appraised, and its present fair market value has been determined to be 16 million dollars. Our best estimate indicates that the cost of the necessary rehabilitation will be in the neighborhood of 8 million dollars. We do not want to borrow the cost of rehabilitation, even if we could, since we feel that interest rates are too high. On the other hand, we do not want to commit 8 million dollars of our own money to one project. As a result, our financial committee has developed the following proposal.

Van Shock will contribute the Building, subject to the purchase money mortgage, to a limited liability company (the company). It will receive a capital account of 4 million dollars and be the sole managing member. It will then privately place an offering of 200 membership units at an offering price of $40,000 each, a total of 8 million dollars if the offering is fully subscribed. In order to make the purchase of the membership units attractive to investors (investor members), the following has been proposed.

All members will receive a preferred return which will be the equivalent of interest at the prime rate on the amount of their respective capital account balances existing from time to time. The first losses up to 10 million dollars will be allocated one-fifth to the managing member and four-fifths to the investor members. Any losses in excess of that amount will be allocated one-half to the managing member and one-half to the investor members. Profits will be allocated first to make up losses previously allocated. Any excess will be allocated one-third to the managing member and two-thirds to the investor members until the allocations to each member equal the amount of the member's preferred return. Finally, the remainder of any profits will be allocated one-half to the managing member and one-half to the investor members. The cash flow of the company (all the receipts of the company less cash expenses, payments of principal and interest on liabilities and appropriate reserves) will be distributed first to the managing member and investor members in the amount of the preferred return to which each is entitled. Second, any excess cash flow up to 12 million dollars will be distributed one-third to the managing member and two-thirds to the investor members. Lastly, any excess cash flow over 12 million dollars will be distributed one-half to the managing member and one-half to the investor members.

Since Van Shock has a great deal of "shelter" at the present time and therefore pays very little, if any, income tax, any tax credits to which the company is entitled because of the rehabilitation will be allocated 100% to the investor members. We plan to use the fastest depreciation rate available for the rehabilitated portion of the building and, as a result, expect the company, during the early years of the operation, to incur substantial losses for income tax purposes while having a fairly substantial positive cash flow. Van Shock plans on charging the company the following fees. For services in organizing the company and conveying the Building to it we will receive 3% of the net fair market value of the Building. For our services in supervising the rehabilitation of the building we will receive a special allocation of the first $80,000 of gross income earned by the company and the distribution of the first $80,000 of the company's cash flow. For our services in managing the operation of the company and the Building we will be paid 2% of the gross rental income received by the company. Lastly, our wholly owned subsidiary, Van Shock Securities, Inc., a registered broker-dealer, will charge the company 2% of the proceeds received from the offering of investor member interests for its services as the company's agent for the sale of the interests.

Please let me know if you have any concerns with the foregoing proposal or any advice with respect to its implementation. We would like you to begin immediately the drafting of the various documents required to carry out the proposal. I suggest we meet next week in order to exchange ideas with respect to the proposal.

Sincerely,

Sam

Samuel Kingsberry
Vice President for Development
Van Shock & Company, Inc.

Note:

See the Note on Opinion Letters following Problem 4P at page 22 and the Note on Limited Liability Companies following Problem 4P at page 22.

Part C

SALE OF A PARTNERSHIP INTEREST

PROBLEM 10P

Your client Samuel Cooper (Sam) has been negotiating with Sarna Klein (Sarna) in hopes of buying her partnership interest in Hot Tubs & Spas Co. (Hot Tubs). Hot Tubs was formed about three years ago by Sarna, Penny Jacklin, Harvey Linderman and Ray Cassart (collectively the partners). The partners each contributed, in cash, one-quarter of the capital required to start the business, and each owns a one-quarter interest in the profits, losses, and capital of Hot Tubs. There have been no transfers of partnership interests, no partners have died and no special allocations have been made. In every year each partner has received the same cash distribution as every other partner, and such cash distribution has always been less than the recipient partner's share of the profits of the partnership for the year involved. The balance sheet of Hot Tubs showing the range of the fair market values of its assets is set out at the end of this problem. Sam recently received the following letter from Sarna.

Sarna Klein
418 Painter
Prescott, Arizona
April 23, Year*

Mr. Samuel Cooper
1711 17th Street
Phoenix, Arizona

Dear Sam:

I have given some thought to our last conversation with respect to your purchase of my partnership interest in Hot Tubs. I agree with you that a fair price for my partnership interest is $69,000. This price results in a value for the assets of the partnership of $276,000.

* See explanatory footnote in Introduction, page vii, note 1.

37

If I were to sell my partnership interest to you for $69,000, I would expect the purchase price to be paid in the following manner. Fourteen thousand dollars would be paid by your assumption of my share of partnership payables and liabilities. The remaining $55,000 would be paid $13,000 in cash at closing and your note in the amount of $42,000, secured by a pledge of the partnership interest and an irrevocable letter of credit, payable in four equal installments of principal and interest at 12% over the four years following the year in which the closing occurs. I prefer receiving the purchase price in installments, as described above, since this will permit me to spread my income tax liability over the five year period, rather than having a great deal of income tax to pay in the year of sale.

In arriving at the $276,000 value of the assets of the partnership and the $69,000 purchase price of my interest, I determined the value of each of the assets of the partnership and the value of my interest in each of the assets. Obviously, the value of the cash is $16,000, and the value of my interest is $4,000. I feel that the value of the installment obligations is $72,000, and the value of my interest therein is $18,000. In my opinion the value of the inventory is $100,000, and the value of my interest therein is $25,000. The value of the furniture and fixtures appears to me to be $56,000, and the value of my interest therein is $14,000. Lastly, I believe that the value of goodwill is $32,000, and the value of my interest therein is $8,000.

If you are in substantial agreement with the understandings and opinions stated in this letter, please let me know. As soon as I hear from you in the affirmative, I will ask my attorney to prepare an agreement providing for your purchase of my partnership interest based on the terms, conditions and understandings expressed herein.

> Sincerely,
>
> *Sarna*
>
> Sarna Klein

Sam has shown you Sarna's letter and asked you to give him your opinion whether he should accept this offer. He has advised you that the suggested purchase price for Sarna's interest seems fair to him. Please advise Sam of any changes which you feel must be made in the terms, conditions and understandings expressed in the letter and any additional items you feel must be added from Sam's standpoint. Please tell Sam the reasons for your suggestions.

Balance Sheet of Hot Tubs & Spas Co.[1]

Assets
(x 1000)

	Adjusted Basis	Fair Market Value Range	
Cash	$ 16	$ 16 -	$ 16
Installment Obligations[2]	64	72 -	80
Inventory	80	88 -	104
Furniture & Fixtures cost 110			
dep. (62)[3]	48	56 -	64
Goodwill	0	24 -	32
	$208	$256	$296

Liabilities
(x 1000)

	Adjusted Basis	Fair Market Value Range	
Trade Accounts Payable[4]	$ 16	$ 16 -	$ 16
Long Term Liability	40	40 -	40
Capital Accounts			
Sarna Klein	38	50 -	60
Penny Jacklin	38	50 -	60
Harvey Linderman	38	50 -	60
Ray Cassart	38	50 -	60
	$208	$256	$296

---

1. The balance sheet is prepared using, in general, the accrual method of accounting.

2. The company has elected to use the installment method as the method of accounting for receivables derived from sales of inventory.

3. Depreciation is computed using the most accelerated method available.

4. Trade accounts payable are accounted for using the accrual method.

Note:

Negotiation

Much of a lawyer's time is spent in negotiation. The suggestions below, although made in the context of formal negotiation, may at times also be useful in informal negotiation engaged in by a lawyer.

Whether the client should be present is an important determination. The client may insist that he conduct the negotiation and simply have you present to advise him. It is, however, ordinarily much wiser for the lawyer to be the negotiator, and there are considerations against having the client present. The client is generally inexperienced in negotiation techniques and may be unaware of the legal consequences of his statements. His absence will shield him from heated controversies and may allow him to preserve a good relationship with the other side. Finally, if he is not there you may have more flexibility, for example, being able to say, "I'll present it to my client, but I doubt that he'll agree."

Learning the other party's limits, expectations and priorities without disclosing yours is advantageous. You can make proposals in the other party's area of acceptability at minimum cost to you or gain leverage by conceding something which matters a lot to the other party but little to you. Disclosures by the other side can be prompted by statements such as "You're the one trying to make the sale" or "You're the one who wants to acquire the assets." Information can be obtained by talking to persons with whom the other party has dealt or by checking public records for prices and interest rates in earlier transactions.

The agenda of items to be negotiated is important, particularly if additional items may not be added once the negotiation has begun. If a party controls the agenda, items that the other party wishes to include may be excluded or discussed in the most helpful order resulting in substantial concessions even before bargaining begins. One of the simplest ways to achieve this control is to present the first draft of an agreement or other key document. This places on the other party the burden of justifying additions to, or changes in, the proposed format. Each time a proposed departure is agreed to, it may be regarded as a concession on your part which will help justify your demands in other areas.

It is best that your first offer be realistic, although it may still be far from the minimum you will accept. This produces professional respect which will be advantageous for the remainder of the negotiation. It also generally establishes your limits, giving credibility to any subsequent statements that there will be no further concessions. There may be gain in bargaining power from successful assertion of a false demand, but there are also risks. Your opponent may agree to the demand to compel you to make a concession in return.

A good settlement involves consideration of the total package. For example, agreements concerning future competition by, or employment of, the seller may do much to make the sale of a business acceptable. But successful culmination of the negotiation is enhanced if agreement on the fundamentals is achieved first. Early disagreement about minor points may create antagonisms which will interfere with later agreement on fundamentals, whereas early agreement on fundamentals will provide a favorable climate for later agreement on less significant points.

Recognition of the other party's relationship with those he represents is important. A statement in the presence of his clients that an attorney has stated the law incorrectly is likely to produce antagonism rather than an acknowledgment of error. If possible, suggest to the other party alternatives to his unacceptable resolutions. If the other party is having trouble convincing his client that the client's demands are unrealistic, your indirect help may be appreciated.

Threats may produce leverage but will work only if the other party is convinced you are not bluffing. A bluff is effective only if it is credible, and a reputation for carrying through on threats will increase your credibility, whereas the repeated use of idle threats may be counterproductive.

Be aware of the tactics used by the other party. For example the other party is usually not protecting your interests against an overly aggressive cohort of his. Your appraisal of the progress of the negotiation should not be affected by apparent disagreements between persons on the other side. Do not be taken in by the other party's desire to use a standard form if the meaning of each and every provision of the form is not clear or acceptable to you. In short, be sure you understand everything to which you agree.

PROBLEM 11P

Glenns Candy Company (Glenns), a limited liability partnership, is one of your firm's best clients. It was formed twenty years ago by Mabel Adamson (Mabel), Vince Rigone (Vince) and Clayton Childs (Clayton), and its registration as a limited liability partnership was filed last year. Each partner contributed, in cash, one-third of the capital needed to start the business. The partnership agreement, prepared by your firm, provides that Mabel, Vince and Clayton each own a one-third interest in capital, profits and losses. The partnership agreement does not contain any provisions dealing with the procedure to be followed upon the death or withdrawal of a partner. To the best of the knowledge of your associates, there have not been any special allocations of income, gain, loss, deduction or credit made by the partnership, nor have there been any transfers of part, or all, of a partnership interest. The foregoing has been confirmed to you by the partners in Glenns who have further advised you that each year each partner withdraws an equal amount in cash, the total of such withdrawals never exceeding the total profits for that year.

  Glenns is a manufacturer, wholesaler and retailer of various kinds of boxed candies. It accounts on the accrual method for income tax and financial accounting purposes. It reports for income tax purposes on the calendar year. The balance sheet of Glenns, including an approximation of the range within which the fair market value of each of its assets would fall, follows.

GLENNS CANDY COMPANY
Assets

	Adjusted Basis (x 1000)	Approximate Fair Market Value (x 1000)	
Cash	$ 30	$ 30	- $ 30
Accounts Receivable	42	42	- 42
Inventory	42	54	- 60
Machinery and Equipment Cost $100 Dep. (40)*	60	68	- 74
Building Cost $240 Dep. (108)**	132	142	- 154
Land	90	110	- 118
Goodwill	-	74	- 82
	$396	$520	- $560

Liabilities and Capital

	Per Books (x 1000)	Approximate Fair Market Value (x 1000)	
Accounts Payable	$ 24	$ 24	- $ 24
Mortgage on Land and Building	120	120	- 120
Capital	252	376	- 416
	$396	$520	- $560

 * Depreciation on the machinery and equipment has been taken using the most accelerated rate available.

 ** Depreciation on the building has been taken using the straight-line method.

Vince, who is getting on in years, would like to sell his partnership interest. Roberta Johnson (Roberta), who has a background in the manufacture and sale of boxed candies, is interested in purchasing it, and Mabel and Clayton have agreed that they will consent to the sale. Vince and Roberta have tentatively agreed on $540,000 as the value of the assets of the partnership and that Roberta will pay Vince $180,000 for his interest. Roberta will pay the purchase price by assuming Vince's share of partnership liabilities in the amount of $48,000 and giving him her note for $132,000 bearing interest at 13% per annum, payable in three equal annual installments and secured by a security interest in the partnership interest. Subsequent to reaching the tentative agreement with Roberta described above, Vince received an agreement prepared by Roberta's attorney providing, among other things, the following:

1. Payment for Capital Interest

1.01. Roberta agrees to pay Vince $120,000 for Vince's capital interest in Glenns Candy Company (partnership).

1.02. Roberta's payment to Vince of the $120,000 referred to in Section 1.01 hereof and the $12,000 referred to in Section 3.03 hereof shall be made by delivering to Vince, at closing, Roberta's note for $132,000 bearing interest at the rate of 13% per annum, payable in three equal annual installments. Payment of the note shall be secured by a security interest in the partnership interest purchased. Roberta shall deliver to Vince, at closing, a security agreement providing for the security interest described in this Section. The note and security agreement shall be in the form attached hereto and marked Exhibits A and B.

2. Assumption of Partnership Liabilities

2.01. In addition to the payment for Vince's capital interest, as described in Section 1.01 hereof, Roberta will assume Vince's position as a partner with respect to partnership liabilities and indemnify and hold Vince harmless against any such liabilities.

2.02. The partnership has total liabilities of $144,000, and Vince's share of such liabilities (which Roberta will assume pursuant to Section 2.01 hereof) is $48,000.

2.03.   At closing, Roberta will deliver to Vince an assumption and indemnification agreement, in the form attached hereto and marked Exhibit C, providing for the assumption by Roberta of, and the indemnification of Vince against, the liabilities as described in Section 2.02 hereof.

3. Covenant Not to Compete

3.01. Vince recognizes that the amount to be paid by Roberta under Article 1 hereof includes a payment for Vince's share of the goodwill of the partnership.

3.02. In order to insure that Roberta receives the full benefit of the share of goodwill purchased, Vince agrees that for a period of three years following the date of closing, he will not engage in the manufacture or sale, at wholesale or retail, of boxed candies in competition with the partnership within 150 miles of the present location of the head office of the partnership.

3.03.   Roberta agrees to pay Vince $12,000 for this agreement not to compete with the partnership.

3.04. At closing, such agreement not to compete shall be delivered in the form attached hereto and marked Exhibit D.

4. Purchase Price of Vince's Partnership Interest and Covenant Not to Compete

4.01.   For federal income tax purposes the purchase price of Vince's partnership interest and covenant not to compete is $180,000 (the sum of the payments Roberta is to make under Article 1 and Article 3 hereof plus Vince's share of partnership liabilities which Roberta is to assume under Article 2).

5. Allocation of Purchase Price to Vince's Share of Partnership Assets and His Covenant Not to Compete

5.01. It is agreed that the $180,000 purchase price of Vince's interest in the partnership and his covenant not to compete shall be allocated (for federal income tax and accounting purposes) to Vince's one-third interest in the assets of the partnership and Vince's covenant not to compete as follows:

	Agreed Value of Asset (x 1000)	Portion of Purchase Price Allocated to Asset (x 1000)
Cash	$ 30	$ 10
Accounts Receivable	42	14
Inventory	60	20
Machinery & Equipment	72	24
Building	150	50
Land	111	37
Goodwill	39	13
Covenant Not to Compete	36	12
	$540	$180

5.02. Roberta and Vince make the allocation set out in Section 5.01 with the knowledge and understanding that it will be used by both Roberta and Vince for federal income tax and accounting purposes. Roberta and Vince declare that the values and the allocation of the purchase price set out in Section 5.01 were determined in good faith in arm's length bargaining.

5.03. Roberta and Vince agree that the purchase of Vince's partnership interest and covenant not to compete will be reported by each for federal income tax purposes in accordance with the values and allocation set out in Section 5.01 and that neither will take a position inconsistent therewith, except with the written consent of the other. However, if the Internal Revenue Service takes a position with respect to either Roberta or Vince that is inconsistent with the values or allocation in Section 5.01, the other party may take a protective position adopting the Internal Revenue Service's contention until the controversy is finally resolved.

* * *

Vince has asked you to represent him with respect to the sale. He has delivered to you the agreement prepared by Roberta's attorney and the current balance sheet of Glenns, both as set out above.

A. Fully advise Vince of the income tax results to him if he sells his partnership interest to Roberta on the terms and conditions provided in the agreement prepared by Roberta's attorney.

B.   Fully advise Vince of the changes you would propose in the agreement prepared by Roberta's attorney in order to produce the best income tax results for Vince. You are to assume that neither Roberta nor Vince will accept a value greater or less than $540,000 for the assets of the partnership, or a purchase price greater or less than $180,000 for Vince's partnership interest, and that other than Roberta's assumption of liabilities, the purchase price is to be paid in installments.

Note:

See the Note on Negotiation following Problem 10P at page 40, the Note on Limited Liability Partnerships following Problem 2P at page 10, and the Note on Legal Drafting following Problem 3P at page 15.

PROBLEM 12P

Quite to everyone's dismay, prior to the execution of any agreement for the sale of Vince's partnership interest to Roberta as described in Problem 11P, Vince passed on to the great candy maker in the sky. Vince's cousin, Helen Fuzak (Helen), has been appointed the executrix of his estate and is his sole heir. Roberta still desires to purchase the partnership interest, and her attorney has submitted to Helen, as executrix and sole heir, substantially the same purchase agreement set forth in Problem 11P. The only changes are: (1) the provisions relating to the covenant not to compete have been deleted; (2) the value ascribed to the covenant, $36,000, and the amount of the purchase price allocated to the covenant, $12,000, have been eliminated; (3) the value of goodwill has been increased to $75,000; and (4) the amount of the purchase price allocated to goodwill has been increased to $25,000. The balance sheet of Glenns remains as set out in Problem 11P.

A.   Advise Helen of the income tax results to her and the estate if the partnership interest is sold to Roberta on the terms and conditions provided in the agreement prepared by Roberta's attorney.

B.   Advise Helen of the changes you would propose in the agreement prepared by Roberta's attorney in order to produce the best income tax results for Helen and the estate. You are to assume that Roberta and Helen will not agree on a value greater or less than $540,000 for the assets of the partnership, or a purchase price greater or less than $180,000 for the partnership interest, and that, other than Roberta's assumption of liabilities, the purchase price is to be paid in installments.

Note:

See the Note on Negotiation following Problem 10P at page 40, and the Note on Limited Liability Partnerships following Problem 2P at page 10.

PROBLEM 13P

The firm with which you are associated has been representing Dr. Joyce Blanchard in the sale of her interest in Bettervision Lens, L.L.C. Bettervision Lens, L.L.C. manufactures and sells to optometrists and ophthalmologists extended-wear soft contact lenses. The company was formed by Dr. Blanchard and five of her colleagues to exploit a patent for extended-wear soft contact lenses which they had acquired from a German company. The negotiations for the sale of Dr. Blanchard's interest have been completed. Dr. Blanchard has asked that your firm send her a letter of advice informing her of the income tax aspects of the sale of her interest. Winfred Dawkins, an associate in the tax department of your firm, has prepared a draft of the letter of advice. You have been asked to review it before the firm mails it to the client.

Klein, Bettis, Hirschbacher & Bingler
Suite 4300
1801 Center Street
Minneapolis, MN   55255

November, 16 Year*

Joyce Blanchard, M.D.
1470 Old South Road
St. Paul, MN   55119

Dear Dr. Blanchard:

You have asked that we advise you of the income tax effects to you resulting from your sale of your interest in Bettervision Lens, L.L.C. (Bettervision). It is our understanding that you and five colleagues formed

---

* See explanatory footnote in Introduction, page vii, note 1.

Bettervision as a limited liability company a few years ago. Bettervision was formed to exploit a patent for extended-wear soft contact lenses which you and your colleagues acquired from a German concern. Each of you contributed, in cash, one-sixth of the necessary capital and each one acquired a one-sixth interest in profits and losses. Until your recent sale there have been no transfers of membership interests, no distributions of assets other than cash have been made, no members have died, no special allocations have been made, and each member has, in every year, received the same cash distribution as every other member. Finally, such cash distribution has always been less than the member's share of Bettervision's profits for that year.

You have sold your one-sixth interest in Bettervision to Dr. Thelma Rycus. The agreed upon purchase price of your interest was $200,000. The $200,000 was paid by: 1) $20,000 in cash at closing; 2) $80,000 by acquiring your interest subject to your share of the liabilities of Bettervision; and 3) $100,000 by means of Dr. Rycus's personal note which was secured by the pledge of the acquired interest and was payable over five years at $20,000 per year plus interest at 10% per annum. The purchase agreement allocated the purchase price among the assets of Bettervision as follows: 1) $5,000 to your interest in cash; 2) $10,000 to your interest in accounts receivable; 3) $30,000 to your interest in inventory; 4) $35,000 to your interest in furniture, fixtures and equipment; 5) $60,000 to your interest in the manufacturing plant; 6) $30,000 to your interest in land; 7) $20,000 to your interest in goodwill and $10,000 of the purchase price to a covenant by you not to compete with Bettervision for the next five years. You have provided us with a current balance sheet of Bettervision which shows the adjusted basis of its assets, its liabilities and the fair market value range in which its assets fall. We have attached that balance sheet to this letter.

In determining a taxpayer's gain from the sale of an interest in a limited liability company, the taxpayer's basis in her membership interest must first be determined. Section 705 of the Internal Revenue Code of 1986, as amended (hereinafter we will refer to sections of the Code simply as sections) provides that a taxpayer's basis in her membership interest is determined by taking into account a number of adjustments on a varying year-to-year basis. Section 705(b), however, permits us to use the total basis of company assets in order to determine your basis in your membership interest. Therefore, dividing the total company basis of $840,000 by six results in a basis for your membership interest of $140,000. Subtracting that basis from the $200,000 purchase price of your interest results in your recognition of $60,000 of total gain on the sale of your interest under Section 1001(a). The next step we must take is to determine how much of this $60,000 of gain is going to be treated as ordinary income and how much is going to be treated as capital gain.

In determining how much of your gain is capital gain and how much ordinary income, one must take account of the assets of the limited liability company which are treated as "hot" assets under Section 751. For the purposes of this letter, "hot" assets are those assets which produce ordinary income on the sale of a membership interest. "Hot" assets usually include accounts receivable, substantially appreciated inventory and depreciation recapture. Since Bettervision uses the accrual method of accounting all the income from its accounts receivable is taken into income when the account arises, subject to only a bad debt reserve. Since all of the income from Bettervision's accounts receivable has been taken into income, the accounts receivable are not treated as "hot" assets. The test to determine whether inventory is substantially appreciated is whether its value exceeds 120% of its basis. Based on the value given the inventory in the purchase agreement, the value of the inventory does exceed 120% of its basis. Therefore, since your share of the inventory basis is $23,000 you will recognize $7,000 of ordinary income on the sale of your membership interest. As mentioned above, the other "hot" asset is depreciation recapture. In your case, Bettervision has depreciation recapture on both furniture, fixtures and equipment and on the manufacturing plant. Since your share of Bettervision's basis for furniture, fixtures and equipment is $25,000, you will recognize $10,000 of ordinary income from this asset on the sale of your membership interest. Likewise, since your share of Bettervision's basis in the manufacturing plant is $52,000, you will recognize $8,000 of ordinary income from this asset on the sale of your membership interest. The sum of the ordinary income resulting on the sale of your membership interest derived through Section 751 is $25,000. Therefore, since your total gain is $60,000, $35,000 of your gain will be treated as capital gain. We regard the amount paid for your covenant not to compete as simply an additional price for your share of goodwill. Therefore, it is not ordinary income to you.

In addition to determining the nature of your gain from the sale of your membership interest, we also should advise you with respect to the amount of your gain which can be reported using the installment method, since a substantial portion of the purchase price will be paid by Dr. Rycus's personal note. Initially, one-sixth of the gain (both capital gain and ordinary income) must be recognized on receipt of the $20,000 in cash. In addition, we must determine whether any of the ordinary income resulting from the sale cannot be reported using the installment method. All capital gain derived from the sale can be reported using the installment method. Therefore, one-sixth of the capital gain should be recognized by you in each year when you receive Dr. Rycus's payment. It appears that the ordinary income which is derived from depreciation recapture cannot be reported using the installment method. Section 453(i) so provides. Therefore, you will have to recognize the $18,000 of ordinary income derived from depreciation recapture in this year. There is not, however, a similar provision with respect to the ordinary income derived from the inventory. While income derived from the sale of inventory cannot be reported using the installment method as provided by Section 453(b), you are selling a membership interest in Bettervision and therefore the $7,000 of ordinary income derived from the inventory can be reported using the installment method. Finally, if you had derived any ordinary income from the disposition of your share of Bettervision's accounts receivable, that ordinary income could not be reported using the installment method. There appears to be no provision in the Internal Revenue Code which requires any different result.

After you have carefully read this letter, we should set up a meeting to discuss its contents. Please call the undersigned when you feel you are prepared for this meeting and we will schedule a meeting at the earliest possible date.

Sincerely yours,

Klein, Bettis, Hirschbacher & Bingler

by

Winfred Dawkins

Winfred Dawkins

Balance Sheet of Bettervision Lens, L.L.C.[1]
Assets (x 1000)

	Adjusted Basis	Fair Market Value Range		
Cash	$ 30	$ 30	-	$ 30
Accounts Receivable[2]	54	56	-	64
Inventory of Lenses	138	176	-	184
Furniture, Fixtures				
and Equipment $250				
(Depreciation)[3] (100)	150	190	-	230
Manufacturing Plant 460				
(Depreciation)[4] (150)	310	340	-	380
Land	158	170	-	190
Goodwill	0	178	-	182
	$840	$1140		$1260

Liabilities (x 1000)

	Adjusted Basis	Fair Market Value Range		
Trade Accounts Payable	60	60	-	60
Working Capital Term Loan	180	180	-	180
Mortgage Loan on Plant and Land	240	240	-	240
Partners' Capital Account	360	660	-	780
	$840	$1140		$1260

1. The company uses the accrual method of accounting.

2. The face amount of the accounts receivable is $64,000. The bad debt reserve is $10,000.

3. Furniture, fixtures and equipment have been depreciated using an accelerated method.

4. The manufacturing plant has been depreciated using the straight-line method.

Note:

See the Note on Limited Liability Companies following Problem 4P at page 22 and the Note on Opinion Letters following Problem 4P at page 22.

Part D

PARTNERSHIP DISTRIBUTIONS

---

1. DISTRIBUTIONS NOT IN REDUCTION OF A PARTNER'S INTEREST

PROBLEM 14P

With the normalization of trade and diplomatic relations in Asia, three of your good clients took advantage of the opportunity to engage in some profitable transactions in Asian art objects (art objects). The three clients pooled their resources in a general partnership (The Partnership) to exploit the potential market for art objects. The three clients are: (1) Hiram Walker (Hiram), an art dealer who buys and sells art objects as an occupation; (2) Indira Garratt (Indira), who is the owner of an art gallery and makes her living on the amounts she charges to exhibit art objects in her gallery and the commissions made on art objects which are sold when on exhibit in her gallery; and (3) Fredrick Tomarees (Fred), a well-to-do art connoisseur who is a partner in an investment banking firm.

During the last five years Hiram, Indira and Fred have sent three expeditions to Asia, led by Hiram, in order to locate and acquire various Asian art objects. Fred provided the start-up financing for the expeditions, Hiram provided his services to lead the expeditions, and Indira contributed the use of her gallery to store, display and sell the art objects to customers in the United States. Each one also contributed $20,000 to The Partnership. The $60,000 was used for the general overhead of The Partnership and certain equipment.

The Partnership has been quite successful. The balance sheet of The Partnership, which also shows the fair market value of its assets, is set out below. The participants are quite pleased with the success of The Partnership and have decided that they would like to continue working with each other in the business of selling art objects. They, however, would like to diversify into other than Asian art objects. In order to do this the participants feel they must reduce The Partnership's inventory of Asian art objects.

Hiram is willing to take $40,000 in fair market value of the remaining inventory as part of his share of The Partnership's profits since he feels that he has the contacts necessary to dispose of this part of the inventory. Fred is also willing to take $40,000 in fair market value of the remaining inventory as part of his share of The Partnership's profits since he would like to use the inventory to decorate the stately country mansion he recently acquired. Indira does not want any of the remaining inventory. Since the distribution of inventory by The Partnership to Hiram and Fred will sufficiently reduce The Partnership's inventory, the participants have agreed that The Partnership should distribute $40,000 of cash to Indira in order to equalize the distributions made to the participants.

Fred, Hiram and Indira have asked you whether there are income tax consequences to them as a result of the distributions described above. Please advise your clients with respect to the income tax effects of the proposed distributions.

Balance Sheet of the Partnership[1]

Assets
(x 1000)

		Adjusted Basis	Fair Market Value
Cash		$ 60	$ 60
Inventory of art objects		120	200
Equipment: cost	40		
dep.[2]	(28)	12	20
Goodwill[3]		18	20
		$210	$300

Liabilities
(x 1000)

	Adjusted Basis	Fair Market Value
Trade accounts payable	$ 30	$ 30
Capital accounts		
Hiram Walker	60	90
Indira Garratt	60	90
Frederick Tomarees	60	90
	$210	$300

1. The Partnership uses the accrual method of accounting.
2. Depreciation is computed using the most accelerated method available.
3. This amount represents the nondeductible cost to The Partnership of certain customer lists.

Note:

See the Note on Interviewing and Client Counseling following Problem 1P at page 4 and the Note on Representing More Than One Party following Problem 2P at page 9.

PROBLEM 15P

Seapines Investment Partnership (Seapines) is a general partnership which invests in securities and real estate and holds its assets for use in trade or business or for investment rather than for sale to customers in the ordinary course of business. Seapines was formed about five years ago by four individuals. Joan Cellicky (Joan) is a securities trader and dealer and an investment adviser. Joan buys and sells securities for her own account and for the accounts of her customers. Homer Pagenel (Homer) is a real estate developer, dealer and agent. Homer buys, sells and develops various kinds of commercial real estate projects for his own account and for the accounts of his clients. Sarah Wellington (Sarah), Joan's and Homer's lawyer, is a general practitioner. Sarah's only investments in securities and real estate have been made through Seapines. The fourth partner is Marc Stewart, M.D. (Marc), a psychiatrist, who is a friend of Sarah's. Like Sarah, Marc's only investments in securities and real estate have been made through Seapines.

Each of the four partners contributed the same amount of cash to Seapines. The partnership agreement provides that the partners each have: (i) the same initial capital accounts; (ii) a one-quarter interest in profits and losses; (iii) the right to receive one-quarter of the value of any distribution made by Seapines; and (iv) the right to receive the amount then in their capital accounts on dissolution and termination of Seapines. Until this year the partners followed the provisions of the partnership agreement with respect to the sharing of profits and losses and distributions of Seapines.

This year, as a result of a drop in the market price of securities personally owned by Joan, which were pledged as collateral for certain bank loans to her, the amount of her bank loans substantially exceeded the value of the securities pledged as collateral. The bank threatened to call the loans if Joan did not adequately secure them with a pledge of additional securities. As a result, Joan has asked the other three partners if they would agree to a distribution by Seapines to Joan of about three-fourths of the securities held by Seapines. The other partners have agreed to the distribution to Joan if, in later years when the financial condition of Seapines so permits, Sarah and

Marc can each receive an equivalent distribution of cash or securities or both and Homer can receive an equivalent distribution of real estate or cash or both. The balance sheet of Seapines, prior to the distribution to Joan, appears below.

Sarah, whose practice in the income tax area is very limited, has prepared the following amendment to the partnership agreement of Seapines to reflect the agreement of the partners described above. She would like your advice with respect to the income tax effects if the amendment to the partnership agreement is carried out as written and your suggestions for any changes or additions to the amendment.

Amendment to
the
Partnership Agreement
of
Seapines
* * *

1.   Section 5.1 of Article V dealing with current distributions of money and property shall be amended by adding the following to the end thereof:

Notwithstanding the foregoing, the following distributions of money or property may be made by the Partnership:

(a) $300,000 in value of securities may be distributed to Joan Cellicky during the Partnership's fiscal year ending December 31, Year*; and

(b)   Upon the agreement of all Partners, which will not be unreasonably withheld, that the financial condition of the Partnership permits such distribution or distributions, the following distributions may be made in any fiscal year or years of the Partnership following the year ending December 31, Year: (i) $300,000 in cash or value of securities or both to each of Sarah Wellington and Marc Stewart and (ii) $300,000 in cash or value of real estate or both to Homer Pagenel.

2.   Section 8.3 of Article VIII dealing with the distribution of the assets of the Partnership on its dissolution and termination shall be amended by adding the following to the end thereof:

---

* See explanatory footnote in Introduction, page vii, note 1.

Notwithstanding the foregoing, if any or all of Sarah Wellington, Marc Stewart or Homer Pagenel have not, prior to dissolution and termination, received the distributions described in Section 1.(b) above, such distributions shall be made prior to the distribution of Partnership assets to the Partners in accord with the amounts then in their capital accounts.

* * *

Balance Sheet of Seapines General Partnership

Assets
(x 1000)

		Basis	Fair Market Value
Cash		$ 100	$ 100
Certificates of Deposit		400	400
Marketable Securities		200	400
Medical Office Building			
Cost	$500		
Depreciation	(150*)	350	450
Dental Office Building			
Cost	$400		
Depreciation	(150*)	250	350
		$1,300	$1,700

Liabilities
(x 1000)

	Basis	Fair Market Value
Term Loan	$ 300	$ 300
Mortgage Loan on Medical Office Building	150	150
Mortgage Loan on Dental Office Building	50	50
Capital Accounts		
Joan Cellicky	200	300
Sarah Wellington	200	300
Homer Pagenel	200	300
Marc Stewart	200	300
	$1,300	$1,700

* Depreciation is computed using the most accelerated method available.

Note:

See the Note on Legal Drafting following Problem 3P at page 15 and the Note on Representing More Than One Party following Problem 2P at page 9.

2. DISTRIBUTIONS IN REDUCTION OF A PARTNER'S INTEREST

PROBLEM 16P

The chair of the tax department in the firm with which you are associated recently received the memorandum set out below from one of the partners in the business department of the firm. The chair of the tax department of the firm has given you the memorandum and asked you to determine the income tax consequences to each of the individuals described in the memorandum resulting from the transactions proposed in the memorandum. The chair of the tax department would like the research done as quickly as possible, since she intends to meet with the individuals in the next two to three days.

Barnes, Reitmeister, Yoshira & Klein
1540 Clubhouse Drive
Davenport, IA   52803

Intraoffice Memo

TO: Amy Garcia

FROM: Arthur Barnes

RE: Reorganization of Shears and Hamilton

We have for a number of years represented Shears and Hamilton, L.L.P. (the partnership), which is a small securities brokerage firm located in Burlington, Iowa. The partnership was formed by Wayland Shears and Thomas Hamilton a number of years ago. Just last year we registered the partnership with the Secretary of State in order to obtain limited liability partnership status. Wayland and Thomas each contributed, in cash, one-half of the capital needed to start the business. The partnership agreement provides that Wayland and Thomas each own a one-half interest in capital profits and losses. There have never been any special allocations of income, gain, loss, deduction or credit, nor has there ever been a transfer of part, or all, of a partnership interest. Each year Wayland and Thomas have withdrawn equal amounts of cash from the partnership, and the total of such withdrawals during any year has never exceeded the total of profits of the partnership for that year.

The partnership buys and sells stock and securities on behalf of customers of the firm. It also buys and sells stock and securities for its own account. The partnership's place of business is located on the ground floor of a small office building which it owns in Burlington. The partnership uses the accrual method of accounting for income tax purposes. It uses the straight-line method to depreciate its depreciable property. The balance sheet of the partnership, at the end of its most recent fiscal year, is attached to this memorandum.

Although the partnership has been quite profitable over the years, Wayland and Thomas feel that its profitability could be increased if a membership on the Midwest Stock Exchange (the Exchange) could be obtained. This would permit the partnership to buy and sell directly on the Exchange floor rather than having to pay a member of the Exchange to execute transactions on its behalf. Membership on the Exchange is quite hard to obtain. Wayland and Thomas, however, heard that Evan Lincoln, an older Iowa City stock broker who has a seat on the Exchange, was interested in associating with a firm since the demands of his sole proprietorship were becoming more extensive than he desired.

After some negotiations, Evan advised Wayland and Thomas that he would like a one-third interest in the partnership in return for: (1) his seat on the Exchange, value—$34,000, basis—$12,000; (2) the small office building he owns in Iowa City, gross value—$180,000, cost—$120,000, adjusted basis—$48,000, subject to a mortgage liability of $100,000 which the partnership would assume; and (3) his office equipment and furniture, value—$36,000, cost—$44,000, adjusted basis—$12,000. Evan has used the straight-line method to depreciate the office building, equipment and furniture. The net value of Evan's proposed contribution to the partnership is $150,000. The partnership would move its head office to Iowa City and use the ground floor of Evan's office building for its place of business, combining the partnership's equipment and furniture with Evan's.

Wayland and Thomas are in agreement with Evan's proposal. They propose to do the following so that each partner's net contribution will be equal to the $150,000 in net value which Evan is contributing. First, the partnership will distribute $80,000 in cash to Thomas and the Burlington office building and land to Wayland. The building and land will be distributed subject to the mortgage liability which Wayland will assume and from which the partnership will be released. Wayland has been active in the real estate business in Burlington and feels certain he can secure tenants for the building. Second, Evan will contribute his assets to the partnership. The partnership will assume the mortgage liability on the Iowa City building. Evan will receive, in return, a one-third interest in the capital, profits and losses of the partnership. Lastly, the partnership's head office will be moved to Iowa City.

As soon as you can, please advise me of the income tax consequences to Wayland, Thomas and Evan if the proposal is carried out as described.

Shears and Hamilton, L.L.P.
Assets
(x 1000)

		Basis	Fair Market Value
Cash		$ 90	$ 90
Accounts Receivable		20	30
Inventory Securities		90	270
Equipment & Furniture	Cost $ 60		
	Dep. (40)	20	40
Office Building	Cost 260		
	Dep. (80)	180	240
Office Building — Land		40	60
Total		$440	$730

Liabilities
(x 1000)

	Book	Fair Market Value
Accounts Payable	$ 50	$ 50
Mortgage Liability on Office Building and Land	220	220
Capital		
Wayland Shears	85	230
Thomas Hamilton	85	230
Total	$440	$730

Note:

See the Note on Representing More Than One Party following Problem 2P at page 9.

PROBLEM 17P

The chair of the tax department of the firm with which you are associated has given you the following memorandum which he received from one of the partners in the real estate department of the firm. He would like your advice with respect to the questions raised in the memo. He expects your advice within a couple of days.

Spain, Denver, Avter & Liscow

Intra-Office Memorandum

TO: James T. McDuff

FROM: Cynthia Browner

RE: Reorganization of Regent Partnership

As you know, we have represented Alvise and Matilda Regent ("Alvise and Matilda") for a number of years. Alvise's principal occupation has been that of a commercial real estate dealer and developer. She has bought, sold, and developed, over the years, a number of office buildings, apartment houses and shopping plazas. Every now and then she came across a development which she felt had long-term investment potential. In such a case, she informed her sister, Matilda, who is a doctor. If Matilda also thought the development had long-term investment potential, the sisters would obtain some financing, which was usually nonrecourse, and acquire the development.

We drafted the partnership agreement for Regent Partnership which was the entity Alvise and Matilda used to acquire the long-term investments. The partnership agreement was straightforward. Alvise and Matilda each owned a 50% interest in profits, losses, and cash flow distributions. They each maintained equal amounts of capital in the partnership and each had an equal voice in the operation of the partnership. They split equally the responsibilities of operating the partnership and the developments it owned.

Recently, however, both Alvise and Matilda have found that the operation of the partnership and its developments takes a great deal more time than they want to devote to it. They have made the acquaintance of a young person, Dana Lozano ("Dana"), who has had a short but very successful career as a real estate dealer and developer. Dana is interested in becoming a partner in the Regent Partnership and assuming the responsibility for the operation of the partnership and its developments. Dana would like to acquire a one-third interest in the partnership. Alvise and Matilda think highly of Dana and are willing to have her acquire this interest and take over the operation of the partnership and its developments. They also would like to change the form of the partnership to a limited partnership with Dana as general partner and themselves as limited partners.

We are considering three alternative ways of reorganizing the partnership. First, Dana could purchase 50% of Alvise's interest and 50% of Matilda's interest. She would pay each sister $125,000 in cash and give each a personal, recourse note for $125,000 bearing a fair market interest rate and payable in equal installments of principal and interest over the next five years. The notes would be secured by a pledge of the purchased partnership interests. Second, Regent Partnership could borrow $250,000 from a bank; the value of the partnership's assets is well in excess of its liabilities. The partnership could then redeem 50% of Alvise's interest and 50% of Matilda's interest by paying each sister $125,000 in cash and giving each the partnership's recourse note for $125,000 bearing a fair market interest rate and payable in equal installments of principal and interest over the next five years. The note would be secured by a security interest in the assets of the partnership.

Finally, Regent Partnership could borrow $250,000 and use the money to pay off the mortgage on the office building and land. Since Dana, Alvise, and Matilda are all agreed that ownership of the office building is not significant to the financial health of the partnership, the partnership could distribute 50% of the office building to Alvise and 50% to Matilda in return for one-half of each one's partnership interest. Alvise and Matilda would then employ Regent Partnership, for reasonable compensation, to manage the office building, which means that Dana would actually manage the office building.

In the second and third alternatives described above, Dana would acquire a one-third interest in Regent Partnership by contributing $250,000 in cash to the partnership and giving it her personal recourse note for $250,000 which would bear a fair market interest rate and be payable to the partnership on the same terms and conditions as the loan between the partnership and the bank described in the second alternative. The note would be secured by a pledge of the acquired partnership interest.

Regardless which alternative is chosen, once the transactions necessary to accomplish it are carried out, Alvise and Matilda will exchange their remaining partnership interests for the two $250,000 limited partnership interests in the limited partnership we will form. Dana will exchange her acquired partnership interest for the $250,000 general partnership interest in the limited partnership.

We and the clients would like to know the income tax effects of each of the above described alternatives. Are the income tax effects of one or more of the alternatives more favorable than those of the other alternatives? Please give me your advice on this matter as soon as possible. I have attached to this memorandum the latest balance sheet of Regent Partnership.

REGENT PARTNERSHIP
ASSETS (x 1000)

		Adjusted Basis	Fair Market Value
Cash		$ 30	$ 30
Marketable Securities		60	60
Furniture and Fixtures	$ 750		
Depreciation	(350)	400	450
Office Building	600		
Accelerated Depreciation[1]	(400)	200	300
Land		180	200
Apartment House	450		
Straight-line Depreciation	(300)	150	200
Land		135	150
Shopping Plaza	1,250		
Straight-line Depreciation	(650)	600	750
Land		385	400
TOTAL		$2,140	$2,540

		Fair Market
LIABILITIES (x 1000)	Per Books	Value
Accounts Payable[2]	$ 10	$ 10
Mortgage on Office Building & Land	250	250
Mortgage on Apartment House & Land	300	300
Mortgage on Shopping Plaza & Land	980	980
Capital		
Alvise Regent	300	500
Matilda Regent	300	500
TOTAL	$2,140	$2,540

1.   All of the depreciation taken is subject to recapture.

2.   The partnership uses the accrual method of accounting for both tax and financial purposes. It does not have any rent receivables.

Note:

See the Note on Interviewing and Client Counseling following Problem 1P at page 4 and the Note on Representing More Than One Party following Problem 2P at page 9.

PROBLEM 18P

Lake Rainard, Co., L.L.C. (the company) is a limited liability company which was formed five years ago by Marsha Prescott (Marsha), a very influential and wealthy real estate developer and dealer, Abraham Epstein (Abe), a wealthy architect and real estate investor and London Properties, Ltd. (London), a substantial Canadian limited partnership which provides equity financing for the acquisition and development of real estate located in the United States. The company was formed to develop the mountain properties surrounding Lake Rainard in the Sawtooth range. Marsha has bought and sold developments similar to the one planned for Lake Rainard. Neither Abe nor London has "dealt" in similar developments.

There have been no transfers of interests in the company since its formation. None of the members have died. No "special" allocations have been made. All distributions made by the company have been made pro rata and no distributions other than cash distributions have been made. Cash distributions made to the members have never exceeded their shares of profit nor has a distribution ever exceeded the basis of a member in his, her or its membership interest.

Marsha, Abe and London each contributed $500,000 in cash to the company in return for their membership interests. The first project developed on the mountain real estate surrounding Lake Rainard consisted of three apartment buildings. The company financed $1,350,000 of the construction costs with a 30 year, 12% mortgage loan from Mountain Federal Savings and Loan Association (S & L) and paid $150,000 of the costs in cash.

The second project consisted of three hundred condominium units in ten separate buildings constructed on the shores of Lake Rainard. The construction costs were financed by a construction mortgage provided by Second Interstate Bank (Second) and $300,000 of equity provided by the company. The company currently owns about 100 completed and unsold condominium units. It also holds purchase money mortgages on 50 units. Second has a security interest in the purchase money mortgages as additional collateral for its construction mortgage. The third project consisted of the development of recreational facilities including a golf course, tennis courts, swimming pools, racquet ball courts, basketball and aerobic facilities and a weight training facility. The $4,000,000 cost of the recreational facilities was financed by a $3,700,000 mortgage loan from the General Electric Pension Trust (G.E.) The mortgage loan had a 30 year term and an interest rate of 14%. The company provided the remaining $300,000 of the cost for the recreational facilities. The recreational facilities were completed three years ago.

The final project scheduled for development on the mountain real estate surrounding Lake Rainard is the commercial area. This area will include retail stores, restaurants, financial institutions, services and entertainment. The projected construction cost of the project is $18,000,000. S & L is willing to provide $14,000,000 of the construction costs through a mortgage loan having a 30 year term and an interest rate of 13%. The company must provide as equity the remaining $4,000,000 of the construction costs. The company raised $250,000 of this amount by selling one of the apartment buildings for a down payment of $250,000 and a purchase money mortgage of $450,000 from the purchaser. The company has invested this $250,000, as well as the remaining $750,000 of the $1,500,000 contributed by the members, in this project and has started construction. Three million dollars must be raised in the near future.

Tokyo Investments, Ltd. (Tokyo), a Japanese controlled investment company, is interested in providing the funds the company needs for the commercial development. Just the other day, Marsha received the following letter from Tokyo.

Tokyo Investment, Ltd.
117 Embarcadero, Suite 418
San Francisco, CA   94107

October 13, Year*

Lake Rainard, Co., L.L.C.
417 Bighorn Avenue
Butte, MT   59701
ATTENTION: Marsha Prescott

RE: Investment in Lake Rainard, Co., L.L.C.

Tokyo Investment, Ltd. (Tokyo) is interested in assisting Lake Rainard, Co., L.L.C. (Rainard) in completing the commercial development at Lake Rainard in accordance with the plans and specifications which have been delivered to Tokyo. It is our understanding that $3,000,000 is required to complete the financing of the commercial development. Tokyo is prepared to invest the $3,000,000 in either of the two manners described below. The choice of Tokyo's method of investment can be made by Rainard. The instruments, documents and agreements providing for the investment will be prepared by Tokyo's attorneys subject to the approval of Rainard.

First, Tokyo is willing to purchase 50% of each member's membership interest for $1,000,000. Each member, however, will have to agree to invest the $1,000,000 purchase price in Rainard for the purpose of completing the construction of the commercial facilities. Tokyo will agree that the first $3,000,000 (plus an amount equal to 12% per annum on $3,000,000) of net cash flow of Rainard after the completion of the commercial area shall be paid pro rata to Marsha Prescott, Abraham Epstein and London Properties, Ltd.

---

* See explanatory footnote in Introduction, page vii, note 1.

In the alternative, Tokyo is prepared to contribute $3,000,000 to Rainard in return for a 50% membership interest in profits, losses, net cash flow and management. Upon the completion of the construction of the commercial facilities, Tokyo will agree that the first $3,000,000 (plus an amount equal to 12% per annum) of the net cash flow of Rainard shall be paid to the three original members.

Please let us know your desires with respect to this investment within two weeks from the date of this letter. When we are notified of your choice, we will instruct our attorneys to prepare the instruments, agreements and documents necessary to reflect our investment. If you have any questions or concerns please do not hesitate to call the undersigned.

Sincerely yours,

Yoko Murita

Yoko Murita, Manager
United States Investments

Marsha, Abe and London have asked your advice with respect to the income tax effects of Tokyo's investment. Advise them of the income tax effects resulting from: (a) Tokyo's contribution of $3,000,000 in return for a 50% membership interest and the distribution to the original three members of the first $3,000,000 plus interest of net cash flow after completion of the commercial area; and (b) Tokyo's purchase of 50% of each original member's interest for $1,000,000, with each original member contributing the $1,000,000 to the company and receiving, after completion of the commercial area, a distribution of $1,000,000 plus interest out of the first net cash flow received by the company. Then, advise your clients which alternative you recommend they choose and tell them the reasons for your recommendation. In order to assist you in your analysis the balance sheet of the company showing the adjusted basis and approximate fair market value of each of the company's assets at the point in time immediately prior to Tokyo's first contribution or purchase has been delivered to you by your clients.

Lake Rainard, Co., L.L.C.
(000 omitted)

Assets

		Adjusted Basis	Fair Market Value
Cash		$ 50	$ 50
Purchase Money Mortgages from Condominium Sales		3,000	4,000
Purchase Money Mortgage from Apartment Building Sale		320	450
Completed But Unsold Condominium Units		6,000	8,500
Apartment Buildings	$1,000		
Depreciation[1]	(170)	830	1,500
Recreational Facilities	4,000		
Depreciation[2]	(1,750)	2,250	3,950
Commercial Facilities Under Construction		2,550	2,550
TOTAL		$15,000	$21,000

Liabilities

	Adjusted Basis	Fair Market Value
Accounts Payable[3]	$ 550	$ 550
S & L Apartment Buildings' Mortgage	1,320	1,320
Second Condominium Construction Mortgage	7,880	7,880
G.E. Recreational Facilities Mortgage	3,700	3,700
S & L Commercial Area Construction Mortgage	1,550	1,550
Capital Accounts		
Marsha Prescott	0	2,000
Abraham Epstein	0	2,000
London Properties, Ltd.	0	2,000
TOTAL	$15,000	$21,000

1.   Apartment buildings have been depreciated using the straight-line method.

2.   Land improvements have been depreciated using an accelerated method.

3.   The company uses the accrual method for both financial and income tax accounting purposes.

Note:

See the Note on Limited Liability Companies following Problem 4P at page 22.

RETIREMENT OR DEATH OF A PARTNER AND TERMINATION OF A PARTNERSHIP

---

1. RETIREMENT OR DEATH OF A PARTNER

PROBLEM 19P

Daniel Yang, one of your associates who specializes in labor law, recently received the letter set out below. Mr. Yang has asked you, as the office income tax expert, to tell him what advice he should give to his friend Jacob Henderschmidt. Mr. Yang anticipates that he will see Mr. Henderschmidt over the weekend and would like to meet with you beforehand in order to learn what advice should be given to Mr. Henderschmidt.

Jacob Henderschmidt
Gemstone Galleries
Sedona, Arizona   86336

October 1, Year*

Daniel Yang, Esq.
Marshall, Tulre & Goins
1412 Court Street
Tucson, AZ 85701

Dear Dan:

Some matters have come up with respect to Gemstone Galleries which have me a bit concerned. I would like your advice with respect to these matters. As you know, Gemstone Galleries is a partnership, which was formed a number of years ago by Annabelle Flick, Derrick Gemstone

* See explanatory footnote in Introduction, page vii, note 1.

69

and me. Each one of us contributed, in cash, one-third of the capital needed to start the business. The partnership agreement provides that Annabelle, Derrick and I each own a one-third interest in capital, profits and losses. The partnership agreement does not contain any provisions concerning the procedure to be followed upon the withdrawal of a partner. There have been no special allocations of income, gain, loss, deduction or credit, nor has there ever been a transfer of part, or all, of a partnership interest. Each year, each of us withdraws an amount of cash equal to that withdrawn by each of the other partners, and the total of such withdrawals during any year has never exceeded the profits of the partnership for that year.

Gemstone Galleries rents space to artists for the exhibition of their work and sells art work on consignment for artists. It has never bought, sold or dealt in art work for its own account. Its income is derived solely from the rental of space to artists and the commissions received when an artist's work held on consignment is sold. The art work listed on Gemstone Galleries' balance sheet, which I have enclosed, was bought for the purpose of providing a gracious setting for the display of other artists' work either on exhibition or held on consignment for sale.

Annabelle is a prominent art dealer. She buys, sells and generally deals in art objects including sculpture, graphics and paintings. She derives a substantial part of her income from the sale of art objects. Derrick is the curator of the local museum of modern art. Although he is an art collector, he has never sold any of his personal art collection. He derives his income from his salary as curator and his share of Gemstone Galleries' profits. As you know, I am a well-known public speaker, raconteur and patron of the arts. I, too, have a personal art collection and have never sold any of the art objects in the collection. My income is derived from fees for public speaking engagements and my share of Gemstone Galleries' profits.

Annabelle is getting on in years and would like to limit the demands on her time. As a result, she would like to withdraw from Gemstone Galleries. The three of us have agreed upon the value of the assets as shown on the enclosed balance sheet. We have discussed three different methods of providing Annabelle with the value of her interest. First, Derrick and I might assume Annabelle's share of partnership liabilities and pay her $80,000 a year plus appropriate interest for the next three years. Second, the partnership might hold Annabelle harmless against the liabilities of the partnership and pay her $80,000 a year plus appropriate interest for the next three years. Third, the partnership might hold Annabelle harmless against the liabilities of the partnership and this year distribute to her the George Woodman Collection, which is a collection of graphics and prints created by George Woodman.

I would like your advice with respect to the tax implications to each of us and the partnership resulting from each of the three alternatives for "buying out" Annabelle's interest.

Say hello to Molly and your children for me. I look forward to seeing them.

Sincerely,

Jake

Jake

Gemstone Galleries

Assets

		Basis (x 1000)	Fair Market Value (x 1000)
Cash		$ 36	$ 36
North African Sculpture Collection		36	72
George Woodman Collection		120	240
Miscellaneous Paintings		12	48
Miscellaneous Sculpture		36	72
Furniture & Fixtures	$120		
(Depreciation)	(72)*	48	72
Gemstone Building	200		
(Depreciation)	(68)*	132	156
Gemstone Building Land		60	84
Goodwill		-	120
Total		$480	$900

Liabilities

	Book (x 1000)	Fair Market Value (x 1000)
Trade Accounts Payable**	$ 12	$ 12
Loan for Furniture and Fixtures	36	36
Mortgage Liability on Gemstone Land and Building	132	132
Capital		
Annabelle	100	240
Derrick	100	240
Jacob	100	240
Total	$480	$900

* Depreciation has been computed using the straight-line method.

** The partnership uses the accrual method of accounting.

Note:

See the Note on Interviewing and Client Counseling following Problem 1P at page 4 and the Note on Representing More Than One Party following Problem 2P at page 9.

PROBLEM 20P

Prior to finalizing the arrangements for Annabelle's withdrawal from Gemstone Galleries, as set forth in Problem 19P, she suffered a stroke and died, despite the heroic efforts of the emergency room personnel at General Hospital. It is now Annabelle's successor-in-interest who wants to withdraw from the partnership. Annabelle's successor-in-interest is Alicia Bloomberg, Annabelle's cousin, who is a very successful corporate attorney without the slightest appreciation of art. Alicia plans to dispose of all the art objects owned by Annabelle as soon as she can. The same methods of "buying out" the partnership interest now held by Alicia, as suggested in Problem 19P, are being considered.

Advise Jacob, Derrick and Alicia with respect to the tax implications to each of them and the partnership resulting from each of the methods of "buying out" Alicia's interest as described in Problem 19P.

PROBLEM 21P

Unique Designs Associated, L.L.P. (Unique Designs) is a limited liability partnership providing architectural services. It was formed twenty years ago as a partnership by Keiji Issuma. Keiji is an outstanding free-lance architect. The other partners are three architects in their early forties, who were all recent graduates of the New School of Environmental Design when the partnership was formed. Keiji owns a 52% partnership interest, and each of the others owns a 16% interest. Your firm recently did the filings necessary for Unique Designs to have limited liability partnership status.

Keiji is considering retiring in another three years and has discovered that the partnership agreement contains no provisions with respect to how a retiring partner, or the estate of a deceased partner, obtains the withdrawal from the partnership of the value of the partner's partnership interest.

Keiji's current adjusted basis in his partnership interest is approximately $400,000. He receives about $120,000 a year in taxable income from the partnership, and he expects his share of earnings to remain at or about that level prior to retirement. Since the partnership deals in services, it finds it convenient to report for income tax purposes on the cash method of accounting and to keep its books on the calendar year. At times the partnership has invested in projects it has designed. The partnership's income, however, is derived in substantial part from its architectural services. The partnership owns the building in which it has its offices. The balance sheet of the partnership for the last complete fiscal year has been made available to you. Keiji does not expect the financial condition of the partnership to change dramatically in the next three years.

Keiji presented the three younger partners with an Agreement to Retire a Partnership Interest which was prepared by Keiji's attorney. The three younger partners have come to you for your advice with respect to Keiji's retirement. They have informed you that they agree with the fair market value of the assets of the partnership as set out in the balance sheet which was made available to you and, as a result, they agree with Keiji on the value of his partnership interest. They, however, desire your advice with respect to the income tax effect on them and the partnership of providing for Keiji's retirement through the agreement which Keiji has presented to them. They would also like to know whether there are any other ways of providing Keiji with the value of his interest in the partnership on retirement and, if there are, whether the income tax effects on them and the partnership are more or less beneficial than the income tax effects resulting from the agreement. The three younger partners would like you to examine the agreement and the balance sheet set out below and get back to them as soon as possible with your advice.

AGREEMENT TO RETIRE

A PARTNERSHIP INTEREST

This Agreement to Retire a Partnership Interest (the "Agreement") is entered into and shall be effective as of _____, Year* by and among Unique Designs Associated, L.L.P., a limited liability partnership (the "Partnership"), and Keiji Issuma (the "Retiring Partner"), and Gerald Shine, Ishmael Alimet, and Paul Klipstein (the "Continuing Partners"), (the Retiring

* See explanatory footnote in Introduction, page vii, note 1.

Partner, the Continuing Partners, and the Partnership are sometimes referred to individually as a "Party" and collectively as the "Parties").

A.　　The Retiring Partner and the Continuing Partners formed the Partnership pursuant to that certain agreement dated October 10, Year-20, which agreement has been amended from time to time (as amended, the "Partnership Agreement").

B.　　The Parties have agreed that the Retiring Partner's entire right, title, and interest in the Partnership (the "Redemption Interest") shall be retired and redeemed by the Partnership and the Retiring Partner shall withdraw from the Partnership, all as set forth herein.

Based on the foregoing, and in consideration of the mutual agreements, covenants, and conditions contained herein, and for other good and valuable consideration, the receipt and adequacy of which are hereby acknowledged, the Parties hereby agree as follows:

1.　　Retirement, Redemption, and Withdrawal. The Redemption Interest shall be retired and redeemed by the Partnership effective as of the close of business on _____, Year, (the "Effective Date"), all in accordance with the provisions set forth in this Agreement. The Retiring Partner shall sell, assign, and transfer the entire Redemption Interest to the Partnership and withdraw from the Partnership as of the close of business on the Effective Date.

2.　　Consideration for Redemption Interest; Indemnification Provisions. In consideration for the retirement and redemption of the Redemption Interest, the Partnership agrees to distribute to the Retiring Partner consideration (the "Redemption Consideration") composed of the following:

(a)　　The Partnership shall distribute cash to the Retiring Partner as follows:

(i)　　$71,760 on _____, Year;

(ii)　　$71,760 on _____, Year+1, plus simple interest on said amount at 10% per annum from the Effective Date through the day immediately prior to the date of payment;

(iii)　　$71,760 on _____, Year+2, plus simple interest on said amount at 10% per annum from the Effective Date through the day immediately prior to the date of payment;

(iv)　　$71,760 on _____, Year+3, plus simple interest on said amount at 10% per annum from the Effective Date through the day immediately prior to the date of payment; and

(v) $71,760 on _____, Year+4, plus simple interest on said amount at 10% per annum from the Effective Date through the day immediately prior to the date of payment.

The Partnership shall have the right to prepay all or any portion of the amounts set forth above at any time without penalty or premium.

(b)   As among the Parties, the Retiring Partner shall be relieved of all responsibility for the liabilities of the Partnership set forth on the Partnership's Balance Sheet attached hereto.   The amounts of such liabilities reflect the amounts outstanding on _____, Year. As soon as practicable after the Effective Date, the Partnership's accountant shall prepare an updated schedule of the outstanding amounts of such liabilities as of the Effective Date and the Partnership shall deliver copies of the updated schedule to all other Parties.   The Partnership shall indemnify, defend, protect, and hold harmless the Retiring Partner from such liabilities.

(c)   As among the Parties, the Retiring Partner shall be relieved of all responsibility for any and all claims, demands, liens, causes of action, suits, obligations, controversies, debts, costs, expenses, damages, judgments, and orders of whatever kind or nature, in law, equity, or otherwise, whether known or unknown, suspected or unsuspected, and whether or not concealed or hidden, excluding only those owing due to the fraud, bad faith, willful misconduct, or gross negligence of the Retiring Partner, which exist on the Effective Date (the "Contingent Liabilities"). The Partnership shall indemnify, defend, protect, and hold harmless the Retiring Partner from the Contingent Liabilities.

(d)   The Redemption Consideration provided for in this Section 2 is the total consideration payable by the Partnership to the Retiring Partner for the Redemption Interest, and the Retiring Partner shall not retain an interest in, or be entitled to receive distributions of, any other Partnership assets.

3.   Continuation of Partnership. The Parties hereby agree that the Partnership shall continue and shall not be dissolved because of the retirement and redemption of the Redemption Interest or the withdrawal of the Retiring Partner.

4.   Tax Matters. The Parties agree that:

(a)   The fair market values of the Partnership's assets (the "Partnership Assets") as of _____, Year are as set forth on the Partnership's Balance Sheet attached hereto.   None of the Partnership Assets are "inventory items" which have "appreciated substantially in value" within the meaning of Code Section 751(d). The Redemption Consideration includes payments for the Retiring Partner's share of the goodwill of the Partnership.

(b)   All amounts considered as distributions to the Retiring Partner pursuant to Section 752(b) of the Code (the "Deemed Distributions") and all distributions to the Retiring Partner of cash (other than interest) pursuant to Section 2(a) hereof shall be treated as follows:

(i)   A portion equal to the Retiring Partner's share of the value of the assets of the Partnership, other than unrealized receivables, shall be treated as a distribution pursuant to Section 736(b) of the Code and corresponding provisions of any applicable state or local tax laws; and

(ii)   The excess, if any, shall be treated as a "guaranteed payment" pursuant to Section 736(a)(2) of the Code and corresponding provisions of any applicable state or local tax laws.

*   *   *

(c)   Of the total distributions to the Retiring Partner described in Section 4(b), all distributions shall be treated first as a return of capital; then as distributions with respect to the Retiring Partner's interest in Partnership property; and finally as guaranteed payments in the amount described in Section 4(b)(ii).

(d)   The Retiring Partner's distributive share of the Partnership's income, gain, loss, and deduction for the taxable year of the Partnership that includes the Effective Date shall be determined on the basis of an interim closing of the books of the Partnership as of the close of business on the Effective Date and shall not be based upon a proration of such items for the entire taxable year.   The Retiring Partner shall not be allocated a distributive share of any Partnership items for any subsequent year except to the extent such allocations are required by or are consistent with the provisions of this Agreement.

(e)   The Parties shall each file all required Federal, state, and local income tax returns and related returns and reports in a manner consistent with the foregoing provisions of this Section 4.   In the event a Party does not comply with the preceding sentence, the non-complying Party shall indemnify and hold the other Parties wholly and completely harmless from all cost, liability, and damage that such other Parties may incur (including, without limitation, incremental tax liabilities, legal fees, accounting fees, and other expenses) as a consequence of such failure to comply.

*   *   *

Balance Sheet of Unique Designs Associated, L.L.P.

Assets
(x1000)

	Adjusted Basis	Fair Market Value
Cash	$ 80	$ 80
Gov. Securities	160	180
Accounts Receivable	-	90
Office Equipment	$100	
(Dep.)*	(60)	40	100
Office Building	320	
(Dep.)*	(190)	130	180
Office Building — Land		100	140
One-third Interest in		
Brisbane Building	200	
(Dep.)*	(100)	100	110
One-fourth Interest in		
Right Arms Apartments	240	
(Dep.)*	(80)	160	180
Goodwill		-	160
	$770	$1,220

Liabilities and Capital
(x 1000)

	Per Books	Fair Market Value
Accounts Payable	-	$ 90
Mortgage on Office	$200	200
Building & Land		
Share of Mortgage on	100	100
Brisbane Building		
Share of Mortgage on	140	140
Right Arms Apartments		
Partners' Capital		
Beginning of Year	$220	
Earnings	240	
(Distributions)	(130)	330	690
	$770	$1220

* Accelerated depreciation is used for equipment and straight-line depreciation is used for real estate assets.

Note:

See the Note on Legal Drafting following Problem 3P at page 15 and the Note on Limited Liability Partnerships following Problem 2P at page 10.

PROBLEM 22P

You frequently have worked on projects under the direction of Eduardo Martinez. Mr. Martinez is one of the young tax partners in the firm with which you are associated. This morning, you found the memorandum set out below on your desk. Attached to the memorandum was a short note from Mr. Martinez. The note stated, "Please take a look at this memorandum and give me your reactions by the end of the week. Louis Goodyear is pressing me for some tax advice." Louis Goodyear is one of the main partners in your firm and the chair of the business department.

Harold, Gonzales, Goodyear & Eisenberg
Interoffice Memorandum

November 10, Year*

TO: Eduardo Martinez

FROM: Louis Goodyear

RE: Retirement of Jean Rheinstein

We have represented Ideal Construction Company, L.L.C. (Ideal) for a number of years. Jean Rheinstein (Jean), Clayton Bullard (Clayton), Mae Held (Mae), and Frank Weiss (Frank) are the members of Ideal. Ideal is a member-managed limited liability company. Ideal constructs homes and multi-residential units. Mae and Frank devote their full time to supervising the operations of Ideal. Jean and Clayton spend part of their time assisting Mae and Frank in the operations of Ideal and are both individually engaged in the business of being real estate dealers and developers. Frequently, when either Jean or Clayton discovered a good opportunity to develop some real estate, they, with Mae's and Frank's agreement, took an option on the real estate in the name of Ideal. Ideal then bought the real estate and constructed the improvements. Sometimes the improvements consisted of rental units. At other times the real estate was subdivided and Ideal

---

* See explanatory footnote in Introduction, page vii, note 1.

constructed single family residences. The subdivided real estate and improvements were then held by Ideal for sale to customers in the ordinary course of business. Other tracts were bought for appreciation and residential lots were sold out of the tracts. Ideal uses the accrual method of accounting and the calendar year for income tax purposes. The members are calendar-year taxpayers who use the cash method of accounting.

No subdivisions have been developed by Ideal, for its own account, during the last few years. The remaining homes and lots in the Ritz Subdivision appearing on Ideal's balance sheet which I have attached to this memorandum are held by Ideal for rental. The subdivision was originally developed by Ideal for sale to customers in the ordinary course of business, but after about two-thirds of the subdivision was sold, the members decided to retain the remainder of the homes in the subdivision and rent those homes to tenants on a year-to-year basis. The homes in the subdivision have been depreciated using the straight-line method.

Ideal's machinery and equipment, the Western Way Apartment Building and the Sea Breeze Fourplex (four connected rental units) have been depreciated using the straight-line method. Ideal, over the years, has provided the financing for many of the purchasers of its unimproved residential lots. It accounts for the sales which it finances by using the installment method of accounting. At the present time each of the members has a basis of about $404,000 in his or her membership interest.

Jean would like to withdraw from Ideal in order to devote more time to her real estate dealership. The members would like to be advised of the best way, in an income tax context, of paying Jean for her interest in Ideal. Jean is willing, subject to your advice, to have: (1) Ideal borrow additional cash secured by its assets and pay her cash for her interest; (2) Ideal distribute to her the remainder of the Ritz Subdivision in return for her interest (she can easily convert the subdivision into cash by selling the homes through her dealership); or (3) the other members pay her cash for her interest. Please let me know, in the next week, the income tax results of each of the above methods so that I can advise Jean and the other members.

Balance Sheet — Ideal Construction Company, L.L.C.

Assets
(x 1000)

		Adjusted Basis	Fair Market Value
Cash		$ 20	$ 20
Accounts Receivable		24	24
Installment Obligations		60	120
Machinery & Equipment	$ 100		
(Dep.)	(46)	54	66
Ritz Subdivision Homes	700		
(Dep.)	(270)	430	440
Land		70	80
Western Way Apartments			
Building	640		
(Dep.)	(176)	464	568
Land		80	120
Sea Breeze Fourplex			
Building	480		
(Dep.)	(128)	352	408
Land		60	50
Goodwill		-	150
Total		$1,614	$2,046

Liabilities
(x 1000)

	Per Book	Fair Market Value
Accounts Payable	$ 30	$ 30
Mortgage Liability — Western Way	520	520
Mortgage Liability — Sea Breeze	364	364
Capital Accounts		
Jean	175	283
Clayton	175	283
Mae	175	283
Frank	175	283
Total	$1,614	$2,046

Note:

See the Note on Representing More Than One Party following Problem 2P at page 9 and the Note on Limited Liability Companies following Problem 4P at page 22.

Problem 23P

Little & Big Screen Associates (L. & B.) is a general partnership formed a number of years ago to make movies and television programs. The five original partners include James Bean (James) and Helen Roark (Helen), respectively, a critically acclaimed movie and television actor and actress, Joseph Gumbaugh (Joseph) and Penny Patton (Penny), highly regarded movie and television directors, and Mira Elkins (Mira), a major producer of movies and television programs. The partners each made an equal contribution to the partnership and each owns a one-fifth interest in partnership capital, profits, losses and distributions. Each partner also has an equal vote in partnership decision making. The partnership agreement does not contain any provisions dealing with the procedure to be followed upon the death or withdrawal of a partner. There have not been any special allocations of income, gain, loss, deduction or credit made by the partnership, nor have there been any transfers of part, or all, of a partnership interest. The foregoing has been confirmed to you by the partners in L. & B. who have further advised you that each year each partner withdraws an equal amount of cash which is never in excess of the partner's share of partnership profits.

The balance sheet of L. & B. showing its adjusted basis for income tax purposes in, and the fair market value of, all of its assets is attached. L. & B. uses the accrual method of accounting for both tax and financial accounting purposes. It uses the charge-off method for bad debts. This means the accounts receivable are shown at their face amount and if a receivable becomes uncollectible it is written off at that time for both income tax and financial accounting purposes. The syndication agreements shown on the balance sheet are agreements with various local television stations which permit, in return for certain fees, the stations to televise programs produced by L. & B. after the programs have been shown on network television. Since L. & B. usually depreciates programs over their network run, for the most part it has no adjusted basis left in the programs when they go into syndication. Royalty agreements are agreements with video companies, various second-run movie theaters, record companies and other suppliers which provide for the payment of fees to L. & B. for the showing of movies produced by it, the selling of records containing the musical scores of those movies or the selling of other items derived from the movies, such as T-shirts. L. & B. usually has no adjusted basis left in its movies to write off against the royalties.

Network programs are those programs produced by L. & B. which are currently being shown on network television. The costs of these programs are depreciated, using the fastest method available, over the period during which they are shown on network television. Movies-in-distribution, as shown on the balance sheet, are those movies which are currently being distributed to first-run movie theaters anywhere in the world. They are depreciated, using the fastest method available, over the period during which they are in distribution. Movies-in-production are just that. They are movies which are currently being made by L. & B. All costs of making the movies are capitalized into their adjusted bases for income tax and financial accounting purposes and the movies are valued at their aggregate cost since they have not been completed.

L. & B. operates out of leased premises. The production facilities include all the tangible personal property required to make television programs and movies, such as cameras, sets and stunt equipment. Production facilities have been depreciated using the fastest available method over the shortest permissible recovery period. The goodwill item shown on the balance sheet is self-generated goodwill. The financing shown on the balance sheet is composed of the loans from various lenders used to pay for the production of the movies and network programs produced by L. & B. The loans are all nonrecourse and are secured by security interests in the movies and network programs made and under production by L. & B.

Penny is the oldest of the current partners and has decided to take life a little easier. She would like to withdraw the value of her partnership interest in L. & B. and retire to her beachfront bungalow in Santa Barbara. She and the other partners agree that the value of her interest is about $2,000,000 as shown on L. & B.'s balance sheet. Penny is willing to spread her collection of the value of her partnership interest over a five-year period. She would like to collect $400,000 plus interest on the unpaid principal balance each year for five years. She also wants to be indemnified against, and held harmless from, all partnership liabilities at the time she receives the deferred payment obligation.

Please advise the partners, including Penny, of the income tax consequences of carrying out Penny's withdrawal from the partnership in the following ways:

1. The current partners, other than Penny, indemnify Penny against partnership liabilities and each purchases one-fourth of Penny's partnership interest by giving her a jointly executed installment obligation for $2,000,000 payable in installments of $400,000 plus interest each year for five years.

2. The partnership indemnifies Penny against partnership liabilities and liquidates her interest in the partnership by giving her its installment obligation for $2,000,000.

3. The partnership indemnifies Penny against partnership liabilities and, in full payment for her partnership interest, distributes to Penny the movie Partners-in-Crime.

Advise the partners and Penny which of the three methods you would recommend that they use, and the reasons for your recommendation.

Little & Big Screen Associates
Balance Sheet (000 omitted)
Assets

			Basis	Fair Market Value
Cash			$ 150	$ 150
Accounts Receivable			400	400
Certificates of Deposit			450	450
Syndication Agreements			0	1,700
Royalty Agreements			0	1,600
Network Programs	Cost	$4,000		
	Dep.	(2,800)	1,200	4,000
Movies-in-Distribution				
Gwen's Ghost	Cost	3,000		
	Dep.	(2,700)	300	1,300
Old Glory	Cost	6,000		
	Dep.	(4,000)	2,000	4,000
Partners-in-Crime	Cost	4,000		
	Dep.	(3,000)	1,000	2,000
Movies-in-Production				
August Reprise			4,000	4,000
Production Facilities	Cost	2,500		
	Dep.	(2,000)	500	2,000
Goodwill			0	500
Total			$10,000	$22,100

Liabilities

	Basis	Fair Market Value
Accounts Payable	$ 400	$ 400
Network Program Financing	3,100	3,100
Movies-in-Distribution Financing	5,000	5,000
Movies-in-Production Financing	3,600	3,600
Capital Accounts		
James Bean	(420)	2,000
Mira Elkins	(420)	2,000
Joseph Gumbaugh	(420)	2,000
Penny Patton	(420)	2,000
Helen Roark	(420)	2,000
Total	$10,000	$22,100

2. TERMINATION OF A PARTNERSHIP

PROBLEM 24P

Your clients, Steven Able, Bernard Bernstine and Tamarra Charles, received the following ruling in response to a ruling request submitted earlier by Joseph Palko, your partner. The request was submitted while you were away on vacation.

U.S. Treasury Department
Internal Revenue Service
Washington, D.C.   20224
Date: Nov. 19, Year*
In Reply Refer to: T:I:I:1:2

Better Craft Homes
1810 Request Street
Topnotch, Utah   84774

Gentlemen:

This is in reply to your letter dated March 13, Year,* requesting a ruling concerning the Federal income tax treatment of the members of your partnership as a result of the transactions described below.

Better Craft Homes is a general partnership organized in Year-7.* The members of the partnership since its inception are Steven Able, Bernard Bernstine and Tamarra Charles. Able owns a one-half interest in the partnership; Bernstine and Charles each own a one-quarter interest in the partnership. The partnership buys land, improves and subdivides it and sells the lots to customers. The partnership uses the calendar year and the accrual method of accounting. The financial statement of the partnership immediately prior to the proposed transactions follows:

* See explanatory footnote in Introduction page vii, note 1.

Assets

	Adjusted Basis (x 1000)	Fair Market Value (x 1000)
Cash	$ 200	$ 200
Accounts Receivable	500	500
Plans, Blueprints	40	100
Machinery (net of depreciation)	300	300
Land	720	1,000
Total	$1,760	$2,100

Liabilities and Capital

		Per Books (x 1000)	Fair Market Value (x 1000)
Current Liabilities		$ 160	$ 160
Mortgage Liability		300	300
Capital			
Able	(50%)	650	820
Bernstine	(25%)	325	410
Charles	(25%)	325	410
Total		$1,760	$2,100

The adjusted bases of the partners in their partnership interests immediately prior to the proposed transactions are as follows: Able — $880,000; Bernstine — $440,000; Charles — $440,000. Even though Able owns a one-half interest in the partnership, he is subject to a very low rate of income tax, whereas Bernstine and Charles are both subject to much higher rates of income tax. A purchaser, Paula Peters, has approached the partners and indicated an interest in acquiring the assets and assuming the liabilities of the partnership.

The partners propose that the partnership use $160,000 of its cash to pay its current liabilities and then dissolve, distributing its assets and liabilities in the following manner. The partnership will distribute to Able the land subject to the mortgage, the plans and blueprints, and $20,000 in cash. It will distribute to Bernstine one-half of the accounts receivable, one-half of the machinery and $10,000 in cash. Charles will receive the same distribution as Bernstine. Able, Bernstine and Charles will retain the cash distributed. Able will sell the land and the plans and blueprints to Peters, who will assume the mortgage. Bernstine and Charles will sell the accounts receivable and machinery to Peters.

Since the transactions described above amount, in substance, to a disposition of the entire continuing business of the partnership, the transactions will be treated as a sale of a partnership interest by each partner [*see Hatch's Estate v. Commissioner*, 198 F.2d 26 (9th Cir. 1952); *Herbert A. Nieman*, 33 T.C. 411 (1959); *Barran v. Commissioner*, 334 F.2d 58 (5th Cir. 1964); *Kinney v. United States*, 228 F. Supp. 656 (W.D. La. 1964), *aff'd per curiam*, 358 F.2d 738 (5th Cir. 1966); and G.C.M. 26379, 1950-1, C.B. 58]; or as a sale of the assets by the partnership, the purchaser assuming the current liabilities and mortgage liability, followed by a pro rata distribution of the cash held prior to the purchase and that received from the purchaser to the partners in termination of the partnership; or as a pro rata distribution of the assets of the partnership to the partners in termination of the partnership followed by a sale by the partners of the land, plans, blueprints, accounts receivable and machinery to the purchaser in return for cash and the assumption by the purchaser of the current liabilities and mortgage liability [*see* Rev.Rul. 72-172, 1972-1, C.B. 265]. Accordingly, the income tax result to Able will be a gain of $170,000, $30,000 of which will be capital gain and $140,000 of which will be ordinary income. Bernstine and Charles will each have $85,000 of gain, $15,000 of which will be capital gain and $70,000 of which will be ordinary income.

Very truly yours,

Jessica Cohen
Jessica Cohen
Chief, Individual
Income Tax Branch

Without attempting to make, other than in general terms, the mathematical computations involved, consider the following:

a.   What did your clients attempt to accomplish by setting up the transactions in the manner they proposed? What are your clients' chances of success if they go ahead with the transactions as planned in spite of the ruling?

b.   Is the ruling correct in stating that no matter how the transactions are handled, other than as your clients proposed, the income tax results will be the same?

c.   Assume that your clients decide to sell their partnership interests rather than going through with the proposed transactions. Can they alter the income tax results stated in the ruling by having the partnership use $60,000 of its cash to pay down the mortgage on the land in order to secure a release from the mortgage of 20% of the land, sell 20% of the land for a $200,000 note and mortgage to an unrelated third party, use the remaining cash to reduce current liabilities and then have Able, Bernstine and Charles sell their partnership interests to Peters who would assume the remaining current liabilities and mortgage liability?*

Note:

Ruling Requests

Obtaining an Internal Revenue Service private ruling as to the tax effects of a contemplated transaction may often be desirable, particularly when the transaction can be restructured if the ruling as to the form initially proposed is unfavorable. When a client is committed to a course of action and the form of the transaction is not very flexible, it may be wise not to seek a ruling. The chance of obtaining a favorable ruling should be weighed against the chance that the Service on audit will assert and successfully pursue an unfavorable position. If there is only a modest chance of obtaining a favorable ruling and virtually no chance that an auditing agent will take an unfavorable position, unless the stakes are quite large one would normally not attempt to obtain a ruling. If a client is committed to a course of conduct, regardless of the tax consequences, there is little reason to seek a ruling if one anticipates that it may be unfavorable.

Issuance of rulings is discretionary. In general, the Service has a cooperative attitude, but there are areas in which it will not rule. These include matters involving factual determinations such as the fair market value of property, issues a court has decided adversely to the government where further litigation is under consideration, completed transactions involving several years, and issues present in a return which has been filed and is under audit. The Service may also

---

* The foregoing problem was suggested by and many of the facts used in the problem were taken from Morris, *Disposition of Partnership Interests: Achieving Capital Gains Treatment,* 25 Tax Lawyer 473 (1972).

refuse to rule on matters involving new Code provisions where regulations have not been issued and on transactions so artificial that they appear to be tax avoidance schemes. The Regulations and various Revenue Procedures define certain areas in which rulings will and will not be issued. Before preparing a ruling request one should always determine whether the Service may or will rule.

The facts pertaining to a proposed transaction for which a ruling is requested should be presented carefully and completely since, if the completed transaction differs from the facts presented, the ruling generally will not be binding on the Service. A preliminary conference on the form of a request may be desirable if the prospective transaction is complicated. This will avoid the embarrassment of submitting a technically faulty request. The Service encourages taxpayers, and many attorneys believe it is advisable, to attach a copy of a favorable ruling to the tax return which includes the transaction.

Under Treasury procedures presently in effect, the request letter should include:

(1) A complete statement of the facts. Alternate plans should not be included. The facts must present a genuinely contemplated transaction since the Service will not rule on hypothetical, as opposed to prospective, transactions. In addition, since most private rulings are available to the public under the Freedom of Information Act, the request letter should indicate which facts, if any, should not be disclosed in the ruling because of the potential adverse effect of disclosure on the taxpayer. Such facts may include the names of the parties to a transaction contemplated that has not been previously publicized and trade secrets.

(2) Names, addresses and taxpayer identification numbers of all interested parties, and the office where the return of each will be filed.

(3) A full and precise statement of the business reasons for the transaction and true copies of all documents to be used in the transaction. The documents must be accompanied by an analysis of the way in which their pertinent provisions bear on the issues.

(4) A statement of whether, to the best knowledge of the taxpayer, any field office or branch office of the Appellate Division is considering an identical issue in connection with an audit.

(5) A precise statement of the issues involved and a discussion of the legal basis for, and the authorities supporting, the taxpayer's requested ruling. If the legal issue involved is easily resolved, the discussion of authorities may be omitted. A proposed draft of the Service's ruling letter may be included to expedite issuance. The request must be signed, under penalties of perjury, by the taxpayer or by his representative whose power of attorney should be enclosed.

A conference in Washington is available and, if desired, should be requested in the letter. Even if it is believed a favorable ruling will be granted, a conference should be requested if it will expedite issuance of the ruling or if there is the possibility of an adverse determination. If it appears at the conference that an adverse determination will be made, it is customary to withdraw the ruling request.

As a general rule, a ruling should be requested when the answer is in doubt, or the transaction is monetarily significant, or the taxpayer is not committed to consummation of the transaction in the form proposed. One should also consider whether the possible benefit from a favorable ruling is likely to be outweighed by what the Service might discover as to other transactions on examination of the taxpayer's past or present records in connection with the request.

3. INCORPORATION OF A PARTNERSHIP

PROBLEM 25P

A little over two years ago Carol Pine, Ken Cruze, and Jack Chong each purchased a 1/3 interest in the Land-O-Pines real estate development partnership from the then-owners. Each one paid $30,000 for her or his interest. There was no Section 754 election made at the time of the purchases. The Land-O-Pines partnership is an accrual method taxpayer which files its tax returns on a July 1-June 30 fiscal year. The partnership subdivides land, installs curbs, sewers, water and utilities and sells the subdivided parcels as homesites. Because of a recession in the local economy, the sale of homesites in the Forrester and Tall Timbers subdivisions owned by the partnership has been quite slow. In fact, the partnership has been operating at about a break-even rate for the last two years. Carol, Ken and Jack, however, are confident that the fair market value of the properties owned by the partnership is realistically reflected in the partnership's balance sheet which appears at the end of this problem. The balance sheet is generally prepared using the accrual method of accounting. The partners anticipate that, with an upturn in the economy, sales will pick up at a brisk rate.

The partners have been doing some thinking about the form of entity which should hold and sell the partnership assets and have concluded that they would be better off if the assets were held and sold by a corporation. Besides limiting their liability and providing for continuity of life, using a corporation would allow them to avoid having the income from the sale of the assets taxed to them personally and permit them to participate in a group term life insurance plan and an accident and health plan. Therefore, Carol, Ken and Jack propose to cause the partnership assets to be transferred to a corporation which they will form in return for all the stock of the corporation and the assumption of the partnership's liabilities. The liabilities currently are recourse liabilities of the partnership.

Since each of them realized capital gains in the amount of $30,000 earlier this year in connection with the disposition of one of their other ventures, they propose that the transfer be handled by having the partnership dissolve and terminate, distributing its assets and liabilities pro rata to Carol, Ken and Jack. They will transfer the assets and liabilities to the corporation in return for the corporation's stock and assumption by the corporation of the liabilities. Carol, Ken and Jack have asked you whether this proposal will accomplish their goals and whether it will produce any undesirable income tax results. If it will not accomplish their goals, or if it produces any undesirable income tax results, they would like your suggestions as to the most beneficial way, in an income tax sense, of carrying out the transfer.

Land-O-Pines Balance Sheet
Assets
(x 1000)

	Adjusted Basis	Fair Market Value
Cash	$ 20	$ 20
Installment Sales[1]	120	130
Forrester Subdivision[2]	200	230
Tall Timbers Subdivision[2]	276	341
Total	$616	$721

1. Homesites are usually sold using the installment method as provided by Section 453 of the Internal Revenue Code. The adjusted basis of this asset is the unrecovered cost of the land sold.   The fair market value is the fair market value of the obligations of the purchasers received for the land, reduced by the payments made. When a payment is received from a purchaser, the fair market value is reduced by the amount of the payment, and the adjusted basis is reduced by the portion of the payment representing recovery of cost. The amount of the payment is added to cash.

2.The cost of land improvements is included in the adjusted basis of each of these assets.

	Liabilities (x 1000)	
	Per Books	Fair Market Value
Accounts Payable	$ 48	$ 48
Forrester Land Development Mortgage	236	236
Tall Timbers Land Development Mortgage	338	338
Capital		
Carol	(2)	33
Ken	(2)	33
Jack	(2)	33
Total	$616	$721

PROBLEM 26P

Raymond Felding (Ray) and Ezra Minor (Ezra) are equal partners in a limited liability partnership known as Medical Circuits Co. (the Partnership). Ray and Ezra each contributed $15,000 to the Partnership when it was formed. The partnership agreement provides that each partner has a 50% share in profits, losses and distributions and an equal voice in making partnership decisions. The Partnership designs and manufactures printed circuit boards which are used in medical diagnostic equipment. The Partnership was formed about five years ago. At that time Ray and Ezra were tenured professors in the Electrical Engineering Department at Midlands University. Ray and Ezra left the university to organize the Partnership since they believed that a substantial amount of money could be made by designing, manufacturing and selling printed circuit boards for diagnostic equipment. Ray and Ezra, however, did not have a great deal of capital with which to start the venture. As a result, the Partnership has been undercapitalized and unable to take full advantage of the potential market. The Partnership's balance sheet appears at the end of this problem.

Harriet Ling (Harri) was one of Ray's and Ezra's brightest graduate students prior to the time they left the university to form the Partnership. Subsequently, Harri received her Doctorate in Electrical Engineering and, as a result of Ray's and Ezra's encouragement, went to work for the Partnership. While the Partnership has not been able to pay Harri very much, she has found the work fascinating. Ray and Ezra believe that Harri is one of the best young designers of circuit boards in the country. While most of the design patents which the Partnership owns were developed by Ray and Ezra, Harri has made a substantial contribution in recent years to the development of design patents. In addition, Harri has developed some time-saving techniques and other unpatentable know-how for working on and with printed circuit boards. Both Ray and Ezra believe that Harri will continue to be productive in future years. To encourage her productivity, and to give her a sense of ownership in the business, Ray and Ezra have agreed in writing to give her 5% of the Partnership's annual net profits.

A few months ago Ray and Ezra met Roberta Klaubman (Roberta), an independently wealthy investor who, after reviewing the operation of the Partnership and the market for its products, concluded that the Partnership could be a very profitable business venture if its capital was adequate to permit it truly to exploit the market. Roberta is prepared to provide that capital, about $180,000, if she can obtain about a one-quarter interest in the venture. She will provide the $180,000 by transferring to the venture securities, which have a fair market value of $180,000 and in which she has a basis of $30,000. Roberta, on the advice of her attorney, believes the venture should be conducted in the corporate form so that each participant's liability will be completely limited and continuity of the enterprise will be assured. Ray and Ezra are in agreement with Roberta's suggestions. In addition, they feel that, because of the valuable contributions which Harri will make to the venture, Harri should receive a small interest in the venture. Roberta's attorney has prepared a Preincorporation Agreement in order to set out in writing the intentions of the parties and their contributions to the corporation to be formed. The parties would like your advice as to the income tax effects if this agreement is carried out as drafted and any suggestions you have for changes or additions to the agreement.

Preincorporation Agreement

The parties hereto, Raymond Felding ("Ray"), Ezra Minor ("Ezra"), Harriet Ling ("Harri") and Roberta Klaubman ("Roberta"), have determined that it is in their mutual interest to form, invest in, and operate a corporation to be known as Medical Circuits, Inc. ("Circuits") to engage in the business of designing, manufacturing and selling printed circuit boards for use in medical diagnostic equipment. The parties hereto believe that it is appropriate to set out their intentions and agreements with respect to the contributions to, interests in, management of and conduct of Circuits.

Now therefore in consideration of the mutual promises and agreements of each of the parties hereto, the parties agree as follows:

Article I
Capitalization of Circuits

1.1 Circuits' authorized stock shall be 7,200 shares of no par common stock.

1.2 No other classes or types of stock shall be authorized without the unanimous consent of the parties hereto.

1.3 The board of directors of Circuits may authorize and issue debt of the corporation when, in their business judgment, the operation of the corporation requires the issuance of such debt.

* * *

Article II
Contributions to and Financial Interests in Circuits

2.1 Ray and Ezra agree to cause Medical Circuits Co. ("the Partnership"), a limited liability partnership in which they are equal partners, to convey to Circuits all of the Partnership's assets subject to its liabilities which Circuits will assume, an agreed net value of $504,000, in exchange for 5040 shares of Circuits' common stock, a price of $100 a share.

2.2 Harri agrees to convey to Circuits her 5% profits interest in the Partnership, which has an agreed value of $30,000, and $6,000 in cash, in exchange for 360 shares of Circuits' common stock, a price of $100 a share.

2.3 Roberta agrees to convey to Circuits 18,000 shares of the common stock of Ideal Life and Casualty Co., Inc., which has an agreed value of $180,000, in exchange for 1,800 shares of Circuits' common stock, a price of $100 a share.

* * *

Article III
Participation in Management and Employment by Circuits

3.1   Each of the parties hereto agrees that upon formation of Circuits they will each execute, and hold their stock subject to, the Shareholders' Agreement attached hereto as Exhibit A which in part provides that each one of the parties hereto will be elected a member of the four-person board of directors of Circuits.

*　*　*

3.3   Ray, Ezra and Harri agree that upon formation of Circuits they will each execute an Employment Agreement in the form attached hereto as Exhibit B which in part provides for a five-year term of employment.

Balance Sheet of the Partnership[1]

Assets
(x 1000)

	Basis	Fair Market Value
Cash	$ 15	$ 15
Inventory of Circuit Boards[2]	90	240
Equipment		
Cost	$600	
Depreciation	(450[3]) 150	210
Patents and Technical Know-how	15	333
Goodwill	0	120
	$270	$918

Liabilities
(x 1000)

	Basis	Fair Market Value
Trade Accounts Payable	$114	$114
Term Loan for Equipment and		
Working Capital	300	300
Capital Accounts		
Raymond Fielding	(72)	252
Ezra Minor	(72)	252
	$270	$918

1. The Partnership accounts using the accrual method.
2. The inventory of circuit boards turns over every three months.
3. Depreciation is computed using the most accelerated method available.

Note:

See the Note on Legal Drafting following Problem 3P at page 15, the Note on Limited Liability Partnerships following Problem 2P at page 10, and the Note on Representing More Than One Party following Problem 2P at page 9.

A Preincorporation Agreement is a form of Preformation Agreement. See the Note on Preformation Agreements following Problem 1P at page 7.

Problem 27P

J. James Bookseller (Bookseller) is the trade name under which a general partnership made up of Tom Fikelis (Tom) and Betty Lewin (Betty), equal partners, has done business for the last thirty years in the city in which you practice. When Tom and Betty formed the partnership each contributed, in cash, one-half of the necessary capital. All withdrawals from the partnership have been in cash. The withdrawals have been equally made and have never exceeded profits. Bookseller is engaged in the purchase and sale of new and used books, including both fiction and nonfiction. Bookseller has been a very profitable business. It owns a small building and conducts its operations on the first floor. The second floor is rented, as office space, to three tenants. The latest balance sheet of Bookseller, prepared using the accrual method of accounting and showing the range of the fair market values of the partnership's assets, is as follows.

J. James Bookseller
(000 omitted)
Assets

	Adjusted Basis	Fair Market Value	
Cash	$ 20	$ 20	- $ 20
Accounts Receivable	30	30	- 30
Inventory of Books	55	60	- 84
Furniture and Fixtures	60		
(Less the most accelerated rate of depreciation available)	(45) 15	30	- 40
Building	100		
(Less Straight-Line Dep.)	(60) 40	50	- 66
Land	20	30	- 40
Goodwill	-	20	- 40
	$180	$240	- $320

Liabilities

	Adjusted Basis	Fair Market Value	
Accounts Payable	$ 20	$ 20	- $ 20
Mortgage on Land and Building	40	40	- 40
Capital Accounts			
Tom	60	90	- 130
Betty	60	90	- 130
	$180	$240	- $320

Marvel Books, Inc. (Marvel) is a recently formed corporation which operates a bookstore in rented space in the fashionable downtown mall. June McCarthy (June), Janice Kahn (Janice) and Marvin White (Marvin) each own one-third of the stock of the corporation. The corporation acquired its furniture and fixtures through the use of the proceeds of an installment loan from First National Bank. In addition, First National Bank has made available to Marvel a working capital line of credit. Marvel has used the line of credit to assist it in acquiring inventory. Marvel has specialized in art, biographies, European literature and comic books. It has done very well during the few years of its existence. June, Janice and Marvin would like to expand Marvel's operations into a full-line bookstore. The latest balance sheet of Marvel, using the accrual method of accounting and showing the fair market value of its assets, is as follows.

Marvel Books, Inc.
(000 omitted)

Assets

		Adjusted Basis	Fair Market Value
Cash		$ 6	$ 6
Accounts Receivable		14	14
Inventory of Books		70	120
Furniture and Fixtures	$45		
(Less the most accelerated rate of depreciation available)	(25)	20	30
Goodwill		-	20
		$110	$190

Liabilities

	Adjusted Basis	Fair Market Value
Accounts Payable	$ 20	$ 20
Inventory Loan	60	60
Furniture and Fixtures Loan	30	30
Stated Capital (150 Shares, no par, one vote per share)	30	30
Earned Surplus (Deficit)	(30)	50
	$110	$190

June, Janice and Marvin have approached Tom and Betty with respect to Marvel's acquisition of Bookseller. The lines and types of books carried by Bookseller are complementary to those carried by Marvel. The lease of the office space on the second floor of Bookseller's building can be terminated and the first and second floor will provide adequate space to house the inventory of the combined company, which will use the name J. James Bookseller. Tom and Betty find this idea quite appealing since they are growing older and would like to be free of some of the responsibilities of operating the business while continuing to have an interest in, and relationship with, a bookstore.

June, Janice and Marvin believe that the assets of Bookseller are worth approximately $280,000. Tom and Betty agree. If this value of assets is used, then the combined value of Tom's and Betty's capital accounts in Bookseller is $220,000. June, Janice and Marvin have proposed that Marvel acquire Tom's and Betty's partnership interests in Bookseller in return for the following consideration: (1) an installment obligation in the amount of $120,000, having an interest rate of 13% and a term of ten years; (2) the assumption of Bookseller's $60,000 in liabilities; and (3) the issuance of 100 shares of preferred stock of Marvel, having a par value of $1,000 a share, a mandatory cumulative dividend of 15% per share, a preference on liquidation of par plus accumulated and unpaid dividends, a redemption price of no less than $1,000 per share plus accumulated and unpaid dividends, and one vote per share. They also propose that a shareholders' agreement be entered into. The shareholders' agreement will provide that no further voting stock will be issued without the unanimous consent of shareholders and that two of the five directors on the board of directors will be elected by the holders of the voting preferred shares.

Tom and Betty find this proposal acceptable in an economic sense. They, however, would like to avoid paying any income tax on the transaction at least until they have received some cash and only as they receive the cash. Please advise Tom and Betty of the income tax effects to them if the transaction is structured as June, Janice and Marvin suggest. Now consider, and advise Tom and Betty of any alternatives to, and modifications of, the proposal made by June, Janice and Marvin which will produce better income tax results for Tom and Betty while conforming as closely as possible to the economic relationship contemplated by June, Janice and Marvin's proposal.

Part F

FAMILY PARTNERSHIPS

PROBLEM 28P

Shadyside Knoll is a resort which has been owned by the Tabor family for a number of years. The current generation of Tabors (Arthur, Denise, Frank and Paula) recently inherited it from their parents. Arthur and Paula have been very active in the business. Arthur has been in charge of internal operations such as purchasing, food preparation, maintenance and repair. Paula has handled external operations such as clientele, financial arrangements, entertainment, advertising, and reservations. Both Arthur and Paula have been paid salaries of $70,000 per annum for their services. Denise is a lawyer, and Frank is an accountant in the small community near which Shadyside Knoll is located. Besides helping out during the busy season and on weekends at the resort, Denise and Frank, in recent years, have taken care of all of the necessary legal and accounting matters for the resort and have received reasonable fees for their services. The resort has been modestly successful; its net income has been in the range of about $240,000 a year, and the Tabors estimate its fair market value at about $1,200,000.

The present generation of Tabors is very close and feels strongly about keeping Shadyside Knoll as a family business. The Tabors have substantial outside income, Denise and Frank from their legal and accounting practices, Arthur as a consulting engineer and Paula as a real estate dealer, the professions they engage in during the off-season. Arthur has two children, 9 and 12 years of age. Denise has a son who is 22 years old, the same age as Frank's daughter. Paula's children are 6 and 10 years old. Both Denise's son and Frank's daughter are interested in participating in the resort business. No one is really sure about the interest of Paula's and Arthur's children, who have displayed interest in being astronauts and park rangers but not resort operators.

Denise and Frank have suggested that a limited partnership be formed for the ownership and operation of Shadyside Knoll. The term of the partnership will be 40 years, and at the end of that term it may be continued by a numerical majority vote of the then-partners. After formation of the partnership, Arthur will sell one-half of his general partnership interest to Denise's son for $10,000 down and a note for $140,000 bearing interest at

10% per annum, secured by a pledge of the partnership interest and payable in equal annual installments over the next 15 years. Denise will give her son the $10,000 down payment. Frank's daughter will purchase one-half of Paula's partnership interest in the same manner. Denise will give to Arthur, as trustee for Paula's children, one-half of Denise's partnership interest in the form of a limited partnership interest. The trust will terminate with respect to each child when the child reaches 21, and the child will receive 1/2 of the limited partnership interest held in trust. At the child's election, within five years after receipt of the interest, it may be converted into a general partnership interest. Frank will give to Paula, as trustee for Arthur's children, one-half of his partnership interest in the form of a limited partnership interest, on the same terms and conditions as Denise's conveyance to Arthur. The result of these transactions will be: one-eighth general partnership interests held by Arthur, Denise, Frank, Paula, Denise's son and Frank's daughter and one-eighth limited partnership interests held by Arthur as trustee for Paula's children and by Paula as trustee for Arthur's children.

Arthur and Paula will be the managing partners and make all day-to-day decisions including the determination of salaries to be paid and income to be retained for the needs of the partnership. All of the general partners will participate in major decisions affecting the partnership, as described in the partnership agreement, such as a sale of all or substantially all of the assets of the partnership. The limited partners will have those rights which are granted limited partners under the Revised Uniform Limited Partnership Act except for the right to remove the general partners. The partners will share in the income and loss of the partnership and partnership distributions in accord with their respective interests in the partnership. If a partner desires to withdraw from the partnership, the partnership will purchase that partner's interest at its then book value.

The Tabors have consulted you as an income tax expert with respect to any income tax problems which may exist now or in the future if the foregoing plan is carried out. What advice and recommendations would you give them?

Note:

See the Note on Interviewing and Client Counseling following Problem 1P at page 4.

Division II

TAXATION OF ORGANIZATIONS
TREATED AS CORPORATIONS

Part A

CONSIDERATIONS PRESENT IN THE
ORGANIZATION OF A
CORPORATION

---

1. IDENTIFICATION AS A CORPORATION

a. Associations Taxable as Corporations

PROBLEM 1C

Sunrise Chemicals, Inc. has, with the cooperation of a local stockbroker, formed the Sunrise Chemicals Junior Executive's Stock Investment Club. The purpose of the club is to provide an opportunity for the junior executives of the company to make investments in the stock market and to participate in a portfolio of securities more diverse than one that any of the junior executives alone could acquire. In order to get the club started, Sunrise Chemicals, Inc. contributed $10,000 per unit to the club for ten units of participation. The club then acquired $100,000 worth of the common stock of Sunrise Chemicals, Inc. The description of the club, as it appears in Sunrise Chemicals, Inc.'s Junior Executive Handbook, is set out below.

SUNRISE CHEMICALS, INC.
Junior Executive's Handbook

* * *

Sunrise Chemicals Junior Executive's Stock Investment Club

* * *

The Sunrise Chemicals Junior Executive's Stock Investment Club ("club") was formed under an agreement which provided that each initial participant received one unit of participation for each $10,000 in cash or fair market value of marketable securities which that participant contributed to the club. Participation in the club is limited to Sunrise Chemicals, Inc. and its junior executives. Each executive currently joining the club must contribute, in cash or fair market value of marketable securities, the book value of the number of units desired, but not less than $10,000 per unit. The books of the club, which are closed whenever new units are issued or existing units are surrendered for purchase by the club, reflect its assets at fair market value rather than cost. Units are freely assignable to any junior executive of Sunrise Chemicals, Inc., anyone in the immediate family of a junior executive and, with the prior approval of the club's Executive Committee, any other person. If a participant desires to withdraw from the club, the club will purchase the participant's units at their then fair market value, which is determined on the basis of the underlying fair market value of club assets.

The securities contributed to and purchased by the club are held in "street name" by the club's broker. The Executive Committee is composed of three members elected for a one-year term at the annual membership meeting. The Committee acts on requests to assign units, negotiates the broker's commission and takes care of most day-to-day matters of the club such as maintaining the club's books.

All decisions with respect to the purchase or sale of securities and the reinvestment or distribution of sale proceeds and dividends are made by majority vote of the participants, with each participant having one vote for each unit he or she owns. The participants meet twice a month for this purpose. The participants also may determine by majority vote if and when the club should be terminated and its assets distributed to the participants. In the absence of such a determination the club continues in existence.

* * *

During the first year of the club's operation, some securities were sold at a $15,000 gain, others were sold at a $12,000 loss and about $10,000 in dividends were collected. All dividends and sale proceeds were reinvested in securities. The fair market value of the securities portfolio currently exceeds cost by about $80,000. The participants in the club seek your advice as to how the club and its participants should be treated for income tax purposes. In addition, they would like your suggestions with respect to any changes they should make in the operation of the club.

PROBLEM 2C

Your client, Ramsey Metal, Inc. (Ramsey), is a Delaware corporation whose principal business consists of mining and processing bauxite minerals resulting in the production of aluminum and aluminum products. Ramsey, in association with the government of Guinea, has recently entered into a business venture in Guinea for the development of bauxite deposits in an area along the Great Scarcies River.

Pete Ashley, the general counsel of Ramsey, has asked you whether Kindia Metal Company (Kindia), the joint venture company Ramsey has formed with the government of Guinea, will be treated, for United States tax purposes, as a partnership or as a corporation. Kindia was created under special enabling legislation passed by the Guinean national assembly. The company was formed with ten participation units, five of which were issued to the Guinean government in exchange for certain land and mineral interests, and five of which were issued to Ramsey in exchange for $20 million and a commitment to provide the know-how and skilled personnel to develop the bauxite deposits and operate Kindia. Under the enabling legislation, Kindia will exist until the bauxite deposits on its land are exhausted. The venture, however, can be terminated at any time after 15 years, by a two-thirds vote of the Guinean national assembly or, with the concurrence of Ramsey, by a simple majority vote of the assembly. In the event of termination, the assets of Kindia, other than the land on which it operates and its mineral rights, will be divided among the holders of "participation units" in proportion to their holding of those interests. On termination the land and mineral interests revert to the Guinean government. During the first twenty years of Kindia's existence, the participation units are not transferable except by permission, by simple majority vote, of the Guinean national assembly. After such time the participation units are freely transferable.

Under the enabling legislation, the profits of Kindia, which are to be exempt from Guinean taxes, are to be divided among holders of participation units in proportion to those holdings. The legislation also provides that the government of Guinea shall not be liable for any losses incurred by Kindia and that Ramsey shall have no liability for losses beyond its initial investment plus $15 million. Neither the land nor mineral interests contributed by Guinea will be subject to claims of commercial or tort creditors.

The enabling legislation further provides that holders of participation units are entitled to designate the holder of one seat on Kindia's governing board for each participation unit held by them. Deadlocks on the governing board are to be broken by the Speaker of the Guinean national assembly. The principal functions of the governing board are to: (1) select the managers of the company who shall have power to negotiate on behalf of, and enter into contracts for Kindia, and otherwise manage its day to day affairs; (2) determine whether profits realized by Kindia shall be retained by Kindia for reinvestment in the business or distributed to holders of participation units; and (3) establish the general business policies of Kindia.

Mr. Ashley indicated that he had first raised the question of the tax status of Kindia with Ramsey's house counsel staff, which felt it best to bring in your law firm to advise Mr. Ashley whether Kindia will be treated as a partnership or as a corporation under the Internal Revenue Code. Prepare yourself to advise Mr. Ashley.

PROBLEM 3C

Herman Stein, one of your quite well-to-do clients, has come in to see you. Herman is 43 years old, married and has three minor children. He derives a substantial income from: (1) his salary as a supervising architect with Well-Built Homes, Inc., a publicly held residential contractor and developer; (2) the profits from his sole proprietorship, D/B/A H. Stein, Architectural Consultation; and (3) securities and improved real estate which he owns. A large portion of his income is taken by the federal government in payment of income tax. Herman has received a brochure from a national organization promising family security and the reduction of income taxes if he adopts the organization's Family Estate Plan. For a modest charge the organization will provide a Family Estate Plan specifically designed for Herman. Herman would like your advice whether the adoption of such a plan would save him income taxes and how the plan would be treated for income tax purposes.

The Family Estate Plan, as generally described by the brochure, is as follows:

Herman, as grantor, would create a trust named "The Stein Family Estate (A Trust)" (hereinafter the Family Estate) which is referred to as a "pure trust," an "equity trust," or a "constitutional trust." Herman would transfer to the Family Estate his personal residence, improved real estate, income-producing securities and his sole proprietorship. In addition, Herman would assign to the Family Estate exclusive use of his "lifetime services," including all remuneration earned by him regardless of its source. In exchange, Herman would receive certificates representing all "units of beneficial interest" in the Family Estate.

At the time of the assignment of his "lifetime services" to the Family Estate, Herman would notify Well-Built Homes, Inc. of the assignment and direct that remuneration which, but for the assignment, would be payable to him should be paid to the Family Estate.

Herman, his wife, and a third party acceptable to Herman would be named as "trustees" of the Family Estate. After the transfer, Herman would retain one-half of the "units of beneficial interest" and assign the remaining units in equal shares to his wife and children. Such "units of beneficial interest," evidenced by certificates, are described in the governing instrument as "transferable." A certificate holder, without the consent of other certificate holders or the "trustees," can transfer any or all of the certificate holder's interest in the Family Estate by sale, exchange, or otherwise.

Under the governing instrument, the Family Estate would continue for a period of twenty years unless the "trustees" unanimously decided to terminate it earlier. Neither the death, insolvency, or bankruptcy of any certificate holder nor the transfer of "units of beneficial interest" in the Family Estate would operate as a termination or dissolution of the Family Estate or in any manner affect the Family Estate or its operations.

The governing instrument would provide that affirmative action, except for the filling of a vacant "trustee" position, which would require a unanimous vote of certificate holders, could be taken only upon a majority vote of the "trustees." The "trustees," in whom the property of the Family Estate is vested, would be authorized to enter into and conduct any legitimate business or commercial enterprise and to conduct all ancillary business activities under the name "Stein Family Estate (A Trust)." A majority of the "trustees" would have the power and authority to make distributions to holders of "units of beneficial interest." The certificate holders would not be personally liable for any liabilities of the Family Estate.

At the first meeting of the "trustees," Herman would be made the general manager of the Family Estate, his spouse would be made secretary, and their compensation would be established.

The trust instrument would provide that a "resolution" of the "trustees" authorizing what they determine to do, or have done, shall be evidence that such an act is within their power. The "trustees'" authority would be similar to that of the executor of an estate wherein the testator directs that the executor is to handle the estate in the manner he thinks best, limited by the terms of the instrument, without the necessity to resort to the court for permission or approval of any transaction.

The trust instrument would provide that Herman and his family could continue to live in the personal residence that Herman transfers to the Family Estate, purportedly for the convenience of the Family Estate in its capacity as Herman's "employer." In addition, the Family Estate would supply the living costs of and provide health care for Herman and his family.

Upon termination, the assets of the Family Estate would be distributed, pro rata, to the certificate holders. The "trustees" may perform and function, severally or collectively, for any purpose on behalf of any individual, group, or combination of individuals holding "units of beneficial interest." If and when the "trustees" exercise their discretion to make a distribution of income or principal to the certificate holders, that distribution would be required to be on a pro rata basis.

The Family Estate would be created in the state in which you practice and in which all parties reside at this time. The property of the Family Estate would also be located in the state. There is no indication that the law of the state would impose, up to the time of Herman's death, any restriction on the actions of the "trustees," in view of the explicit grant of unfettered discretionary powers in the instrument. The certificates of beneficial interest which Herman owns at his death would be subject to probate administration in the state. The Family Estate itself would not be subject to probate administration.

Note:

See the Note on Interviewing and Client Counseling following Problem 1P at page 4.

PROBLEM 4C

In Problem 8P you were advised of Van Shock & Company, Inc.'s plans to form a limited liability company and to offer 200 membership units in the company pursuant to a private placement in order to raise part of the financing necessary to rehabilitate the DeNevar Building. Review the facts given to you in Problem 8P and determine whether your firm can give an opinion, as part of the private placement memorandum, that, for income tax purposes, the limited liability company will be treated as a partnership and the purchasers of membership units will be treated as partners.

Note:

See the Notes on Opinion Letters and Limited Liability Companies following Problem 4P at page 22. See the Note on Private Placement Memoranda following Problem 6P at page 30.

PROBLEM 5C

Rebecca Williams, the senior partner in the income tax department of the firm with which you are associated, recently received the following memorandum and attachments from one of the partners in the securities department of the firm. She would like you to consider the question raised in the memorandum and advise her of your conclusions.

TO:	Rebecca Williams *Nelson*
FROM:	H. Nelson Bruce
RE:	Oliver Enterprises, Inc.
DATE:	March 10, Year*

Oliver Enterprises, Inc. ("Oliver") is a new corporate client of the firm. It has been engaged in the business of equipment leasing for the last four to

* See explanatory footnote in Introduction, page vii, note 1.

five years. Oliver operates in the following manner. Two to three times a year Oliver forms a new limited partnership. Oliver contributes a nominal amount of cash for a two percent interest in the partnership as the general partner. The remaining 98% interest in the partnership is then sold as limited partnership interests to no more than 35 investors for a total purchase price of about $3 million. In the last few years Oliver has, itself, purchased between 10% and 20% of the limited partnership interests offered for sale to investors. Once all of the limited partnership interests are sold, Oliver causes the limited partnership to purchase sophisticated, high-tech equipment for about $10 million. The $3 million raised from the sale of limited partnership interests is used as equity and the remaining $7 million is borrowed on a recourse basis from a banking institution. The equipment is then leased for relatively short terms to major companies who have a need for such equipment.

Oliver is compensated by the various limited partnerships for its services as general partner and for supervising the maintenance and servicing of the leased equipment owned by the limited partnerships. All the gross income that Oliver receives as a result of this compensation, as well as the cash distributions that it receives as a general and limited partner of the various limited partnerships, is invested by it in general and limited partnership interests in subsequently formed limited partnerships. As a result, apart from its general and limited partnership interests, some of which are quite valuable, Oliver has very little in the way of net worth.

Oliver has requested our legal assistance with the formation of, and sale of the limited partnership interests in, the first limited partnership to be formed by it this year. In connection therewith, we have been asked to give our opinion that the limited partnership will be treated as a partnership for income tax purposes. I have attached the relevant portions of the limited partnership agreement that we propose to use. I would like your advice whether we can give the opinion requested.

**CERTIFICATE AND AGREEMENT
OF
LIMITED PARTNERSHIP
OF
EDINBOROUGH LEASING, LTD.**

* * *

ARTICLE I
Name and Certain Definitions

* * *

1.3 "Capital Account" shall mean, when used with respect to any Partner, the initial capital contribution of the Partner (as shown under the "Initial Capital Contribution" column of the signature pages to this Agreement), increased by: (i) the amount of all additional contributions to the capital of the Partnership made by such Partner; and (ii) the amount of all Net Gains credited to the account of such Partner and decreased by: (i) the amount of all Net Losses charged to the account of such Partner; and (ii) the amount of all distributions made to such Partner.

1.4 "Capital Contribution" shall mean $200 with respect to the General Partner and, with respect to all other Partners, the amount shown under the "Initial Capital Contribution" column opposite each Partner's name on the signature pages hereto, plus any additional capital contributions the Partner may subsequently make to the Partnership.

* * *

ARTICLE II
Management and Accounting

* * *

2.6 On vote of the holders of 90% of the Limited Partnership Interests, the General Partner may be removed and a successor General Partner appointed.

* * *

ARTICLE III
Contributions and Accounts

* * *

3.2 Each Partner shall be entitled to recover the amount in his Capital Account and his Capital Contributions solely at the time or times provided for herein and solely from the assets of the Partnership (including any contributions required to be made by Partners under the following sections of this Article III), and no other Partner shall have any personal liability therefor.   Except as otherwise provided in this Agreement, no Partner shall have a right to receive a distribution of property, other than cash, from the Partnership.

3.3 The General Partner shall contribute to the Partnership, upon the Partnership's dissolution and termination, any deficit then existing in the General Partner's Capital Account.

* * *

ARTICLE IV
Allocation of Net Gains and Net Losses

4.1   Net Gains and Net Losses shall be allocated among the Partners in the following manner: 2% of any Net Gain or Net Loss shall be allocated to the General Partner and 98% of any Net Gain or Net Loss shall be allocated to the Limited Partners.

* * *

ARTICLE VII
Transfer of Partnership Interest

* * *

7.3 The Partnership interest of a Limited Partner may be assigned in whole, or in part, including all, or part, of the interest in the gains, losses and distributions of the Partnership, only if, prior thereto, the General Partner consents in writing to such assignment.   In addition, the General Partner shall have the sole and absolute discretion to refuse to consent to any assignee of a Limited Partner becoming a substituted Limited Partner.

* * *

ARTICLE VIII
Retirement, Etc.

8.1   The retirement, insanity, death, dissolution, insolvency or bankruptcy of, or any other event with respect to, a Limited Partner shall not dissolve the Partnership.

8.2   The General Partner's bankruptcy, insolvency, dissolution, retirement, withdrawal or removal from the Partnership may cause the dissolution of the Partnership.

* * *

ARTICLE IX
Dissolution and Termination

9.1 The Partnership shall be dissolved and terminated upon the earliest to occur of the following: (a) the occurrence of the bankruptcy, insolvency, dissolution, retirement, withdrawal or removal of the General Partner unless, within 90 days after the occurrence of any such event, 90% of the remaining Partners agree in writing to continue the business of the Partnership and appoint a new General Partner; or (b) March 3, Year+20.* Upon dissolution and termination, the property owned by the Partnership shall, with reasonable promptness, be sold, distributed or otherwise disposed of and the Partnership liquidated subject to the provisions of this Agreement. Upon dissolution and termination, except as otherwise required by law, the assets of the Partnership (including any net proceeds from dispositions of assets pursuant to the preceding sentence) shall be used and distributed in the following order: (i) to pay or provide for the payment of all Partnership liabilities and liquidating expenses and obligations; and (ii) to distribute to the Partners the amount then in their Capital Accounts.

Note:

See the Note on Legal Drafting following Problem 3P at page 15. See the Note on Opinion Letters following Problem 4P at page 22.

b. Avoiding Corporate Status

PROBLEM 6C

A. Your client, Real Estate Endeavors, Ltd. (Endeavors), a limited partnership, is well-known in the community as a developer of shopping plazas, commercial office buildings and apartment buildings. The general partners have found in recent years that when they have attempted to obtain options on or title to various parcels of real estate in order to put together a suitable tract for development, the owners, knowing the partnership's reputation, have usually demanded quite a high price for their real estate. The partners therefore propose in the future to organize a number of corporations for each new development, hoping thereby to disguise the identity of the partnership and obtain options or title to property at lower prices. Immediately after such corporations, acting as nominees for Endeavors, have obtained all options or real estate necessary for development, the options or the real estate will be conveyed to the partnership for development.

The corporations will never issue any stock except for qualifying shares which will be nominally held by a member or members of your law firm on behalf of Endeavors. The funds necessary to acquire the options or real estate will be contributed to the corporations by Endeavors as capital contributions. There will be only an initial meeting of each of the corporations. At that meeting the general partners in Endeavors will be elected directors and officers of the corporations and then will authorize and execute an agreement between the corporations and Endeavors providing that the corporations are only nominees of Endeavors and that immediately upon obtaining all options or real estate necessary for a development, such options or real estate will be conveyed to Endeavors.

The partners of Endeavors ask whether the corporations will be treated as taxable entities and, if so, what the effect of that treatment will be. What would be your advice if you found that: (1) the corporations acquired only options, and when options on all the necessary real estate were acquired, the corporations transferred the options to Endeavors, which then exercised them; (2) the corporations acquired only the necessary real estate and transferred it to Endeavors; or (3) the corporations acquired both options and real estate and transferred the options and real estate to Endeavors?

B. What would be your reaction to the above issue if, with respect to one corporation which had acquired three of six parcels necessary for a development but was having difficulty obtaining the other parcels, Endeavors determined, that in order to obtain some return on its investment, the corporation should lease the parcels acquired as a used car lot until all the necessary parcels were obtained? You may assume that the nominee agreement referred to above is in existence and that the corporation immediately distributed any rent received from the parcels to Endeavors.

C. Your client has found that many of the financial institutions in the area are unwilling to make mortgage loans to a partnership because of the state usury law's limitation on the interest which can be charged. The financial institutions, however, are willing to make such loans to a corporation since, in this state, corporate borrowers are excluded from the limitations of the usury law.

The financial institutions are also willing, after the loan is made, to permit the corporation to convey the property subject to the mortgage to

Endeavors, without an assumption by Endeavors of the mortgage liability. The general partners of Endeavors feel that this is a good procedure because they personally will have no liability for the loan. Will the use of a corporation to borrow money and grant a mortgage affect your conclusions as to the treatment of the corporation for income tax purposes?

PROBLEM 7C

XYZ Manufacturing Corporation has, for the last 20 years, been a successful manufacturer of alphabet building blocks for children. Eighty percent of its stock is owned by various members of the Zancovitch family. The other 20% is owned by seventy of XYZ's employees, all of whom are unrelated to the Zancovitch family. Alex Zancovitch and his sister, Hilda, are the principal shareholders and executive officers of the corporation. They are both getting on in years and, having decided to retire, want to get their money out of the corporation.

Both Alex and Hilda are impatient people, and they want to have the corporation liquidated and dissolved immediately. At their insistence, the Board of Directors and shareholders of the corporation adopted a resolution authorizing the officers to file a certificate of dissolution and authorizing liquidation of the corporation's assets. Because of the large number of employee-shareholders, the Directors felt that a later sale of the assets would be unduly burdensome if the assets were distributed directly to the shareholders. Therefore, the Directors, with the shareholders' approval at a duly convened meeting, appointed themselves trustees of the corporation's assets for the benefit of the shareholders.

A certificate of dissolution was duly filed, and all corporate assets, except for cash not required for continued operations, were distributed to the Directors in their capacity as trustees for the benefit of the shareholders. The cash not required for continued operations was distributed directly to the shareholders. The trustees, apparently unable to locate a buyer, continued to operate the business and to employ the same employees. The agreement between the trustees and the shareholders was that all the net income from such operations, other than that needed for further operations, would be currently distributed to the shareholders pro rata.

The Zancovitches have asked for your advice whether the XYZ Corporation should file a final income tax return for the period ending on the date of dissolution and liquidation.

If, instead of the Directors with shareholder approval appointing themselves as trustees, the shareholders had met and themselves appointed the trustees, would this have any bearing on your advice? If the trustees, when they received the assets in liquidation, were negotiating a sale of the assets and the sale in fact occurred within 6 months thereafter, would this affect your advice?

What would be your reaction if, at the time of liquidation, there were no prospects for sale and the trustees operated the business for three years and then sold the assets? Under these facts, are there any income tax problems for the Zancovitch family, the other shareholders or the corporation other than the question whether XYZ can file a final tax return? If so, what are they and what dangers do they present?

Note:

See the Note on Interviewing and Client Counseling following Problem 1P at page 4.

PROBLEM 8C

You are a Senior Technician Reviewer in the Office of the Assistant Chief Counsel of the Internal Revenue Service. One of your colleagues has prepared a Private Letter Ruling to be sent to the taxpayer, Mustafah Investments, Inc. You have been asked to review the Private Letter Ruling and determine whether the position taken in the Private Letter Ruling is proper.

May 17, Year*

Hakkim Mustafah
Mustafah Investments, Inc.
1475 La Salle Street
Chicago, IL   60601

Dear Mr. Mustafah:

This is in reply to your letter of February 1, Year and subsequent correspondence requesting a ruling on the classification of a trust as a liquidating trust for federal tax purposes.

* See explanatory footnote in Introduction, page vii, note 1.

The information that you gave us states that Mustafah Investments, Inc. (Mustafah) was created and operated as an investment company by you and your brother, Nazir Mustafah. Mustafah has made a number of investments and presently holds some corporate securities, some corporate debentures, and a number of real estate interests. Mustafah currently has a number of contingent debts and unliquidated claims outstanding. You and your brother each own 50% of the stock of Mustafah.

Early in Year-2, your brother indicated his desire to withdraw from Mustafah. As a result, you determined that Mustafah's purposes could no longer be carried out after the loss of funds sufficient to satisfy the interest of your brother. Accordingly, Mustafah adopted a plan of dissolution and liquidation in which Mustafah was to liquidate its assets for reasonable value over a reasonable period of time. At the conclusion of this period Mustafah was authorized to create a liquidating trust, to be known as the Trust, in order to receive: (1) those assets which could not be sold for a reasonable value; and (2) certain liquid assets to provide for payment of creditors whose claims at that time were still contingent or unliquidated. Accordingly, in Year, you determined that the transfer of some of Mustafah's remaining assets to the Trust had become appropriate.

The terms of the Trust provide the following: (a) the Trust is organized for the primary purpose of liquidating the assets transferred to it from Mustafah and paying creditors' claims as they become determinable and liquidated with no objective to continue or engage in the conduct of a trade or business; (b) the existence of the Trust shall terminate upon the earlier to occur of (i) the sale of all the assets of the Trust transferred to it from Mustafah and the payment of all determinable and liquidated creditors' claims and (ii) the expiration of seven years following the commencement date of the Trust. However, notwithstanding the foregoing, if the Trust contains installment obligations, such as those described in Section 453(h) of the Code, which arise from the sale of property of Mustafah, the Trust term may be extended, solely with respect to those obligations, for a period that is reasonably necessary to collect and distribute payments made with respect to the obligations. The investment powers of the trustee of the Trust are unlimited but the trustee presently intends only to exercise the powers to invest in demand and time deposits in banks or savings institutions, or temporary investments such as short-term certificates of deposit or Treasury bills. The Trust will not receive transfers of any listed stocks or securities, any readily-marketable assets, or any operating assets of a going business other than those assets necessary to provide for the payment of contingent or unliquidated claims. The Trust will not receive or retain cash in excess of a reasonable amount to meet unliquidated or contingent claims. The Trust will not receive transfers of any unlisted stock of a single issuer that represents 80 percent or more of the stock of such issuer or any general or limited partnership interests.   Except for the retention of a reasonable amount of proceeds or income to meet unliquidated or contingent claims, the Trust may elect to distribute at least annually to all beneficial owners any proceeds from the sale of assets or income from investments.

The following representations have been made by you with respect to the Trust: (a) the Trust does not now contain any installment obligations such as those described in Section 453(h) of the Internal Revenue Code but it may receive such installment obligations on the sale of assets conveyed to the Trust; (b) the trustee of the Trust will make continuing efforts to dispose of the Trust's assets, to make timely distributions, and not to prolong unduly the duration of the Trust; and (c) you are the trustee of the Trust.

Section 301.7701-4(d) of the Procedure and Administration Regulations provides that certain organizations that are commonly known as liquidating trusts are treated as trusts for purposes of the Code. An organization will be considered a liquidating trust if it is organized for the primary purpose of liquidating and distributing the assets transferred to it, and if its activities are all reasonably necessary to, and consistent with, the accomplishment of that purpose. A liquidating trust is treated as a trust for purposes of the Code because it is formed with the objective of liquidating particular assets and not with the purpose of carrying on a profit-making business that normally would be conducted through business organizations classified as corporations or partnerships. However, if the liquidation is unreasonably prolonged or if the liquidation purpose becomes so obscured by business activities that the declared purpose of the liquidation can be said to be lost or abandoned, the status of the organization will no longer be that of a liquidating trust.

The Internal Revenue Service will issue a ruling that an organization is classified as a liquidating trust if the conditions described above are met. The Trust complies with the conditions.

Accordingly, based on the representations made and the facts as presented, the Trust will be classified for federal income tax purposes as a liquidating trust owned by its beneficiaries. The beneficiaries will be treated as if they had received a distribution of the assets and had then contributed them to the Trust.

Except as specifically set forth above, no opinion is expressed concerning the federal tax consequences of the facts described above under any other provision of the Code.

This ruling is directed only to the taxpayer who requested it. Section 6110(j)(3) of the Code provides that it may not be used or cited as precedent.

In accordance with the power of attorney on file with this office, a copy of this letter is being sent to your authorized representative.

Sincerely yours,

J. ELLEN HINES

Senior Technician Reviewer Branch 2
Office of the Assistant Chief Counsel
(Corporate Transactions)

Enclosures: 2

Note:

See the Note on Ruling Requests following Problem 24P at page 88.

2. FORMATION OF A CORPORATION

PROBLEM 9C

One of the general partners of the firm with which you are associated recently received the following letter from Marc Cohen, for whom the firm has done some work from time to time. The partner would like your assistance in preparing a reply to the letter.

Lakeside Inn
1050 North Shore Drive
South Haven, Michigan

September 3, Year*

Evelyn Brinkerhof, Esq.
Baker, McKittrick & Hayes
501 Ship Street
St. Joseph, Michigan

Dear Ms. Brinkerhof:

I have operated Lakeside Inn, a summer resort, as a sole proprietorship since inheriting it from my parents about fifteen years ago. Lakeside is in an excellent location for a summer resort. The lodges, kitchen, dining room and cabins are attractive and in good repair but are in need of modernization such as air conditioning, color TV sets and better lighting. In addition, the resort property, although well-maintained and in good repair, requires the addition of certain facilities such as a swimming pool, tennis courts, club house and lounge in order to compete effectively with the more recently established resorts in the area. I estimate that the total net value of all the assets which currently make up Lakeside is about $600,000. The assets, my adjusted basis in them, and their value is as follows:

Item	Adjusted Basis (x 1,000)	Value (x 1,000)
1. Kitchen Utensils, Silverware, Dishes, Linen	$ 0	$ 48
2. Furniture and Fixtures	66	132
3. Equipment	24	120
4. Buildings	132	288
5. Land	126	372
	$348	$960

* See explanatory footnote in Introduction, page vii. note 1

The land and buildings are subject to a mortgage liability in the amount of $360,000. The kitchen utensils, silverware, dishes and linen were expensed in the year in which they were purchased. The furniture, fixtures and equipment have an estimated remaining actual useful life of about ten years.

The buildings have an estimated remaining actual useful life of about twenty years. All depreciable assets have been depreciated using the straight-line method and the shortest available useful life. I have determined that the modernization and new facilities described above will cost about $600,000. I have not saved much money over the years, and the most I can invest is about $12,000.

Conveniently, my college roommate, Ned Alterman, recently inherited a substantial amount of money. Ned is prepared to invest $600,000 in Lakeside. Ned and I estimate that, once the modernization is accomplished and the new facilities are added, Lakeside will produce, after the deduction of reasonable salaries for Ned and me and all other proper deductions for income tax purposes, about $66,000 in net taxable income per year. We would like to share equally in the capital and profits of Lakeside once Ned has made his investment.

I recognize that upon Ned's investment in Lakeside some form of entity will be needed for the operation of the resort. Ned and I like the limited liability, centralized management, transferability and continuity of life inherent in the corporate form. Please advise us whether there are any income tax problems or concerns which might arise from the formation of a corporation to own and operate Lakeside and the conveyance of the money and assets described above to the corporation. We would like the income tax treatment accorded each of us, while operating Lakeside, to approximate each one's economic position.

Please let me hear from you at your earliest convenience.

Very truly yours,

Marc Cohen

Marc Cohen

Note:

See the Note on Interviewing and Client Counseling following Problem 1P at page 4.

PROBLEM 10C

H. Boyd Pickens (Boyd) is a well-respected practicing architect. About five years ago he became fascinated with the possibilities of computer-assisted design. He abandoned the practice of architecture and formed a small proprietorship, Design Programs Co. (Design), for the development and sale of programs for computer-assisted architectural design. In the ensuing years Design has developed programs to assist in the design of mechanicals, structural components, electricals and foundations. Each of the programs has been copyrighted in the name of Design.

Because of a lack of capital, Design has been slow to acquire an inventory of programs and aggressively sell them. Design has an adequate inventory of the first programs developed — those for mechanicals and electricals — and these programs have sold quite well. Its lack of capital, however, has kept Design from manufacturing an adequate inventory of any of the newer programs and from mounting an aggressive sales campaign for any of its programs. In fact, while its prospects are very bright, Design has lost money in all of the last five years. Loans from United Bank were used to fund the creation of some of the programs. While the loans remain on the books of Design as a liability, the costs of creating the programs were deducted for financial and income tax purposes as research and development expenses. Boyd presently operates Design out of leased facilities. Design, however, owns all its machinery and equipment. The balance sheet of Design at the end of its most recent fiscal year, prepared using the accrual method of accounting, appears at the end of this problem.

Word has spread in the trade that Design's programs are the best and most highly-advanced programs for computer-assisted design available anywhere. While most of the program development has been done by Boyd, he has been assisted by two employees of Design, Mable Kyle and Harris Ledstone (Mable and Harris), who both have dual degrees in architecture and computer science. In order to induce Mable and Harris to become employees of Design, their employment agreements provide that they are each entitled to receive 11% of each year's profit, if any, earned by Design. While Mable and Harris have not as yet received anything pursuant to that clause of their employment agreements, they anticipate that it will produce a great deal of money for them in the future. All the remaining ten employees of Design are compensated on an hourly basis.

Jane Clark and Howard Nettles (Jane and Howard), who are both partners in a large venture capital firm, have heard of the good reputation and high repute of Boyd and Design. While it appeared to them that Design was not a candidate for investment by their firm, they felt that they might personally take a chance and invest in Design in order to provide the working capital that the company needed. In their judgment, an investment of about $400,000 would provide the necessary capital so that, after a couple of years of start-up losses, a substantial return could be made on the investment. Jane and Howard also feel that, in order to be profitable, Design should own its own building to avoid the constant rent expense. Their friend, Raiso Yamata, owns a small two-story building which would be perfect for the operations of Design. The fair-market value of the land and building is $300,000. The building is subject to a mortgage liability of $100,000 and Raiso's adjusted basis in the land and building is $90,000. Raiso has agreed to convey the land and building to Design when and if Jane and Howard make their investment of $400,000. Jane, Howard and Raiso, after reviewing the operations of Design, agreed with the fair market values set out on the balance sheet of Design appearing at the end of this problem.

Jane, Howard and Raiso have proposed to Boyd that Design be incorporated and that the parties enter into the following pre-incorporation agreement.

PRE-INCORPORATION AGREEMENT

The parties hereto, H. Boyd Pickens ("Boyd"), Mable Kyle ("Mable"), Harris Ledstone ("Harris"), Jane Clark ("Jane"), Howard Nettles ("Howard") and Raiso Yamata ("Raiso"), have determined that it is in their mutual interest to form, invest in and operate a corporation to be known as Design Programs, Inc. ("Design") to engage in the business of formulating, designing, manufacturing and selling computer-assisted architectural design programs. The parties hereto believe that it is appropriate to set out their intentions and agreements with respect to the contributions to, interests in, and management and conduct of Design.

In consideration of the promises and agreements of each of the parties hereto, the parties agree as follows:

ARTICLE I
Contributions to Design

1.1 Boyd agrees to contribute to Design those assets listed on the balance sheet of Design Programs Co., which is attached to this agreement as Exhibit A, and Design agrees to assume the liabilities listed on that balance sheet. The parties agree that the assets of Design Programs Co. have the fair-market value and adjusted basis listed on the balance sheet.

1.2 Mable and Harris each agree to convey to Design their respective rights, contained in their employment agreements, to each receive 11% of the annual profits of Design Programs Co.

1.3 Jane and Howard each agree to invest $200,000 in Design.

1.4 Raiso agrees to convey to Design a two-story office building that he currently owns. The agreed fair-market value of the office building is $300,000. Raiso's adjusted basis in the office building is $90,000. The office building is subject to a mortgage liability of $100,000 which Design agrees to assume.

ARTICLE II
Interests in the Company

In return for each party's contribution, investment or conveyance to Design, the party will receive the interest in Design indicated below.

2.1 In return for their combined investment, Jane and Howard will receive: (a) a 30-year note of Design having a principal amount of $361,000 and bearing interest at 12% per annum; and (b) three hundred and ninety shares of voting stock of Design which will have a liquidation preference and stated price of $100 a share and a cumulative dividend of 9% per annum. Each share of stock will have one vote.

2.2 In return for Raiso's conveyance to Design, Raiso will receive: (a) a 30-year note of Design in the principal amount of $161,000, bearing interest at 12%; and (b) three hundred and ninety shares of the common stock of the corporation, having a liquidation preference and price of $100 a share and a cumulative dividend of 9% per annum.

2.3 In return for Boyd's contribution to Design, Boyd will receive: (a) a 30-year note of the corporation, subordinate to the notes given to Jane and Howard and Raiso, bearing interest at 9% and having a principal amount of $161,000; and (b) three hundred and ninety shares of the common stock of the corporation, having a liquidation preference and price of $100 a share, subordinate to the liquidation preference of Jane's and Howard's and Raiso's stock, and a cumulative dividend of 6% per annum.

2.4 In return for Mable's and Harris's contribution to Design, they will each receive 160 shares of the common stock of Design. While the stock they receive will be entitled to one vote per share, it will have no liquidation preference nor will it be entitled to a cumulative dividend.

ARTICLE III
Management of the Company

3.1 Jane, Howard, Raiso, Boyd and either Mable or Harris will be elected to the Board of Directors of Design.

3.2 Boyd will serve as the President of Design, Mable will serve as Vice-President—Product Development and Harris will serve as Vice-President—Manufacturing. Howard will be elected the Secretary of Design. Boyd, Mable and Harris will enter into employment agreements with Design in the form attached hereto as Exhibit B.

* * *

BALANCE SHEET OF DESIGN PROGRAMS, CO.
Assets
(in 000's)

		Basis	Fair Market Value
Cash		$ 5	$ 5
Accounts Receivable		10	10
Inventory of Design Programs		40	70
Machinery & Equipment	$100		
Depreciation	(55)	45	60
Copyrighted Programs		-	160
Goodwill		-	45
		$100	$350

	Liabilities	
	(in 000's)	
	Basis	Fair Market Value
Accounts Payable	$ 30	$ 30
United Bank Loan	120	120
Proprietor's Capital	(50)	200
	$100	$350

Boyd would like you to advise him of any income tax concerns or problems you foresee if Jane's, Howard's and Raiso's proposal is carried out.

Note:

See the Note on Preformation Agreements following Problem 1P at page 7. See also the Note on Legal Drafting following Problem 3P at page 15.

PROBLEM 11C

In Problem 2P, you were asked for your advice with respect to the steps which should be taken to form a limited liability partnership for Olive Mayer, Jefferson Wellknown, Jackson Wellborn and Ralph Guidinghand. The partnership was to be known as Creative Associates. A short while after obtaining your advice, the four clients returned to your office. They had second thoughts about operating the business in partnership form. They are seriously considering operating the business in corporate form, using the name Creative Associates, Inc. They have told you that each one proposes to make the same contribution to the corporation as he or she proposed to make to the partnership. In return, each expects to receive 25% of the common stock, be one of the four directors, and also be one of the officers.

Advise your clients of the steps which should be taken in the formation of the corporation in order to produce the best income tax results for all concerned. What ethical considerations are present in your representing all four of the incorporators?

Note:

See the Note on Representing More Than One Party following Problem 2P at page 9.

PROBLEM 12C

In Problem 16P you assisted the chair of the tax department in the firm with which you are associated in determining the income tax consequences to Wayland Shears and Thomas Hamilton of bringing Evan Lincoln into their limited liability partnership as a one-third partner. Apparently, Messrs. Shears, Hamilton and Lincoln had second thoughts about the transaction proposed in Problem 16P and the partner in the business department of the firm has sent a new memorandum asking for the tax department's advice on the income tax consequences of a new transaction which the parties have proposed. The chair of the tax department has again asked you to determine those tax consequences. She has given you the memorandum set out below.

Barnes, Reitmeister, Yoshira & Klein
1540 Clubhouse Drive
Davenport, IA   52803

Intraoffice Memo

TO: Amy Garcia

                        Art

FROM: Arthur Barnes

RE: Reorganization of Shears and Hamilton

Wayland Shears and Thomas Hamilton have expressed some concerns about their brokerage firm remaining in the limited liability partnership form when Evan Lincoln is brought into the partnership. They have asked us whether there would be any significant income tax problems in the use of a corporation as their form of business entity when Evan Lincoln is brought into the business. They have told me that Evan Lincoln would contribute the same assets for a one-third common stock interest in the corporation as he would have in the partnership. The limited liability partnership of Wayland and Thomas would contribute to the corporation its assets subject to its liabilities, other than those assets and liabilities which were going to be distributed to Wayland and Thomas in the prior proposal.

In return for the assets, the corporation would issue to the limited liability partnership two-thirds of the common stock of the corporation and assume its liabilities. The limited liability partnership would remain in existence owning two-thirds of the stock of the corporation and the assets and liabilities which were going to be distributed to Wayland and Thomas in the prior proposal.

As soon as you can, please advise me of the income tax consequences to Wayland, Thomas and Evan if the modified proposal described above is carried out.

Note:

See the Note on Representing More Than One Party following Problem 2P at page 9. See also the Note on Limited Liability Partnerships following Problem 2P at page 10.

PROBLEM 13C

Jean Reinhard and Joseph Glid are presently highly paid engineers employed by General Electric Company. They are both subject to the highest marginal income tax rate. They derive their income primarily from their salaries, but both also have substantial investment income. They have, in their spare time, developed a device called the Tricometer, which is capable of automatically adjusting light intensity in a room as external illumination increases or decreases. Jean and Joe have determined that the market for this device will be very large and plan to form a corporation to produce and sell the device. Each will own 50% of the corporation's stock. There are a number of expenses which must be incurred with respect to the Tricometer. First, they must obtain a trademark for the Tricometer. Second, they must obtain a trade name — "Tricometer." Third, they must have the Tricometer patented. Finally, they will incur about $10,000 in other expenses in organizing the corporation.

Jean and Joe have come to you for your advice whether they should pay these expenses individually and then assign the trademark, trade name and patent to the corporation. Or, should they first form the corporation and have it pay the expenses out of the money they contribute to it together with their know-how and rights in the Tricometer, in exchange for their 50% interests in the corporation? Or, should they pay the Tricometer expenses

1st option: assign
2nd option: exchange
3rd option: License

individually, license the corporation to use the trademark, tradename and patent for reasonable fees to be paid to Jean and Joe, and have the corporation pay its organization expenses out of money which they contribute to the corporation? Advise them as to the best procedure from an income tax standpoint.

PROBLEM 14C

Major Oil Company (Major), pursuant to its attempt to establish retail outlets in western Colorado, proposes to form a subsidiary, Major Western Colorado, Inc. (Western), which will have only voting common stock and to which it will transfer certain marketing assets in exchange for all of Western's stock.

Major has determined that there are about 100 independent garage owners and gasoline retailers in western Colorado. Immediately after forming Western, Major proposes to approach these independent businesses and offer up to 50% of Western's stock in return for transfers to Western by them of their business assets, including the garages, any franchises, etc. The stock will be distributed in proportion to the value of the assets exchanged, and individual interests may range from .01% to a maximum of 3% of the outstanding stock of Western. The individuals will continue to operate their establishments but will sell only Major products and will receive salaries and bonuses from Western. They will also participate in Western's profit-sharing, medical, and life insurance plans.

The officers of Major and some of the prospective individual stockholders of Western have asked for your advice as to the income tax consequences of carrying out the transaction described above. What is your advice? How should the transaction be carried out to maximize everyone's chances for tax-free treatment? What would be your reaction if you discovered that some of the independent garage owners agreed to take in exchange for their assets only: (1) Western long term debt; or (2) Western short term debt? Is there any reason why you should not represent both Major and Western's prospective individual stockholders?

Note:

See the Note on Representing More Than One Party following Problem 2P at page 9.

PROBLEM 15C

Wallboard, Inc. (Wallboard) presently manufactures, sells and markets various building materials for home construction. Its stock is divided equally among four individual stockholders. Wallboard's manufacturing plant is leased from Wallboard Services, Inc. (Services). Twenty percent of Services' stock is held by Wallboard, and the balance is divided equally among the four stockholders of Wallboard.

The stockholders of Wallboard have decided, for business reasons, to have Wallboard's present sales and marketing operations carried out by Services. The stockholders would like to have Wallboard contribute all its assets related to sales and marketing (which have a fair market value substantially in excess of their adjusted basis) to Services which would also assume the existing employment agreements between the sales and marketing personnel and Wallboard.

In return for these assets, Services would issue to Wallboard certain of its authorized but unissued common stock. After the transaction, Wallboard will hold 60% of the stock of Services and the balance of the stock will be divided equally among the four stockholders of Wallboard.

Advise Wallboard, its stockholders and Services of the income tax consequences of the foregoing proposal. Do you have any suggestions for the modification of the proposal to improve the likelihood of tax-free treatment?

PROBLEM 16C

Prepare yourself to respond to the following letter which the chief of your division in the state Attorney General's office received from the Secretary of Commerce of New Jersey.

Emily G. Johnston
Secretary of Commerce
State of New Jersey

September 10, Year*

Thomas V. Glynn, Esq.
Assistant Attorney General
One Independence Plaza
Trenton, New Jersey   08610

Dear Mr. Glynn:

This letter confirms my telephone conversation with you of yesterday in which I asked for your assistance in formulating a reinvigorated industry search program. As you know, for some years now the State of New Jersey has had an industrial recruitment program run by this office. As a part of our recruitment activities, the state and various local governments offer financial inducements to industries for locating within the state and in local communities.   These inducements frequently take the form of direct subsidies such as land on which factories are built, cash used to construct new buildings or to purchase machinery and equipment, and in-kind contributions of new materials and cash. The use of such inducements is unrestricted except for the requirement that they be used to start a new business in a given area.

It is my understanding that when the State of Alabama succeeded in getting Daimler-Benz to locate its Mercedes-Benz plant in Alabama, a critical part of its strategy was that it offered to provide its assistance in the form of land and plant, whereas a competing state offered to provide its assistance in the form of cash and inventory. As I noted yesterday, I believe that because of tax considerations Daimler-Benz found the Alabama offer to be more advantageous.

I would very much appreciate an explanation of the tax consequences and advantages of the Alabama offer and would also like your advice as to the form that New Jersey subsidies should take to minimize any negative tax impact on the recipients.

* See explanatory footnote in the Introduction, page vii, note 1.

Should you desire any additional information on our industrial recruitment program, please do not hesitate to call me on my direct line (842-7412) or my executive assistant Butch Pryor (842-7448).

Very truly yours,

Emily G. Johnston

Emily G. Johnston
Secretary of Commerce

PROBLEM 17C

Snowpyle Corporation is engaged in the development of Snowpyle Mountain as a destination ski area. It owns most of the real estate suitable for development on and near the mountain and has developed a portion of this real estate with residential condominium units. You have assisted it in carrying out its development plans.

Snowpyle Hotel, Inc., a wholly owned subsidiary of Snowpyle Corporation, has constructed a combination hotel-conference center and athletic facility (the hotel) as a complement to the residential development. Since purchasers of residential units will acquire, as a result of the purchase of a unit, a membership in the athletic facility and access to the conference facility, the presence of the hotel, in your client's estimation, increases the value of the residential condominium units. Your client, however, misjudged the construction costs and the gross income of the hotel and, as a result, the facility needs about $2,000,000 in capital in order for it to have a stable financial base.

Mountain-Ventures, Inc. (Mountain-Ventures), a real estate investment subsidiary of Hanover Manufacturers Bank, has offered to buy the remaining real estate owned by your client on and near Snowpyle Mountain which can be developed with residential condominium units. The proposed purchase price is $10,000,000. Snowpyle Corporation's adjusted basis in the remaining real estate is $5,000,000. Mountain-Ventures, however, has proposed that the purchase be conditioned on Snowpyle Corporation's investment in Snowpyle Hotel, Inc. of $2,000,000 of the purchase price in order to provide a stable financial base for the hotel facility. Marguerite Chapin, a substantial stockholder in, and executive vice president of, Snowpyle Corporation, has drafted a letter to Mountain-Ventures rejecting its offer and making a counter-offer. She has asked your advice with respect to the income tax consequences of her counter-offer.

Snowpyle Corporation
180 Easter Street
Grand Junction, CO   81503

November 13, Year*

Curt Stein
Executive Vice President
Mountain-Ventures, Inc.
1720 Bleaker Street
Modesto, CA   95351

Dear Curt:

We have received your offer for the purchase of all undeveloped real estate which we own on and around Snowpyle Mountain which is suitable for development as residential condominium units. While the terms and conditions, for the most part, seem reasonable, we are concerned about the requirement that $2,000,000 of the $10,000,000 purchase price must be invested by us in Snowpyle Hotel, Inc. in order to provide a stable financial base for the hotel-conference center and athletic facility (the hotel).

Since it is our belief that the presence of the hotel will increase the marketability and value of any residential condominium units developed by you, in the event that you purchase from us the above-described real estate, we feel it is in your interest to make a $2,000,000 investment in Snowpyle Hotel, Inc. to be used to provide financial stability for the hotel. If you agree to make this investment, we, of course, will consider a reduction of approximately $2,000,000 in the purchase price of the real estate.

Please let me know if this proposed change in the terms of your offer is acceptable to you.   If so, I will instruct our attorneys to begin the preparation of the many documents needed in order to effectuate this transition.

Very truly yours,

Marguerite

Marguerite Chapin
Executive Vice President
Snowpyle Corporation

---

* See explanatory footnote in the Introduction, page vii, note 1.

3. CAPITAL STRUCTURE AND FINANCING OF A CORPORATION

PROBLEM 18C

Ed Keane, an old client of your firm and a highly successful entrepreneur, telephoned to make an appointment to discuss with you the capital structure of a new corporate venture he is planning to undertake. He also mentioned that, if you had time, he would like to discuss the tax consequences of raising some additional capital for Tartan, Inc., one of his existing companies. Prepare yourself to interview and advise Mr. Keane.

Note:

See the Note on Interviewing and Client Counseling following Problem 1P at page 4.

PROBLEM 19C

A. Your clients, Frank Rose and Tom Heyden, have operated the F & T Machine Shop as a partnership for a number of years. Each of them holds a 50% interest in the partnership. The fair market value of the assets of the partnership at replacement cost exceeds liabilities by about $180,000. To obtain the advantages of limited liability, continuity of life and centralized management and to facilitate their estate plans, your clients now propose to incorporate.

Because of the tax advantages of debt as opposed to stock, your clients' accountant has advised them that the assets of the partnership should be contributed to the corporation in return for $30,000 of common stock (3,000 shares), with the rest in long-term debt. Because of the corporation's future requirements for outside credit, it is proposed that the debt take the form of 40-year 9% debentures, with interest payable annually only out of each year's earnings on a noncumulative basis. If interest in any one year is not paid, the debenture holders will have the right at the next annual meeting to elect a majority of the directors of the corporation. The debentures will be subordinated to debts owed to general creditors and will be convertible into common stock at the rate of $6,000 of debt for 25 shares of stock.

The accountant also suggested that the debentures have a face amount of $240,000 even though your clients will only contribute the equivalent of $150,000 for them. He advised your clients that if the business thrives and the debentures eventually are retired at face value, the $90,000 excess over your clients' cost will be taxable at capital gain rates. Although Frank and Tom intend to retain both the stock and debt for a number of years, both of them contemplate eventually giving the stock to their children who participate in the business and leaving the debt to their surviving spouses or children who do not participate in the business.

Advise your clients of any income tax problems with this form of financial organization of the corporation.

B.   After discovering that Commercial National Bank would not continue to extend credit to the business as it had in the past if Frank and Tom proceeded with the capitalization outlined in Part A, Frank and Tom decided that the partnership's assets should be contributed to the corporation solely in return for $90,000 of the no par common voting stock of the corporation (3,000 shares) and $90,000 of the $30 par value, 8% cumulative dividend, nonvoting preferred stock of the corporation (3,000 shares). They, however, would like to have the benefits of Section 1244 of the Internal Revenue Code in the event the stock they receive ever becomes worthless and the benefits of Section 1202 if they ever sell the stock at a gain. Prior to organizing the corporation, a young associate in your office has prepared a tentative draft of the minutes of the first meeting of the board of directors of the corporation. It is the associate's intention to have the directors conduct the meeting pursuant to the draft and adopt the draft as the minutes of the meeting, thereby assuring the availability of Sections 1202 and 1244. You have been asked to review that portion of the draft dealing with the transfer of the assets to the corporation to make sure that Sections 1202 and 1244 treatment will be available. The associate has informed you that after the exchange of assets for stock, the partnership will be terminated and the stock distributed to Frank and Tom in equal amounts. The associate also informed you that the partnership has an adjusted basis of $150,000 in the assets which it will transfer to the corporation.

Excerpt from the Minutes of the First Meeting of the Board of Directors of F & T Machine Shop, Inc.

The Chairman stated that the Corporation was authorized by its certificate of incorporation to issue 10,000 shares of common stock and 10,000 shares of preferred stock and that, other than the three shares of common stock held by incorporators who surrendered that stock at the beginning of today's meeting, all its authorized shares were at present unissued. He further stated that F & T Machine Shop, a partnership composed of Frank Rose and Tom Heyden as equal partners, was interested in acquiring stock of the corporation.

Upon motion duly made, seconded, and unanimously carried, it was:

RESOLVED, that the Corporation offer for sale 3,000 shares of its authorized common stock and 3,000 shares of its authorized preferred stock in accordance with the Plan attached hereto.

Mr. Rose and Mr. Heyden, on behalf of F & T Machine Shop, stated that it would accept the 6,000 shares offered pursuant to said Plan and that it would pay for them by transferring to the Corporation, in such manner as may be necessary to transfer title, certain assets used by it in the conduct of its business having a fair market value of at least $300,000, subject to assumption by the Corporation of certain partnership liabilities totaling $120,000. The directors thereupon determined that the corporation accept title to such assets, and agree to assume the liabilities in the above amount, in exchange for the issuance to F & T Machine Shop of 3,000 shares of the common stock and 3,000 shares of the preferred stock of the Corporation. The following resolutions were duly made, seconded and unanimously adopted:

RESOLVED, that the Corporation, pursuant to its Plan (a copy of which is attached) to offer 3,000 shares of its common stock, and 3,000 shares of its preferred stock, issue the 6,000 shares to F & T Machine Shop, a partnership, in exchange for transfer to the Corporation of the partnership assets listed on the attached Schedule A, subject to the assumption by the Corporation of the partnership liabilities listed on the attached Schedule B. It is hereby declared that all such assets are necessary for the use and lawful purposes of this Corporation.

RESOLVED FURTHER, that the proper officers of this Corporation are hereby authorized and directed, as part of such exchange, to execute, in the name and on behalf of this Corporation, a "Bill of Sale and Agreement" to be dated as of today, and to provide for the transfer and assignment of the said assets to this Corporation and the assumption by this Corporation of said liabilities.

RESOLVED FURTHER, that upon transfer to the Corporation, by F & T Machine Shop, of good title to all assets described in Schedule A, the proper officers of this Corporation are hereby authorized and directed to execute and deliver, in the name and on behalf of this Corporation and under its corporate seal, a certificate or certificates to F & T Machine Shop for an aggregate of 3,000 shares of this Corporation's common stock and an aggregate of 3,000 shares of this Corporation's preferred stock.

Plan to Offer 3,000 Shares of the Common Stock Without Par Value and 3,000 Shares of the $30 Par Value Preferred Stock of F & T Machine Shop, Inc.

1. The Corporation hereby offers for sale, at $30 per share, 3,000 shares of its common stock without par value and 3,000 shares of its $30 par value, 8% cumulative dividend, nonvoting preferred stock. It being intended that both the common and preferred stock qualify as qualified small business stock under Section 1202(c) of the Internal Revenue Code of 1986, as amended.

2. Such price shall be paid either in cash or in property having a fair market value equal to $30 per share.

3. The maximum amount to be received by the Corporation in consideration for the stock to be issued pursuant to this Plan is $180,000 in cash or in fair market value of property.

4. This offer shall be made to such person or persons as the Board of Directors of the Corporation may select, but no shares shall be sold or offered for sale to the public, and no steps shall be taken under this Plan which would constitute this offering as a public offering within the meaning of the Blue Sky Laws of any state or the Federal Securities Act of 1933, as amended.

5. The Corporation represents and warrants that it is a qualified small business which engages in the active conduct of a trade or business pursuant to Sections 1202(d) and (e) of the Internal Revenue Code of 1986, as amended.

6. This offer shall expire upon the sale of all the stock authorized to be issued pursuant to this Plan, or at the end of two years from the date of the adoption of this Plan, whichever is earlier.

7. It is intended that the stock offered pursuant to this Plan qualify under Sections 1202 and 1244 of the Internal Revenue Code of 1986, as amended.

Note:

See the Note on Legal Drafting following Problem 3P at page 15.

Corporate Resolutions and Stock Offering Plans

The business corporation acts in most states require that the board of directors approve the issuance of the stock of a corporation and, probably, the acquisition of major assets by a corporation. The corporate resolutions set out above are designed to reflect the required action by the board of directors of the corporation. A careful attorney, when preparing for a meeting of the board of directors, may prepare in advance of the meeting the resolutions to be adopted by the board of directors. This will insure that the board of directors take all necessary and appropriate actions. The Plan to Offer Stock, while not absolutely necessary for either Section 1202 or 1244 treatment, serves as a memorial of the issuance of the stock and the status of the corporation at the time of the issuance of the stock.

PROBLEM 20C

Your client, International Pulp, Inc. (IPI), a large producer of wood and paper products, whose stock is traded on the New York Stock Exchange, is involved in extensive discussions with its investment advisors, Reed, Harris and Balk, about several significant financial matters. John Martin, who is IPI's vice president for finance, has received the following preliminary memorandum from Mary Rosen, a partner at Reed, Harris and Balk. Mr. Martin would like to know the income tax consequences to IPI of the various matters discussed by Ms. Rosen.

<u>*Memorandum*</u>
<u>*International Pulp, Inc.—New Financing Package*</u>

Mary J. Rosen

International Pulp, Inc. (IPI) is in need of three distinct financing arrangements to cover several contingencies.

Below, under the appropriate headings, will be found a preliminary discussion which will be used to establish guidelines for dealing with each of the various financing arrangements.

<u>*Refinancing*</u>. Approximately twelve months from now, IPI will have to retire $10,000,000 in face amount of existing long term debt. Since the company treasury does not contain sufficient liquid funds to enable it to retire this debt and, at the same time, satisfy normal operating requirements, it is proposed that the debt be refinanced by one of four different alternatives.

The existing debt bears interest at a rate of five percentage points below the current market rate, and the company is reluctant to refinance by a means which will cause it to incur increased fixed charges. Consequently, in developing the refinancing alternatives, primary emphasis has been placed on the development of financing arrangements which will keep new fixed charges equal to present fixed charges on existing debt.

(a) <u>*Straight Debt Alternative*</u>—Issuance of $10,000,000 in face amount of conventional subordinated debentures to replace existing debt will cause IPI to incur $500,000 per year in additional fixed charges. If IPI were to seek to obtain $10,000,000 from creditors with a fixed charge equal to the present interest charge, it would have to issue debt with a significantly larger face amount thereby resulting in a significant discount on the debt at issuance. For example, by offering $13,000,000 of ten-year conventional subordinated debentures with an interest rate of three percent below that on the existing debt, the fixed charge for interest on the new debt would be equal to the present fixed charge, and IPI would suffer approximately a $3,000,000 discount resulting in its receiving only $10,000,000 for the debt. The obvious disadvantage of this alternative is that, rather than offering the debtor a reduction of costs, it merely offers it a deferral of costs since IPI would have to repay $13,000,000 when the debt falls due.

(b) <u>*Convertible Debt Alternative*</u>—Because of the value attached to convertibility, debt instruments carrying such a privilege can be issued bearing interest at a below-market rate. The discount which is obtained is reflective of the value which investors attach to the privilege. This value, of course, is contingent on a variety of factors such as: (1) the conversion price; (2) the number of years the privilege is available; and (3) the investment community's appraisal of the investment potential of the security into which the debt is convertible. Convertible debt sometimes is said to be preferable to both straight debt and to equity as a device for raising additional corporate financing. Because of the conversion feature, it is cheaper for the corporation than is straight debt. Moreover, since the conversion is available only at a price significantly in excess of the existing traded value of the equity into which it is convertible, conversion will cause the old shareholders to suffer less dilution than they would have suffered had the new investors originally been issued stock at the old price in exchange for their investment.

I estimate that IPI could issue $10,000,000 of twenty-year convertible debt with a fixed cost equal to the interest cost of its present debt if it allowed the debt to be convertible into IPI common stock for the next ten years at the rate of 25 shares of IPI (currently listed at $20 per share) per $1,000 of face amount of debt.

(c) *Warrants-Debt Alternative*—Issuance of debt instruments with warrants attached is somewhat comparable to the effect of the issuance of convertible stock. In a warrant-debt package, the market, however, assigns a separate value to the debt and to the warrant. Consequently, one normally would issue debt in an amount less than the amount sought to be raised by the offering, with the balance being raised by the warrant component. Therefore, even if the debt bears interest at the normal market rate, it can be structured to have the same fixed charge as the greater amount of debt which is to be retired, since the new debt will be for a lesser amount. The value assigned to the warrant, like the convertibility feature, is dependent on a variety of factors such as the number of months or years during which the warrant will be exercisable, the price at which it is exercisable and the investment potential of the underlying security.

As a ballpark figure, I would suggest that, if each $1,000 bond carried with it the right to purchase, for five years, ten shares of IPI stock at $40 per share, we would be able to raise $10,000,000 with an offering of $8,000,000 of conventional twenty-year subordinated debt bearing interest at the market rate. This would result in no increase in the fixed charge associated with the existing debt.

The advantage of such a package over the convertible debt package is that, if the warrants are not exercised, IPI need pay back only $8,000,000 and will be the beneficiary of a $2,000,000 windfall. The disadvantage in drawing a comparison with convertible debt is that, if the stock rises sufficiently to cause the warrants to be exercised, the corporation still will be left with $8,000,000 of debt. This, however, must be offset partially by the consideration that, if all warrants were exercised, IPI will have received $3,200,000 in new capital, which could be used to meet a part of the principal of the debt to be retired. This $3,200,000 is $1,200,000 more than the amount which would be realized by issuing presently the 80,000 shares of IPI stock which will be needed to back up the proposed warrant issue.

(d) *Common Stock Alternative*—Because of the potential for growth and increase in dividends, it is seldom necessary that common stock have the same yield as debt of an equal amount. Due to the growth potential for IPI and its industry group, the general financial health of the company, and its record of paying dividends, the dividend yield on existing IPI stock is approximately two-thirds of the yield on the soon-to-be retired debt. Thus, by issuing $10,000,000 of new common stock, IPI could reduce its fixed obligation to investors and avoid having to confront the periodic necessity of arranging for retirement or refinancing of a large debt obligation. The principal disadvantage of this alternative is the dilution of equity interest the existing shareholders will confront.

Baxter Forest, Inc. Acquisition

IPI is interested in acquiring Baxter Forest, Inc. (Baxter) from Aetna Insurance Co. (Aetna), which acquired the stock in Baxter in a corporate reorganization of the now defunct American Home Supplies Co., of which Aetna was a major creditor. The Baxter holdings are worth approximately $62,500,000, and Aetna is anxious to dispose of them as soon as possible. IPI is interested in acquiring either all of the Baxter stock or all of its assets. Aetna has proposed that IPI acquire either the Baxter stock or assets in exchange for $50,000,000 in IPI 25-year debentures, which will bear interest at the current rate and which will be secured by a lien on the Baxter assets. In addition, Aetna, which is looking for some form of an equity kicker, proposes that it be given warrants authorizing it to purchase 500,000 shares of IPI stock for $40.00 per share exercisable over the next five years.

The Baxter holdings should generate sufficient cash flow to enable IPI to accept this offer. Moreover, since the new debt will only cause IPI's debt/equity ratio to rise to 2.2 to 1 in an industry where 3 to 1 is quite common, the new debt should not cause the market to react adversely toward IPI's current common stock value.

The financial issues represented by the warrants are identical to those represented by the warrants mentioned above under the heading of *Warrants-Debt Alternative*.

In closing out discussion of this issue, I would like to suggest that IPI attempt to reduce debt carrying costs on any new IPI debt to be issued to Aetna by reducing the interest payable and commensurately increasing the face amount of the debentures. For a discussion of this, refer to the discussion above under the heading *Straight Debt Alternative*.

Pressedboard Joint Venture

Northwest Lumber, Inc. (Northwest), a small producer of wood building supplies, has developed a newly patented procedure for making pressedboard at a considerable savings over current technology. Northwest is unable to exploit its patent, which has an estimated value of $3,000,000, without considerable outside assistance. Northwest proposes that IPI join with it in a corporate venture to manufacture pressedboard under the patent. IPI owns an idle plant worth about $9,000,000 which, with an expenditure of $1,500,000, could be converted to produce pressedboard under the Northwest patent. Since operating funds of about $1,500,000 would also be needed, Northwest proposes that IPI also provide these. At present, there are a number of alternatives before IPI. First, Northwest proposes that a new company be formed called Wonder Pressed Board, Inc. (Wonder) and that IPI contribute to it the plant and $3,000,000 in cash and that Northwest contribute to it the patent. Since Northwest would like to benefit, as fully as possible, from the potential of the patent, it has proposed that the common stock be divided equally between it and IPI. In addition, IPI would be given $9,000,000 of Wonder debentures, which would bear interest at the market rate but which would also allow IPI to name an additional director to the Wonder board of directors. Northwest proposes that the debt be forty-year debt so that the company can operate unimpaired by concerns of repaying the debt for many years. David Adler, who is in charge of IPI's acquisitions team, is not very interested in accepting this proposal. He informed me that IPI would probably accept a package in which it took seventy-five percent of the stock in Wonder in exchange for its plant and $3,000,000 in debt with a twenty-year term in exchange for $3,000,000 in cash with the balance of the Wonder stock going to Northwest in exchange for the patent. Nonetheless, Mr. Adler indicated that IPI would actually prefer to hold no debt and instead own eighty percent of the stock in Wonder with Northwest owning the balance. I have suggested to him that, if Northwest rejects both of these offers, he consider proposing that IPI offer to purchase the patent for $3,000,000 and go it alone. In that case, I would suggest that Wonder be organized with $1,500,000 of stock being issued to IPI and $13,500,000 of 20-year subordinated debt which bears interest at the market rate. This structure would leave IPI totally in control of Wonder and leave Wonder with all the tax advantages which debt has over stock.

PROBLEM 21C

You have handled most of the tax questions for the small law firm that you joined immediately after graduating from law school and passing the bar examination. One of your colleagues who handles most of the financing transactions for the firm recently received the following memorandum from one of the business lawyers in the firm. Your colleague has evaluated the financing aspects of the suggestions made in the memorandum. She would like your advice as to the tax consequences of the financial suggestions made in the memorandum. She would like your advice by Monday of next week since the meeting with the client's executive officers is planned for the following Tuesday morning.

Poindexter, Lujan & Thau
4116 Central Street
Portland, OR   97203

Intraoffice Memorandum

TO: Katrina Trujillo

FROM: Stacy Kelly   *S.K.*

RE: Ideal House, Inc. Acquisition of New Machinery

Ideal House, Inc. ("Ideal House") was formed about five years ago by ten individuals skilled in the production of manufactured housing. Each individual purchased one-tenth of the stock in the corporation for $90,000. The ten individuals hoped that, through the combination of their skills as employees of Ideal House and the use of the latest equipment in the manufactured housing industry, Ideal House would become one of the leading producers of manufactured housing in the region. Ideal House acquired its equipment and plant through the use of part of the equity contributed by the ten shareholders in combination with bank financing.

While the performance of Ideal House has been acceptable over the five-year period, it has failed to meet the expectations of the ten individuals. Ideal House's cash flow has been positive in every year, but its profit has been minimal or nonexistent as a result of the depreciation which it has taken on its plant and equipment. The balance sheet of Ideal House, at the end of the fifth year, is attached to this memorandum.

The ten individual shareholders have come to the conclusion that Ideal House requires the latest in computer-assisted machinery to reach its potential. The cost of such machinery is about $900,000. The shareholders do not believe that the cost of the new machinery can be financed by a third-party lender, since the performance of Ideal House, up to this point in time, does not inspire great confidence.   In addition, the shareholders are concerned about obligating Ideal House to pay a substantial interest charge each year. The shareholders, however, are personally prepared to make the needed funds or machinery available to Ideal House. Each shareholder will make available the proportion of the $900,000 which the shares of stock he or she owns bears to the total stock outstanding.

The shareholders and I would like your advice with respect to the financial and income tax aspects of the various ways that we have determined that the funds or machinery can be made available to Ideal House and your advice with respect to which means of making the funds or machinery available would produce the best result for the shareholders. The shareholders have informed me that they would like to receive a modest return on their investments, and if possible, at least some of the shareholders would like to have their investments repaid by Ideal House when it has sufficient funds available.   The alternatives which the shareholders and I have considered are the following:

1.   The shareholders each might buy additional shares of common stock for an amount per share equal to the common stock's value based on the current fair market value of Ideal House's assets, less its liabilities. These shares would be redeemable at the same price at the discretion of the board of directors of Ideal House.

2.   The shareholders each might buy some nonparticipating preferred stock for the same price per share as indicated in paragraph 1. The stock would have a preferred dividend of 7% per annum, payable if earned and cumulative if not paid, with a redemption and liquidation preference of the amount paid for the stock plus accumulated and unpaid dividends.

3.   The shareholders each might buy her or his proportionate share of an issue of bonds of Ideal House. To reduce the fixed charges, the face amount of the bonds would be $1,200,000 at 6.5% per annum interest, but the shareholders would only pay $900,000 for them.   The bonds would be subordinate to all other debt of the corporation.

4.   Nine hundred thousand dollars of convertible, variable rate bonds might be offered to the shareholders. If this option was chosen, each holder of a bond could convert the bond into common stock of Ideal House at a conversion price per share

equal to the present fair market value per share plus 20% of the fair market value. The interest paid on the bonds would be 5% per annum plus an amount equal to the annual dividends, if any, which would have been paid on the common stock of the corporation into which the bonds were convertible if the bonds had been converted before the corporation paid the dividends. The convertible debt would be subordinate to all third-party debt of the corporation.

5. A package of $600,000 of debt at 10% per annum and $300,000 of warrants might be offered to the shareholders. The warrants would give the holders the right to purchase common stock of Ideal House at the present fair market value plus 20%. The debt would be subordinate to all third-party debt of the corporation.

6. The shareholders might persuade a third-party lender to loan the $900,000 to Ideal House at 8% per annum if each shareholder would pay his or her proportionate share of 6 points up front to the lender and guarantee his or her proportionate share of the loan. The corporation would reimburse the shareholders for the points paid when the corporation repaid the third-party's loan.

7. The shareholders might personally buy the equipment for $900,000 and then sell it to the corporation for a note of the corporation in the principal amount of $900,000 at a 6.5% per annum interest rate.

8. The shareholders might personally buy the equipment and lease it to the corporation for an annual rental equal to about 6.5% per annum of $900,000. The lease would grant the corporation an option to buy the equipment at the end of the lease term for $900,000.

Balance Sheet of Ideal House, Inc.

Assets (x 1000)

		Adjusted Basis	Fair Market Value
Cash		$ 30	$ 30
Accounts Receivable		120	120
Inventory		240	390
Furniture, Fixtures,			
Equipment	$ 900		
(Depreciation)	(840)	60	360
Plant	1500		
(Depreciation)	(900)	600	1200
Land		300	450
		$1350	$2550

Liabilities (x 1000)

	Adjusted Basis	Fair Market Value
Trade Accounts Payable	$ 150	$ 150
Equipment Loan	300	300
Mortgage Loan for Plant and Land	750	750
Capital		
Stated Capital 30,000 Shares		
Outstanding	900	900
Earnings and Profits	(750)	450
	$1350	$2550

PROBLEM 22C

A. The McArthur Hotel was one of the most elegant and noteworthy hotels in your community during the '60's and '70's. Lately it has become quite rundown, and the current owners have been losing money operating it. Six of your clients, including some of the most influential and wealthy individuals in the community, have decided that the purchase and renovation of the McArthur Hotel not only would remove an eyesore and preserve a community landmark, but also might produce substantial income for the investors. After working with an architect, hotel management consultants and engineers, your clients have determined that the project will require $6,000,000, consisting of $4,000,000 needed to purchase the hotel and present furnishings, $1,200,000 for renovation, $400,000 for new furnishings, and $400,000 for working capital.

Your clients have arranged the financing of the purchase and renovation with Western Savings Bank. The bank will loan $4,200,000 for a term of 30 years at a market interest rate, requiring level quarterly payments of principal and interest, secured by a first mortgage on the land and building and a security interest in present furnishings. The cost of the new furnishings will be financed by a $360,000 loan from First Guaranty Bank having a term of eight years, a market interest rate, level quarterly payments of principal and interest and a security interest in the new furnishings. The working capital will be provided partially by a term loan from First Guaranty Bank in the amount of $240,000 for a term of ten years, at an interest rate two percentage points above the prime rate and requiring level quarterly payments of principal and interest.

Your clients plan to form a corporation called McArthur Hotel, Inc. to purchase, renovate and operate the hotel. All the loans described above will be made to the corporation. The remaining $1,200,000 needed for the project will be provided by your clients. In exchange for $200,000, each will acquire one-sixth of the no par common stock of the corporation and a $120,000 note of the corporation payable at the end of 15 years, with interest payable annually at the prime rate charged by First Guaranty Bank. These notes will be expressly subordinate to the First Guaranty Bank term loan. The opening balance sheet will be as follows:

McArthur Hotel, Inc.

Assets

Cash	$ 400,000
Furnishings	800,000
Building	3,720,000
Land	1,080,000
Total	$6,000,000

Liabilities	
Loan for Furnishings	$ 360,000
Term Loan for Working Capital	240,000
Loan for Acquisition & Renovation	4,200,000 *Liab*
Notes Payable to Shareholders	720,000
Capital	
Stated Capital *(stock)*	480,000 *Equity*
Total	$6,000,000

Your clients would like your advice as to the likely tax consequences, both now and in the future, of the above proposed financial structure. They would also like to know whether their stock will be eligible for treatment under Sections 1202 and 1244 of the Internal Revenue Code.

B. After obtaining your advice with respect to the questions they asked in Part A, your clients proceeded to organize McArthur Hotel, Inc. along the lines described in Part A and carried out the purchase of the hotel and its renovation in the described manner. Five years later, they informed you that their income projections were much too optimistic, and it has taken longer than they anticipated to build up the hotel's clientele. Over the five years, the corporation has incurred losses of $508,000, although it has paid the interest on the shareholders' notes in every year. Your clients are reasonably confident that, in the next few years, the corporation will begin to show a profit if it can secure additional working capital of $320,000. It can secure $200,000 of this amount from First Guaranty Bank if your clients will personally guarantee the loan, which they plan to do. In addition, they will provide the remaining $120,000 by each purchasing a $20,000 note of the corporation, payable at the end of ten years, with interest payable annually at two percentage points above First Guaranty Bank's prime rate. These notes will be subordinated to the above First Guaranty Bank loan.

Your clients would like your advice as to the likely tax consequences, both now and in the future, of the above proposal. The financial statement of McArthur Hotel, Inc. at the end of the fifth year, but before the infusion of the new working capital, follows.

McArthur Hotel, Inc.

Assets

	Per Books	Fair Market Value
Cash	$ 160,000	$ 160,000
Accounts Receivable	160,000	160,000
Furnishings	$ 800,000	
(Depreciation)	(360,000) 440,000	480,000
Building	3,720,000	
(Depreciation)	(478,000) 3,242,000	3,400,000
Land	1,080,000	1,190,000
Total	$5,082,000	$5,390,000

Liabilities

	Per Books	Fair Market Value
Accounts Payable	$ 80,000	$ 80,000
Loan for Furnishings	165,600	165,600
Term Loan	154,400	154,400
Loan for Acquisition & Renovation	3,990,000	3,990,000
Notes Payable	720,000	720,000
Capital		
Stated Capital	480,000	480,000
Surplus (Deficit)	(508,000)	(200,000)
Total	$5,082,000	$5,390,000

4. SUBCHAPTER S ELECTION

PROBLEM 23C

Jean Reinhard and Joseph Glid, your clients, some of whose problems you considered in Problem 13C, have decided to organize Tricometer Corporation. Only common stock, which is to be held equally by Jean and Joe, will be issued. The corporation is expected to have net taxable income of $100,000 a year for the first few years, after paying salaries of $60,000 each to Jean and Joe, who seek your advice whether the corporation should elect S corporation status.

Both Jean and Joe are married and file joint returns with their respective spouses. Jean and Joe each earn about $120,000 per year at General Electric where they are employed, and their spouses each earn about $100,000 per year from their respective jobs. In addition, both couples derive a substantial amount of income from their respective investments. Assume alternatively that they continue their employment with General Electric and operate Tricometer only during their free time, or that they quit their jobs with General Electric and devote all of their time to Tricometer. In the latter case, their taxable income would consist of their salaries from Tricometer and investment income of roughly $4,000 each.

Consider also the income tax ramifications of the following alternatives if the corporation elects S corporation status: (1) Jean and Joe conveyed the trademark, trade name and patent to Tricometer; (2) Tricometer by purchase acquired these assets for their fair market value; or (3) Jean and Joe acquired these assets and entered into an agreement with the corporation permitting it to use these assets in return for certain royalties.

If Tricometer elected S corporation status and Jean and Joe consented, prepare yourself to advise them of the effect on Tricometer's S corporation status of each of the following occurrences:

(1) Jean sells one-half of her stock to Tom Peters, a regional investment banker who refuses to consent to the election;

(2) Joe sells his stock to Southwest Properties, Inc., an investment banking firm operating in the corporate form;

(3) Joe conveys one-half of his stock to a trust under which income is distributed to his daughter Donna for twelve years after which the trust is terminated and the corpus returned to Joe;

(4) Joe conveys all the stock to himself as custodian or guardian for his three minor children;

(5) Jean dies, and the stock is temporarily transferred to her estate prior to distribution;

(6) Jean dies, and the stock is distributed to a marital trust. The Trust agreement provides that the income is distributed annually to Jean's surviving spouse for his life and, at his death, is distributed in a manner designated by Jean, in this case to her issue *per stirpes*; or

(7) Jean contributes her stock to a trust under which income is paid to her children for their lives and on their death the remainder is distributed to a charity.

Considering your conclusions, what might you suggest as appropriate provisions to be included in a shareholders' agreement between Jean and Joe as to the maintenance of S corporation status?

PROBLEM 24C

F & T Machine Shop (F & T), which you previously encountered in Problem 19C, elected S corporation status on its formation with the consent of Frank and Tom, its sole shareholders. In recent years, the corporation has experienced financial difficulties, and Frank and Tom have been considering various ways to secure $260,000 in new equipment and working capital. To their surprise, Phineus Trap, an old friend, has offered to invest the $260,000. In exchange, Phineus proposes that he be given one of three different investment packages. The three alternative packages are set forth in some detail in a document entitled "Outline of Investment Proposal," which is set forth below. To protect his investment, Phineus is insistent that, under each alternative, he have a representative named to the F & T board of directors. The document below was prepared by Phineus's attorney and was sent to you by Frank and Tom, who seek your advice on this matter.

TO: Frank P. Rose and Thomas L. Heyden
FROM: Phineus H. Trap
DATE: October 4, Year*
RE: Outline of Investment Proposal

Phineus H. Trap, hereafter referred to as "Investor," will invest $260,000 in F & T Machine Shop, Inc. (the corporation) under one of three alternative investment proposals set forth below.

Proposal One—In exchange for $260,000, the corporation will issue to Investor $260,000 in face amount of twenty-year debentures which shall be fully subordinate, bear interest at two points below the rate for twenty-year Treasury notes and be convertible into common stock at a ratio which will enable Investor, if all the debentures are converted, to own sixty percent

* See explanatory footnote in Introduction, page vii, note 1.

of the common stock of the corporation then issued and outstanding. In addition, the bylaws of the corporation, which presently provide for appointment of three directors, shall be amended to provide for the appointment of a fourth director, who shall be an individual appointed by Investor or his assigns until such time as the above debt shall be retired or converted.

Proposal Two—In exchange for $260,000, the corporation will issue to Investor: (1) $200,000 in face amount of twenty-year debt bearing interest at two points above the Citibank prime rate. The debt shall be secured by all assets acquired with the proceeds of the debt as well as all of the corporation's current assets which are not pledged to secure existing debt; and (2) warrants, exercisable for five years, to acquire from the corporation an amount of common stock equal to thirty percent of the stock now owned by Messrs. Rose and Heyden. In addition, the by-laws of the corporation shall be amended to contain a provision similar in effect to the provision mentioned in Proposal One.

Proposal Three—In exchange for $260,000, the corporation will issue to Investor $180,000 in face amount of ten-year notes, which shall have terms similar to those outlined in Proposal Two. In addition, there will be issued to Investor a sufficient number of shares of common stock so that he will hold twenty-two percent of the common stock of the corporation, and all other investors will hold a total of seventy-eight percent of the common stock. To assure Investor a place on the corporation's board of directors, one of the four following alternatives will be implemented:

(1) after issuance of the stock to Investor, all shareholders shall convey their stock to Security National Bank as trustee under a voting trust requiring that, at each of the next ten annual shareholders' meetings, the trustee shall vote all the stock so as to insure Investor or his assignee (or a designee of his assignee) and Messrs. Rose and Heyden or their assignees (or designees of their assignees) membership on the corporation's board of directors;

(2) after issuance of the stock to Investor, all shareholders shall enter into a shareholders' agreement providing that, for the next ten years, each shareholder will vote his stock at each annual meeting for the election as directors of Investor and Messrs. Rose and Heyden or their assignees or designees of their assignees;

(3) prior to the issuance of the stock to Investor, the existing shareholders shall cause the charter of the corporation to be amended to authorize two classes of stock. Class A stock shall have the right to elect one director, and Class B stock shall have the right to elect two directors. The Class A stock issued to Investor and the

Class B stock (into which the existing stock of the corporation shall be converted) shall be held by the shareholders in the proportions outlined above. All other rights of Class A and Class B stock will be identical; or

(4) prior to issuance of the stock to Investor, the existing shareholders will amend the corporate charter and by-laws to provide for cumulative voting for directors and for an increase in the number of directors from three to four.

Caveat—This document is being provided by Investor solely for the purpose of facilitating discussion among the parties. It is not a formal offer of terms, the acceptance of which will give rise to a binding agreement among the parties.

PROBLEM 25C

William Fergus, the Executive Vice-President for Finance of American Cable Network, Inc. (American), has asked your advice with respect to the legal feasibility of a proposal sent to him by Miwah Sasaki, his chief assistant for financial matters. Ms. Sasaki's proposal is set forth in a memo in which she outlines a new method for financing future enlargements of American's cable network.

TO: William J. Fergus
FROM: Miwah Sasaki
RE: Financing of new cable television systems

As I mentioned to you in our conference of last week, I have heard a number of rumors that several of our competitors (National Cable and Fox Video) have been employing a new financing arrangement for expansion of their cable systems. I have made a number of inquiries, and although I have learned some general information, I have not been able to come up with the full details of the arrangement.

Apparently, the technique involves the formation of a corporation which holds the franchise for expansion in a new market. This corporation is owned exclusively by individual shareholders who are residents of the new market area and who elect S corporation status for the corporation. All management and services of and for this corporation are provided on a contract basis by the interested cable company (the sponsoring company), which holds options on all the stock of the individuals, exercisable at a price in excess of the original subscription price (e.g., 120% of issue price). The individuals also hold rights to put the stock to the sponsoring company at a price close to, but below, the subscription price (e.g., 90% of issue price). The individual shareholders are all high-bracket taxpayers who have substantial passive income, and the basic thrust of the plan is to enable such individuals to use, on their personal income tax returns, the start-up passive losses experienced by all new cable systems, which typically last from three to four years. The losses used by the individuals are ordinary passive losses which reduce their bases in the stock. When the sponsor comes into possession of the stock either on exercise of the option or the put, the individuals then realize long term capital gains on the difference between their adjusted bases in the stock and the proceeds they receive from the sponsor. Apparently, this swapping of ordinary passive losses for capital gains lies at the heart of the economic advantage realized by individuals in the arrangement. In addition, the individuals assist in securing the availability of cable television for the markets in which they reside, and if the venture is successful, they stand to make a good return on their investments while the exposure to loss is limited because of the put.

The sponsoring cable company has the advantage of establishing a viable expansion of its network without having to make any investment for a number of years. Moreover, if the venture proves a disaster, the investment made by the sponsor is made at the lower figure (the put), is a deferred investment, and on abandonment is taken as an ordinary loss on the stock of an affiliated corporation.

PROBLEM 26C

On June 1, Year-2,* June Pagnano and Albert Breyer formed Deer Valley Silver Company (Deer Valley), an S corporation whose principal business consisted of the retail sale of jewelry at the Deer Valley Ski Resort. Since the company's principal sales activities took place during the winter months, with an extraordinary amount of the sales occurring during the Christmas holiday season, the company was formed with a fiscal year ending on September 30. Deer Valley was formed by Albert contributing $90,000 in cash to the corporation and June contributing $9,000 in cash plus $81,000 of jewelry designed by her in which she had a basis of $15,000. In exchange for

* See explanatory footnote in Introduction, page vii, note 1.

their contributions, they each were issued 500 shares of Deer Valley or 50% of the common stock of the corporation.

During its first fiscal year, which covered only the four months prior to September 30, Year-2, Deer Valley experienced an expected start-up loss of $60,000. During its second fiscal year, Deer Valley realized net taxable income of $150,000, all derived from sales of jewelry. Until this point, Deer Valley's financial affairs were relatively simple with all income derived from sales of jewelry occurring in rented quarters. In the last fiscal year, which ended on September 30, Year, Deer Valley realized $270,000 in net income and saw its financial affairs become somewhat complicated. In addition to the sales transactions and related deductions of rent, utilities, and salary to both owners of $90,000 each, Deer Valley experienced the following financial transactions which were not considered in computing the $270,000 of income mentioned above. First, it realized a loss (capital or ordinary) of $15,000 on the sale by it of certain gold futures contracts. Next, it suffered a $12,000 loss on the sale by it of some land it had purchased shortly after its founding to secure reserved parking space for customers. In thanks for its successful start, the corporation made a gift of $30,000 to the University of Minnesota from which its founders had both received their college degrees. In that year, Deer Valley also purchased for $36,000 a computer, a cash register, counters and various pieces of equipment used in the jewelry shop. In addition to its income from sales of jewelry, Deer Valley also realized $9,000 of interest on certificates of deposit and $6,000 of interest income on tax exempt municipals in which spare cash was invested.

No distributions were made by Deer Valley in its first two fiscal years, but during its last fiscal year, on August 15, Year, the corporation distributed to each shareholder $30,000 in cash and $12,000 of inventory consisting of raw silver in which it had an adjusted basis of $9,000.

June and Albert, who had previously prepared their own tax returns, consult you to determine how they should report the results of Deer Valley's operations for the fiscal year ending September 30, Year. They also seek your advice as to the amount of adjusted basis which each has in his or her Deer Valley stock as of October 1, Year.

PROBLEM 27C

The chair of the tax department in the firm in which you recently became an associate has received a letter from a friend of his, who is a partner in a regional accounting firm.   The letter asks for his assistance in determining whether a $100,000 net operating loss, which the accountant came up with, is the proper income tax result for the last year of the taxpayers. He has given the letter to you and asks for your evaluation of the propriety of the $100,000 net operating loss.

Arthur Andrews & Co. L.L.P
1417 Calumet
South Bend, IN   46628

February 1, Year*

Harlan Tashnick
Kohn, Tashnick & Bitterman
410 Lincoln Drive
South Bend, IN   46601

Dear Harlan:

RE: Space Age Communications, Inc.

A little over a year ago, four individuals, none of whom is a nonresident alien, determined to form Space Age Communications, Inc. (the corporation).   The corporation was formed on the first day of the year. Shortly after formation, the corporation elected, and the shareholders consented to, subchapter S treatment of the corporation. I tentatively have determined that the corporation has incurred, for its first year of operation, a $100,000 net operating loss. I am, however, concerned because of all the legal complexities involved in computing this amount, especially in the context of a subchapter S corporation. The corporation, which uses the accrual method, keeps its books and files its tax returns using the calendar year.

The shareholders, who are all highly trained and sophisticated telecommunication engineers and are all active in the business of the corporation, have attempted to take advantage of the fast-growing field of satellite telecommunication. They have developed and conveyed to the corporation a system by which the computers of large national and international businesses, with branches located in various parts of the nation and the world, can communicate directly with one another within minutes by the use of satellite telecommunications. Each of the individuals invested $150,000 in the stock of the corporation. The corporation, on the 31st of

---

* See explanatory footnote in Introduction, page vii, note 1.

March following its formation, purchased, for $2,500,000, 60 hours a week of telecommunication time for a five-year period (the expected remaining life of the satellite) on the most recent commercial communications satellite launched (satellite access agreement). The corporation paid $250,000 in cash and a five-year note in the amount of $2,250,000 for the time. The note was nonrecourse as to the corporation and its shareholders, but its payment was guaranteed in full by the Federal Communications Commission, which is eager to promote competition in the satellite telecommunications field. The note also was secured by a security interest in the telecommunications time purchased.

The other $350,000 invested by the shareholders was used by the corporation to purchase a general partnership interest in a limited partnership, Southwest, Ltd. (Southwest). Southwest was formed to finance, construct and own ground facilities for satellite telecommunications located near Tucson, Arizona. The acquisition and construction cost of the facilities, $1,200,000, was financed by the partnership through: (1) the use of the $350,000 investment by the corporation; (2) an additional $350,000 contributed by 35 investors in Southwest who are different individuals from the investors in the corporation and each of whom bought their limited partnership interest for $10,000; and (3) a $500,000 recourse loan from the First National Bank of Tucson. Southwest used the $1,000,000 to construct $500,000 of tangible personal property and $500,000 of real property improvements. It used $200,000 to acquire the real estate. Construction was complete by the end of the first quarter of the corporation's first year. The corporation has a 50% interest, and the limited partners, combined, have a 50% interest, in Southwest.

On March 31, Southwest entered into an agreement with the corporation whereby Southwest leased the facilities to the corporation, and it undertook the operation and management of the facilities. The rent paid by the corporation under this agreement is $400,000 a year. The agreement has a five-year term. The corporation uses its rights under this agreement and under the satellite access agreement to make available time on the satellite to other businesses for an access charge of $100,000 a year plus a use charge of $60 a half-hour. A number of businesses have purchased access for various periods and have paid, and made prepayments of, the user charges due under their contracts with the corporation.

I have determined the financial income of the corporation, using the accrual method of accounting, in the following manner.

Income (Loss) Space Age Communications, Inc.
(000 omitted)

Receipts

Share of Income of Partnership (See Exhibit A below)	$ 90
Access Charges	
Received $600,000—allocated to first 3/4 year	425
User Charges	
Received $550,000—allocated to first 3/4 year	350

Expenses

Expense and Maintenance	(90)
Rent paid to Southwest—3/4 of a year	(300)
Interest paid	(325)
Amortization of Investment in Satellite Time	(375)
	($225)

Exhibit A Income (Loss) of Southwest, Ltd.
(000 omitted)

Receipts

Rental Income—3/4 of a year	$300

Expenses

Interest Expense-- Real Property Improvements	
($50,000 total—$13,000 capitalized pursuant to	
Section 263a)	(37)
Interest Expense—Personal Property	(34)
Depreciation—Personal Property	(34)
Depreciation—Real Property	(15)
	$180

     You can assume that my allocation of access and user charges paid to the corporation and the rent paid by the corporation to Southwest for the 3/4's of a year of operation were done properly. While the corporation's income statement shows a loss of $225,000, I have taken the position that only $100,000 of the loss is available to the shareholders since that amount is the extent of the corporation's investment which is "at risk" under the "at risk" rules.

     I calculated the "at risk" limitation in the following manner. Since the 60-month satellite access contract only gave the corporation access for the last nine months of the year, only 9/60 of the $2,500,000 cost can be taken as a deduction for that year, resulting in a $375,000 deduction for amortization of the satellite access contract. Furthermore, since only

$250,000 in cash and no recourse debt was invested in the satellite access contract, the amount of amortization allowed under the "at risk" rules must be reduced to $250,000 (rather than the $375,000 shown on the income statement), thereby producing a taxable net loss for the corporation of $100,000 rather than the $225,000 loss shown on the income statement.

Please let me know if you have any concerns or problems with my computation of the net operating loss suffered by the corporation. If you do, I would like to get together with you early next week so that you can explain your concerns to me.

Sincerely yours,

Marisa Devough
Marisa Devough

PROBLEM 28C

Barbara Carter owns all the stock of Barbara's Boutique, Inc. (Boutique), which operates a boutique out of a small downtown building owned by Boutique. The balance sheet of Boutique, which is a C corporation, is set forth below:

Barbara's Boutique, Inc.
(x 1000)

Assets	Book Value or Basis	Fair Market Value	Liabilities	
Cash	$ 60	$ 60	Payables	$ 80
Securities	52	60	Loan	40
Accounts Receivable	40	40	Paid-In Capital	60
Inventory (LIFO)	100	140	Retained Earnings	160
Personalty counters, etc.)	8	40		$340
Building	50	80		
Land	30	200		
Goodwill	-0-	100		
	$340	$720		

Boutique, which is a calendar year taxpayer, has accumulated earnings and profits of $160,000 and has always used the straight-line method for determining all depreciation. Although the company uses the LIFO method, if it had used the FIFO method, its basis in the inventory would be $130,000. For the last two years, Boutique, which has paid Barbara an annual salary of $60,000, has realized net taxable income of about $80,000 on gross annual sales of $400,000. Barbara does not anticipate that these figures will change much for the next few years.

Barbara has long been interested in locating the store in a suburban mall, and she recently received an offer to purchase the land and building owned by Boutique for $280,000. Because of Boutique's low basis in these assets, she is reluctant to have Boutique accept the offer because of the impact which the "corporate double tax" would have on the proceeds. If economically feasible, however, she would like it to accept the offer and relocate in a mall.

Barbara informs you that her brother, Paul, who is a third-year law student, suggested that she cause Boutique to: (1) elect S corporation status effective at the beginning of the next calendar year; (2) defer the sale until that year; (3) distribute the proceeds of the sale to Barbara in the year of sale; and (4) revoke the S corporation status effective for the next succeeding calendar year. As an alternative to items (3) and (4), Paul suggested that Barbara consider causing Boutique to: (1) sell the land and building for the purchaser's installment obligation, which would have a term of eleven years, have interest only payable during the first ten years, provide that the full amount of principal would be payable at the end of the eleventh year and would be secured by a mortgage on the land and building; (2) continue the S corporation status through the year in which the installment obligation is paid in full, distributing interest and principal payments to Barbara; and (3) revoke the S corporation status effective for the year following the year in which the installment obligation is paid in full.

Barbara would like your advice on the tax consequences of following Paul's suggestions.

PROBLEM 29C

One of the young partners in the tax department of the firm recently received a letter from a passing acquaintance. She has given you the letter and asks that you brief her with respect to the issues involved so that she will be prepared to meet with her acquaintance and properly advise him in the next few days.

Edmundo Lapetina
714 Brock Way
Middletown, CT 06547

November 13, Year*

Christina Tucker, Esq.
417 Center Street
Middletown, CT 06547

Dear Ms. Tucker:

I hope you remember our conversation at a PTA meeting a month ago. I am a faculty member at Wesleyan University and have been doing research in medical engineering. I mentioned to you that I was working on a device which can be used for testing X-ray machines, and I had applied for a patent on that device. I have just been awarded the patent. I would like your assistance in forming a corporation to exploit and manufacture the patented device.

I estimate that the new corporation will lose money for its first year or two of operation. If the device proves as good as I believe it to be, the company will realize substantial profits thereafter. The manufacture of the device is a fairly complicated, customized operation, which I and my wife, Maria, intend to carry out in our basement. Because of the loss potential, I would like to consider using an S corporation. When the corporation starts generating income, I would like to see to it that a significant portion of the income is taxed to my minor daughter, Helen, who, at present, owns no income-producing assets.

The only assets which the company will require at its inception are: (1) the patent; (2) machine tools and equipment, which I own; (3) rent-free use of the basement; (4) $30,000, which Maria and I will contribute; and (5) our services. To avoid complicated record-keeping and FICA and FUTA

---

* See explanatory footnote in Introduction, page vii, note 1.

taxes, neither Maria nor I (we both have substantial incomes) intends to be paid a salary. I would like your advice as to how best to realize my goals.

Sincerely yours,

Edmundo Lapetina

Edmundo Lapetina

5. COMPARISON OF THE SUBCHAPTER S CORPORATION WITH OTHER CONDUIT FORMS

PROBLEM 30C

Five of your more successful clients have just asked for your advice. In the past, the clients have invested jointly in a number of real estate development projects such as apartment and office buildings, shopping plazas and the like. You have always recommended that an unincorporated conduit form of entity, such as a general or limited partnership, a limited liability partnership or a limited liability company, be used, at least initially, to own and operate these investments. Your general explanation of the reason for this recommendation was that, despite having to give up at least two of centralized management, limited liability, free transferability and continuity of life that go with the corporate form, the income tax benefits gained through the use of an unincorporated form of entity are well worth the cost.

Your clients have heard, in casual discussions with other persons engaged in real estate development, that an S corporation is taxed like a partnership and that the shareholders who work for such a corporation can obtain, to some extent, tax-free fringe benefits which are not usually available to participants who work for their unincorporated form of entity.

Your clients are in the planning stages of a small office building project. They estimate that the office building will produce an aggregate $450,000 tax loss during the first five years of operation. It will, however, produce a positive cash flow starting the second year of operation and when, in the sixth year of operation, it begins producing taxable income, the amount of cash flow will exceed substantially the amount of taxable income for the sixth through the twelfth year. Your clients' total equity contribution toward the purchase of the land and the construction of the office building will be in the neighborhood of $600,000. The remainder, $2,400,000, of the estimated cost of purchase and construction will be borrowed from Western Savings Bank, secured by a first mortgage on the land and building. Some of the clients will take an active role in management, and some will take a passive role. In addition, some may sell, transfer or otherwise dispose of their interest in the venture prior to the end of the life of the venture.

While your clients realize that an S corporation is not treated just like other unincorporated forms, they would like you to contrast and compare, with particular reference to your clients' proposed venture, the treatment of an S corporation with the treatment of a general, limited and limited liability partnership and a limited liability company with particular reference to the following areas:

1. The eligibility of the entity for use in carrying on the proposed business activity;

2. The ability of the participants in the entity to separate their interests in future earnings from their interests in capital and their interests in capital and earnings from their interests in management;

3. The determination of the bases of the participants in their interests in the entity;

4. The taxation of the income of the entity to the participants;

5. The pass-through of the tax losses of the entity to the participants;

6. The ability to have the participants share the income of the entity in a manner different from that used to share the losses and the ability to change the sharing ratios during the life of the entity;

7. The treatment of the tax losses of the entity which cannot, in the year incurred, be passed through to the participants;

8. The income tax treatment of pro rata current distributions of money by the entity to the participants;

9. The income tax treatment of non-pro rata distributions of money by the entity to the participants; and

10.   The ability of the participants to transfer or dispose of the "tax attributes" of their interests in the entity when they sell, transfer or otherwise dispose of some, or all, of such interests.

Note:

See the Note on Limited Liability Partnerships following Problem 2P at page 10 and the Note on Limited Liability Companies following Problem 4P at page 22.

PROBLEM 31C

At one time, Dakota Beach was a thriving summer resort community on the shores of Cavern Lake. Over the years, it has fallen into disrepair and has lost most of its vacation trade. The area, however, still possesses many natural amenities which would be attractive to vacationers such as the clear deep lake, mild climate and attractive rolling countryside. The accommodations presently located in Dakota Beach, including the once-elegant Grand Hotel, are quite outmoded and decrepit. Stephanie Kowalski (Stephanie), Matthew Dugan (Matthew) and Rose Clipman (Rose), residents of Dakota Beach, think they have found a way of building up the vacation trade.

Stephanie owns, as a sole proprietor, the Grand Hotel, which she inherited from her parents a number of years ago. While many of the accommodations and amenities presently in the hotel are quite outmoded, the hotel buildings are basically very sound and solid structures. To attract more vacation trade, at least $1,200,000 in renovations would have to be made to the hotel to bring the accommodations and amenities up to the standard expected in a first-class hotel. Stephanie, Matthew and Rose feel that the present fair market value of the hotel buildings is about $1,000,000, and the value of the land on which the buildings are situated is about $220,000. Stephanie has an adjusted basis in the hotel buildings of $500,000 and a basis in the land of $100,000. The hotel buildings and land presently are unencumbered, and Stephanie does not owe any debts with respect to the operation of the hotel except about $20,000 in trade accounts payable left over from last summer's operation.

Matthew is a very well-to-do land speculator. He has acquired most of the land surrounding the Grand Hotel and between it and the lake. The old cottages, which were located on some of the land, have been demolished since they had little value as vacation accommodations. Matthew financed a substantial portion of the purchase price of the land and has increased the amount of liabilities to which the land is subject in order to pay the carrying costs of the land such as taxes, interest on the liabilities, etc. Matthew, Stephanie and Rose feel that the fair market value of Matthew's land is about $2,400,000. The land is subject to liabilities of $1,200,000, and Matthew's basis in the land is $900,000.

Rose is the former executive vice-president and manager of Sea Pines Resort in Hilton Head, South Carolina. She is noted as one of the most innovative resort planners and managers in the country. She has developed plans for the renovation of the Grand Hotel and for recreation and vacation oriented uses of Matthew's land. The plans contemplate, as mentioned above, making the Grand Hotel a first-class facility and improving Matthew's land with a variety of recreational facilities to be available to guests of the hotel. Facilities such as a golf course, tennis courts, swimming pools and health and athletic clubs will be constructed. The cost of such facilities is estimated to be about $2,600,000.

For Rose's plan to be carried out, the Grand Hotel and Matthew's land must be owned, or at least controlled, by the same entity. The entity, using the Grand Hotel and Matthew's land as a capital base, might be able to finance the renovations to the hotel for $1,200,000 and the construction of the recreational facilities for $2,600,000 — a total of $3,800,000. Rose would contribute $600,000 of her savings to the entity for this purpose. She believes that $1,200,000 can be raised from about thirty outside investors in exchange for the equivalent of a one-quarter interest in the entity, and the remaining $2,000,000 can be borrowed from a bank. Consequently, Stephanie and Matthew have each agreed to contribute the Grand Hotel and the land to an entity, and in return, each will receive a one-quarter interest in the entity. Rose will contribute the plans and $600,000, arrange for the investors and the bank financing, and supervise the renovations and the construction of the recreational facilities in return for a one-quarter interest in the entity. The projections of taxable income and loss indicate that the entity will lose, for tax purposes, an aggregate of about $800,000 over the first five years of operations. The cash flow of the entity, however, will be positive after the first year.

Stephanie, Matthew and Rose have considered using, as a business entity to own and operate the renovated Grand Hotel, either a limited partnership with Rose as the general partner, a limited liability company or an S corporation. They have asked for your advice. What problems will they face if they decide to form and use a limited partnership or a limited liability company? What if they choose to form and use an S corporation? Which would you recommend and why?

PROBLEM 32C

The firm with which you are associated does a lot of work for construction contractors. As a result, a number of the firm's partners are specialists at construction law. One of those specialists recently sent a memo to one of the partners in the tax department of the firm. That partner has given you the memorandum plus its attachments and asks that you advise her with respect to your recommendation of the form of entity which should be chosen by the clients described in the memorandum.

Hollingsworth, Midu & Marshall
1717 14th Street
Billings, MT 59102

Intraoffice Memorandum

TO: Sylvia Loh

FROM: Richard Heath   *Rick*

RE: Combination of Amax Construction, Inc. and Betterbilt Construction Corp.

Amax Construction, Inc. ("Amax") and Betterbilt Construction Corp. ("Betterbilt") are corporations which engage in the general contracting business. The two corporations are located next door to one another at 1830 Sycamore (Amax) and 1840 Sycamore (Betterbilt). At these locations, both of the corporations have substantial buildings which contain their offices, maintenance areas for equipment, storage areas for construction materials which cannot be kept out of doors, employee cleanup and locker areas, and dispatch and communication rooms. Both corporations store their vehicles and equipment at their respective locations when the equipment and vehicles are not in use. Lastly, both corporations store their inventories of construction materials and supplies which can be kept out of doors, such as aggregate, asphalt and sand, in large piles at these locations.

Amax and Betterbilt have been competitors for the past ten years. Amax is wholly owned by Justinian Sweet ("Sweet"). One hundred percent of the stock of Betterbilt is owned by Rosiland Lucas ("Lucas"). During the last couple of years, Sweet and Lucas have been discussing combining their businesses. A combination of their businesses would make a lot of sense since the business strengths of each corporation complement the strengths of the other. Sweet and Lucas and I have given the combination of their businesses some thought, and it appears to us that the most feasible approach would be to form a third entity ("new entity") to which each corporation would transfer all its property. Also, the new entity would assume all of the liabilities of each corporation. Both Sweet and Lucas want to keep Amax and Betterbilt in existence to hold the interests in the new entity. Sweet and Lucas and I would like your advice with respect to what form of entity they should choose for the new entity.

Both Amax and Betterbilt have elected S corporation status, and Sweet and Lucas have both consented. Sweet and Lucas, since they want to avoid paying the "double" corporate income tax, would like Amax and Betterbilt to continue as S corporations, if possible, after the new entity is formed. Sweet and Lucas also desire that Amax's and Betterbilt's shares of the income of the new entity be transferred tax-free or with a minimum of tax, if possible, to Amax and Betterbilt. The results of the new entity suffering financial reverses and having to be liquidated or put into bankruptcy also have been considered by Sweet and Lucas and me. They believe that it is very important for Amax and Betterbilt to be able to treat the loss of their investments in the new entity as an ordinary rather than a capital loss.

Sweet and Lucas would like to take the opportunity presented by the formation of the new entity to bring some of their key employees into ownership positions in the business. The employees do not have much in the way of assets to contribute to the new entity, probably no more than $2,000 or so apiece. The four individuals whom Lucas and Sweet have in mind, two from Amax and two from Betterbilt, are very valuable employees and have been with their respective employer for a number of years. Sweet and Lucas believe that one way to help assure the successful operation of the new entity is to make sure these employees have a stake in its success. For the foregoing reasons, Sweet and Lucas have determined that each of the four employees should have about a 6% interest in the new entity. Amax and Betterbilt each will receive a 38% interest in the new entity in return for each one's contribution of assets.

Both Amax and Betterbilt are going to transfer to the new entity all of the assets, and the new entity is going to assume all the liabilities shown on the balance sheets attached hereto. In addition to the assets shown on the balance sheets, both Amax and Betterbilt are going to transfer to the new entity construction contracts which they are presently working on, or which have been awarded to one or the other but upon which work has not yet begun.   Amax will contribute about $400,000 in value of construction contracts, and Betterbilt will contribute about $600,000 in value of construction contracts.

As mentioned above, Sweet and Lucas and I would like you to advise us with respect to the form of entity which should be used for the new entity.   I have advised them that some possible choices are: 1) an S corporation, 2) a general or limited partnership, 3) a limited liability partnership, or 4) a limited liability company.

Balance Sheet of Amax Construction, Inc.[1]
(in $,000)
Assets

		Basis	Fair Market Value
Cash		$ 50	$ 50
Inventory of Building Materials		100	140
Construction Equipment			
Original Cost	$220		
Depreciation[2]	(100)	120	180
Building			
Original Cost	750		
Depreciation[2]	(430)	320	380
Land		110	150
Total		$700	$900

Liabilities

	Basis	Fair Market Value
Trade Accounts Payable	$ 80	$ 80
Working Capital Loan	200	200
Mortgage on Land and Building	440	440
Capital		
1,000 Shares No Par Value		
Common Stock	10	10
Surplus (Deficit)	(30)	170
	$700	$900

---

[1] Balance Sheet Prepared Using the Accrual Method of Accounting
[2] Depreciation Computed Using the Straight-Line Method

Balance Sheet of Betterbilt Construction Corp.[1]
(in $,000)
Assets

		Basis	Fair Market Value
Cash		$ 70	$ 70
Inventory of Building Materials		60	100
Construction Equipment			
Original Cost	$180		
Depreciation[2]	(90)	90	130
Building			
Original Cost	440		
Depreciation[2]	(240)	200	280
Land		90	120
Total		$510	$700

Liabilities

	Basis	Fair Market Value
Trade Accounts Payable	$ 40	$ 40
Working Capital Loan	280	280
Mortgage on Land and Building	250	250
Capital		
500 Shares No Par Value		
Common Stock	50	50
Surplus (Deficit)	(110)	130
	$510	$750

[1] Balance Sheet Prepared Using the Accrual Method of Accounting
[2] Depreciation Computed Using the Straight-Line Method

Note:

See the Note on Limited Liability Partnerships following Problem 2P at page 10 and the Note on Limited Liability Companies following Problem 4P at page 22.

Part B

CORPORATE DISTRIBUTIONS

---

1. DIVIDENDS AND OTHER NON-LIQUIDATING DISTRIBUTIONS

a. Cash and Property Dividends

PROBLEM 33C

Jane Maise, Phylis Jordan and Ray Misourka formed Empire Pharmaceuticals, Inc. (Empire) last year. Each paid $120,000 for one-third of the stock. The corporation acts as a manufacturer's representative and wholesaler of pharmaceutical supplies. It used the investment by its stockholders, a line of credit from 10th National Bank, and a mortgage loan from Etnor Life Insurance Company to acquire its opening inventory and a small combination office and warehouse building and generally to get started in business. The corporation uses the accrual method of accounting and used, during its first year, FIFO for inventory and the most accelerated rate of depreciation available for the office and warehouse. For its first year it reported $75,000 of taxable income after deducting salaries, interest, general business expenses and depreciation, and it accrued $15,000 in federal and state income taxes on such sum. Empire's financial statement at the end of its first year was as follows:

EMPIRE PHARMACEUTICALS, INC. ᴵˢᵗ yᴿ
Assets

Cash		$ 60,000
Municipal Bonds		60,000
Accounts Receivable		145,500
Inventory		270,000
Office & Warehouse Building	$240,000	
(Depreciation)	(12,000)	228,000
Office & Warehouse Land		90,000
		$853,500

Liabilities

Accounts Payable	$111,600
10th National Bank Line of Credit	60,000
Etnor Life Ins. Co. Mtg.	261,900
Capital	
Stated Capital - *par value of the stock*	90,000
Capital Surplus - *Amt pd. above par, also 30k contrib p capital*	270,000
Earned Surplus - *sum of earnings not distributed as dividends*	60,000
	$853,500

To date, the current year has not been as good as Empire's first year. In fact, Jane, Phylis and Ray expect Empire to show an overall economic loss. Its gross income for income tax purposes will probably be about $9,000 less than its deductions for salaries, interest, general business expenses and depreciation. The corporation has received but does not intend to include in gross income: (1) undeveloped land worth about $30,000, conveyed by the County Industrial Development Commission in return for Empire's promise to locate in the local industrial park in the near future; (2) $4,500 of interest on the municipal bonds it holds; and (3) a $6,000 account payable which was forgiven by a supplier and with respect to which Empire plans to file a consent to adjustment of basis under Section 1017.

In addition to the deductions mentioned above, the corporation plans to deduct a $30,000 contingency reserve set up for earthquake damage. The area in which its office and warehouse are located is prone to serious earth tremors, and it cannot obtain insurance to cover this risk. The corporation also plans to deduct a $1,000 reserve for anticipated bad debts on its current accounts receivable.

To meet some of its financial needs during this year, Empire sold some of its municipal bonds at a $15,000 loss. Since it has never realized any capital gains, it plans to carry over this loss. Even though prohibited by statute, the corporation, as is the custom in the trade, paid $15,000 in kickbacks to various suppliers. On the advice of its accountant, it does not plan to claim these payments as a deduction on its income tax return. Finally, Empire's accountant has advised it that $9,000 of the current year's interest paid on loans made pursuant to its line of credit from 10th National Bank may be disallowed as a deduction because, rather than selling all its municipal bonds this year, the corporation chose to borrow through its line of credit.

The last few months of the year should produce a fairly good cash flow despite the anticipated loss for the entire year. Jane, Phylis and Ray would like to get some cash out of the corporation for personal use. They realize that a year-end bonus of $15,000 each will, at best, be taxable to them at ordinary rates. They ask you whether their personal income tax positions will be any better if the corporation declares a $45,000 dividend.

bonus or dividend ?

Note:

See the Note on Interviewing and Client Counseling following Problem 1P at page 4.

PROBLEM 34C

Duncan McMillan, the president of Athens International, Inc. (Athens), has asked for your assistance in determining the tax consequences of several strategies which he is considering employing to recognize the valuable contribution of Athens' investors. Athens, which is principally engaged in the business of manufacturing quality jewelry, is owned by two individual shareholders, Mr. McMillan and Helen Hughes, the company vice president, and two corporations, Consolidated Investments Inc. (Consolidated), and Rich Properties, Inc. (Rich). Each of the four investors owns twenty five percent of Athens' common stock, having paid $100,000 for it 10 years ago. Athens has been very successful and has accumulated

each owns - 25% of common per book 10 yrs ago

earnings and profits of $1,500,000 and current earnings and profits of $150,000. Mr. McMillan is considering distributing to each investor $50,000 in value using one or a combination of the following:

(1)   cash which is on deposit in Athens' accounts;

(2) $200,000 in value of gold inventory which has a basis of $160,000 in the hands of Athens; and

(3) $200,000 in value of silver inventory which has a basis of $230,000 in the hands of Athens.

Ms. Hughes has suggested that rather than distributing any of the above, the Board of Directors of Athens should pay Ms. Hughes and Mr. McMillan a bonus of $50,000. The bonuses would be deductible by Athens. Consolidated and Rich could be compensated by loaning them, for one year, an amount of money (about $400,000) interest-free which will result in transferring to each corporation $50,000 in value.

Scott Munn, a bright young recent law school graduate who works for you, has advised Mr. McMillan that the above strategies are fraught with undesirable tax consequences. Since Mr. McMillan caught Mr. Munn on his car phone while Mr. Munn was on his way to the airport for a meeting in Tokyo and was not able to get a full explanation, he has turned to you to explain the tax consequences of the above to him.

PROBLEM 35C

Bill Powers, an associate in your law firm, has prepared the following memorandum to assist you in advising Ridgewood Garden Supply, Inc. (Ridgewood) with respect to a distribution of property to its investors. You must review his memorandum to determine what advice should be given to Ridgewood.

Memorandum Re:
Ridgewood Garden Supply, Inc.
Dividend and Sale of Realty

William Powers   Sept. 23, Year*

    You have asked me to investigate various means whereby, in the context of a sale of corporate assets, investors in Ridgewood Garden Supply, Inc. (Ridgewood) could receive a distribution of $100,000 each from Ridgewood with minimal tax consequences.

    Miriam Novak, Patricia Baloyra, Robert Lanier and Morris Realty, Inc. (Morris) each own 250 shares (25 percent) of the common stock of Ridgewood which for the last fourteen years has conducted a landscaping and garden supply business. Each of the investors, who are Ridgewood's original incorporators, have an adjusted basis of $25,000 or $100 per share in the stock which they own. Mrs. Novak, Ms. Baloyra and Mr. Lanier are all employed by Ridgewood and have received decent salaries for their efforts. Unfortunately, after allowing for salaries and other expenses, Ridgewood has been somewhat less than a break even operation resulting in its having an $80,000 deficit in accumulated earnings and profits. Mrs. Novak, who is Ridgewood's president, has told me that, absent unexpected events such as the possible sale of its realty which will be discussed below, she anticipates that Ridgewood will realize no current earnings and profits this year.

    Despite its lack of operating success, the investors in Ridgewood are satisfied with their investments. It has been a source of gainful employment for its three individual investors and Morris has always been able to obtain attentive, prompt service from Ridgewood for prospective home sellers and for homes under management by Morris. In addition, the ten acres of land on which Ridgewood conducts its business is located in the Westwood area where property values have soared. This has resulted in the value of the Westwood land increasing from $60,000 to $800,000 during Ridgewood's ownership. The present fair market value was established by an offer that Ridgewood received from Village Builders, L.L.C. (Builders) which is anxious to acquire the land for a condominium project. Mrs. Novak has indicated that the investors would like to accept Builders' offer. A new, suitable business site could be purchased on the edge of town for approximately

---

* See explanatory footnote in Introduction, page vii, note 1.

$100,000, thus leaving the investors with a considerable profit and the business intact and operational.

In analyzing Ridgewood's situation and considering various alternative courses of action, I have explored the following: (1) allow Ridgewood to sell the Westwood land this year and distribute $100,000 per shareholder to the four investors in the form of a cash dividend; (2) have Ridgewood borrow sufficient money to enable it to pay a dividend of $100,000 to each of the four shareholders this year and have the sale of the Westwood land take place either (a) this year following payment of the dividend, (b) next year, or (c) this year using the installment method to defer recognition of income until next year; or (3) distribute an undivided one-eighth interest in the Westwood land to each shareholder. They and Ridgewood would then sell their respective interests in the land to Builders.

I will discuss the tax consequences of each of these alternatives, but before doing so I will make several observations about matters which will be of general application.

General Observations — Under Sec. 301 and Sec. 316 of the Internal Revenue Code of 1986, as amended (the Code), corporate distributions are taxed as dividends to the extent of accumulated or current earnings and profits of the payor. Under Sec. 301(c)(2) and (3), that portion of any distribution which is not a dividend is treated as a recovery of basis to the extent of the shareholder's adjusted basis in his or her stock and any excess is, assuming the stock is a capital asset, taxed as a capital gain. Under Sec. 243, corporate shareholders are entitled to deduct from the amount of any distribution taxed as a dividend either 100, 80, or 70 percent of such amount. The 100 percent deduction is available only to small business investment companies and corporations which are members of an affiliated group (requiring, among other things, corporate ownership of 80 percent of the stock of the payor). If the corporate shareholder owns at least 20 percent of the stock of the payor, as does Morris, the 80 percent deduction applies and where it owns less than 20 percent, the 70 percent deduction applies.

Sale Followed by Distribution — As mentioned above, under Sec. 301 and Sec. 316 of the Code, distributions are taxed as dividends only to the extent of earnings and profits. The Code does not define earnings and profits. Most commentators indicate that to determine the amount of earnings and profits, one should start with net taxable income for federal purposes, make the adjustments called for by Sec. 312, and use common sense to determine the pool of available earnings and profits from which distributions can be made. *See e.g., Boris Bittker & James Eustice, Federal Income Taxation of Corporations and Shareholders*, ¶ 8.03 (6th ed. 1994).

It is anticipated that, in the absence of a sale of the Westwood realty, Ridgewood would have no current earnings and profits and would have a deficit of $80,000 in its accumulated earnings and profits account. Sale of the Westwood realty would generate taxable income of $740,000 for Ridgewood. I estimate that this would result in a combined state and federal tax liability of $260,000. In computing current earnings and profits of Ridgewood, both state and federal taxes should be deducted. Therefore, Ridgewood's current earnings and profits would equal $480,000. A per shareholder distribution would result in Miriam, Patricia and Robert each being taxed on the full $100,000 received as a dividend. Since Morris owns 25 percent of the stock of Ridgewood, under Sec. 243 it would be entitled to a deduction of $80,000 (or 80 percent) on its $100,000, resulting in only $20,000 being taxed to it.

Dividend Followed by Sale — Section 316(a)(2) indicates that current earnings and profits are computed as of the close of the taxable year and without regard to the earnings and profits at the time a distribution is made. This means that, if Ridgewood sells the Westwood realty this year for $800,000 after it has made a distribution of $100,000 per shareholder, it will not matter that there were no current earnings and profits at the time of the distribution. Dividend status for the distribution will be determined at year end with the result that the distribution of $100,000 per shareholder will be taxed in the manner indicated under the heading of Sale Followed by Distribution.

If Ridgewood were to defer the sale of the Westwood property until next year and borrow $400,000 to enable it to distribute $100,000 to each shareholder this year, none of the distribution would be treated as a dividend since this year Ridgewood would have neither current nor accumulated earnings and profits. Each shareholder would treat $25,000 (the amount of each one's adjusted basis in the stock) as an untaxed recovery of capital. The balance, $75,000 per shareholder, would be taxed as long term capital gains. This would be advantageous to all shareholders and indeed preferable to a sale followed by a distribution. Under this alternative, all shareholders would reduce their basis in the stock of Ridgewood to zero. See Sec. 301(c)(2).

If the investors in Ridgewood are reluctant to defer the sale to another year out of fear that Builders might change its mind or the value of the realty might drop resulting in a reduced sale price, I suggest that Ridgewood consider selling the property to Builders this year using the installment method with payment due next year. Since Ridgewood would have no current taxable income from the sale, the sale would not have any impact on Ridgewood's earnings and profits for this year. Ridgewood could then borrow the $400,000 necessary to fund a distribution of $100,000 per shareholder. The distribution, as outlined above, would be treated by each shareholder as a $25,000 tax free recovery of capital and a $75,000 capital gain with the stock held in Ridgewood having an adjusted basis of zero after the distribution.

Distribution of Interest in Property — Under Sec. 301(b)(1) the amount of any distribution of property is its fair market value. Moreover, under Sec. 311(b)(1), a corporation distributing property to its shareholders is required to recognize gain on the distribution as if the distributed property were sold to the distributee shareholders for its fair market value. This means that a distribution to each shareholder of a one-eighth interest in the Westwood realty which is worth $100,000 would generate a gain of $92,500 ($100,000-$7,500 adjusted basis of one-eighth interest) to Ridgewood. The aggregate $370,000 gain to Ridgewood, after allowing for combined state and federal tax liability of $130,000, would result in Ridgewood's earnings and profits being increased by $240,000 ($370,000-$130,000). Moreover, when the shareholders and Ridgewood sell their interests in the Westwood realty to Builders, Ridgewood will recognize $370,000 of gain on the sale of its one-half interest. After deducting Ridgewood's combined state and federal tax liability of $130,000, the sale will result in an additional increase in its current earnings and profits of $240,000. Since the total of $480,000 of current earnings and profits would be sufficient to cause the full property distribution of $100,000 per shareholder to be taxed as a dividend, the result to the shareholders would be the same as it was under the heading of Sale Followed by Distribution above.

Recommendation — As the above discussion indicates, the most advantageous tax treatment to the Ridgewood shareholders would be obtained by either: (1) arranging for a $100,000 per shareholder distribution in a year preceding the sale of the Westwood realty; or (2) arranging for an installment sale of the realty with no payment being made until a year after the distribution of $100,000 per shareholder has been made. Either of these two approaches would avoid dividend treatment for the Ridgewood shareholders and result in only $75,000 of the $100,000 received by each shareholder being taxed as long term capital gains, a real advantage when compared to taxation of $100,000 per shareholder as a dividend.

Note:

Memoranda

The memorandum is a basic element in the representation of most clients. It is the foundation for negotiations, opinion letters, pleadings and motions, and trial and appellate briefs. It also assists in the drafting of other documents such as contracts and wills. The time spent in research for, and writing of, a memo is likely to save time and money later.

Whether a memo is written at the request of a senior partner or for your own use, its purpose is the same — to produce a reliable and complete statement of the facts and applicable law. It must be objective, as concerned with the weaknesses as with the strengths of a client's situation. The purpose is not to find arguments to support a preferred conclusion. Wishful thinking should never distort analysis.

It is more important to be thorough than concise, though precision is desirable. In discussing decided cases, state enough facts, issues and procedural points to insure that decisions and quotations will be presented in their true context. Your research should be as complete as possible. If there are limitations of time or economy, or if you feel that further exploration is not needed, so indicate in the memo. Include accurate and complete citations so that there will be no need to retrace your steps in preparing other documents.

A memo generally deals with a specific problem. To deal effectively with that problem, you must thoroughly understand the relevant facts. Make your resolution of the problem as complete as possible leaving no loose ends. Unless otherwise directed, include your recommendations for future tactics or strategy. Do not attempt to pass the buck for concrete answers and recommendations to the person who requested the memo.

There is no particular standard form for a memo, although many firms develop their own. The memo appearing in the problem is in somewhat informal style. A formal memo may include, in the following order: (1) the questions to be discussed; (2) brief answers or recommendations; (3) a complete statement of the relevant necessary facts; (4) an analysis of the applicable law, including citations; and (5) conclusions of law and an appraisal of how firmly the authorities support such conclusions. For efficient filing and indexing it is desirable to include in prominent fashion the name of the client and the particular matter under consideration.

Good organization is critically important. Plan the memo before writing it. Preparation of a detailed outline including authorities is often a good idea. Be aware of where you are headed and why you cite a particular case or use a particular argument. Liberal use of headings and subheadings will help, particularly when making cross-references or subsequently referring to the memo.

PROBLEM 36C

Janice Carillo and Ruth Schlinger formed Speculation Corporation (Speculation) ten years ago. At present they each own 30% of the stock of Speculation (30 shares each), Wise Investments, Inc. (Wise) owns 35% of the stock (35 shares), and the balance (5% or five shares) is owned by Thomas Glynn. Both Wise and Thomas acquired their interests four years ago by purchase from Janice and Ruth. The adjusted basis in the stock owned by each of Speculation's owners is shown in the parentheses which follow his or her name: (1) Janice ($180,000); (2) Ruth ($240,000); (3) Wise ($700,000); and (4) Thomas ($100,000).

Speculation is currently involved in the operation of an intra-city express mail service and the ownership and rental of real estate. The net worth of the corporation is presently about $4,800,000. Approximately one-half of its assets are dedicated to the operation of the express mail service. One-quarter of its assets consist of two apartment houses, Regency Park and Lindell Manor, which constitute the corporation's real estate operations. The remainder of the corporation's assets consists of $1,200,000 in cash and certificates of deposit. Speculation has a deficit in accumulated earnings and profits of $160,000. It currently has a net loss of $20,000 half-way through its tax year, and, in the absence of the distributions proposed below, it would be expected to finish the year with a deficit in current earnings and profits of $40,000.

Regency Park is rented to Geriatrics, Inc. on a net lease basis for use as a senior citizens' residence. The lease, which has nine years until expiration, was entered into last year as part of a restructuring of the real estate operations of Speculation. It obligates Geriatrics, Inc. to pay all operating expenses and real estate taxes assessed against the property. Prior to entering into the lease with Geriatrics, Inc., Speculation had operated Regency Park as a traditional, residential apartment house for which it collected the rents and provided basic maintenance services.

Since its opening eight years ago, Lindell Manor, Speculation's other apartment house, has been operated as a luxury apartment structure. Speculation has provided 24 hour doorman service and a 12 hour per day reception service. It also has provided the tenants with package pick up facilities, and contact with commercial housekeeping, dry cleaning and laundry services all of which are provided through Speculation approved independent contractors. There is a modest fitness facility in Lindell Manor which is available to all tenants and is staffed by a Speculation employee on week-ends and evenings.

Last year, when it became clear that the Lindell Manor units could be operated more profitably as professional offices, Speculation, as units became available through vacancy or at the end of a lease, began to switch units over to professional tenants. Approximately 45% of the units are now commercial providing almost 60% of total rent receipts. The balance of the receipts, approximately 40%, come from the 55% of the units dedicated to residential use. Since the new professional tenants are somewhat upscale and were attracted to Lindell Manor primarily because of its personalized services, Speculation intends to continue providing the same level of personal services currently provided to residential tenants and is also considering expanding the hours in which the fitness facility is staffed to better accommodate the needs of commercial tenants who would use the facility during the lunch hours or in the late afternoon.

Each of Speculation's apartment houses has a fair market value of $600,000 and an adjusted basis of $120,000. If sold for their fair market value, it is estimated that Speculation would incur a combined state, local and federal income tax liability of $180,000 on each apartment house. The buildings are not subject to any liabilities, and each currently produces annual gross rents of almost $120,000.

Janice, who is president of Speculation, and Ruth, who is its executive vice-president, serve as the corporation's chief operating officers. They seek your advice with respect to the following matter.

Wise, which is in need of liquid assets, has recently been lobbying for payment of a large dividend. Bryan Bromberger, Wise's president, suggested at a Speculation shareholders' meeting that Speculation's Board of Directors pay a dividend of $10,000 per share. If that would deprive Speculation of too much of its liquid assets, Mr. Bromberger suggested that the Board consider paying Wise and Thomas a cash dividend of $10,000 per share and distributing to Janice and Ruth an in-kind dividend of a 50% interest in either Regency Park or Lindell Manor. Thomas, who is a shrewd venture capitalist, strongly objected to the proposal for an in-kind dividend. He indicated that although, in this particular case, he would not object to a cash dividend of $10,000 per share, he generally was opposed to taking his profits out of an investment in the form of a dividend. He preferred to receive his reward in the form of a capital gain when he sold his stock. Mr. Bromberger said that he could see that the shareholders would be in for a long day if he and Thomas were to thrash out their differences. Prior commitments dictated that the shareholders' meeting end at that moment.

Janice and Ruth, who are highly skilled entrepreneurs but have only a fundamental knowledge of tax law, seek your advice in preparing for a resumption of the shareholders' meeting next week. Please advise them as to the basic tax considerations which are driving the positions of Bryan and Thomas and the tax consequences of each of the proposals. In addition, please consider whether it would be "cheaper" in a tax sense to meet Wise's cash needs by Speculation making an interest free loan of $10,000 to it.

PROBLEM 37C

Your client owns 30 shares of the common stock of Mark IX, Ltd., a manufacturer and retailer of contemporary furniture. Mark IX, Ltd. makes and sells furniture such as dining room chairs at $200 each, desks at $1,000 to $5,000 each, and easy chairs and couches at $600 to $8,000 each. Its usual markup is about 40%. Your client received the following communication from Mark IX, Ltd. on December 3rd of this year.

Rights Offering

December 3, Year*

To the Shareholders of Mark IX, Ltd.

Mark IX, Ltd. is distributing to its common shareholders Rights to purchase any of the furniture it manufactures at 20% below retail price. For each Right received one may, for example, purchase a $200 dining room chair or a $2,000 couch at 20% below retail price.

Enclosed is a list of the furniture items available and their current retail prices. Also enclosed is a Certificate with detachable coupons. Each coupon represents one Right for each share of common stock held by you on the record date.   *Client has 30 coupons*

Your Rights are expected to have value, and you may transfer one or more if you do not wish to exercise them. Any shareholder or transferee

---

* See explanatory footnote in Introduction, page vii, note 1.   *Sounds like an option*

desiring to exercise Rights shall mail the coupon or coupons, together with a description of the furniture selected from the enclosed list and your check in the amount of the retail price of that furniture less 20%, to Mark IX, Ltd., Shareholder Relations Division at the address shown below.

To transfer any of your Rights, detach the coupon or coupons and fill out the endorsement form on the back of each.

The Rights will expire at 5:00 P.M. California time one year from the date shown above, and your Certificate and coupons will be valueless thereafter. Accordingly, you are urged to act promptly.

Very truly yours,

James Marquis

James Marquis
Manager, Shareholder
Relations Division
Mark IX, Ltd.
1405 Sunset Street
Los Angeles, California   90026

The Rights were issued because Mark IX, Ltd., which previously had paid cash dividends of at least $6.00 per share, had a critical need for working capital this year and therefore decided to forego the cash dividend and issue the Rights to mollify shareholders. The corporation uses LIFO for inventory and has accumulated earnings and profits of $1,000,000 and current earnings and profits of $80,000. The corporation and your client are calendar year taxpayers.

Your client asks whether he has income as a result of his receipt of the Rights Certificate and coupons, and if so, when and how much. Consider the consequences of: (1) use of a coupon by your client, prior to January 1st, to purchase a desk which retails at $1,000; (2) use of a coupon by your client, after January 1st, to purchase a bookcase which retails for $2,000; (3) a gift of ten Rights to your client's favorite nephew and his wife to assist them in furnishing their new home; and (4) a sale of fifteen Rights for $1,200 to an accountant who is opening an office. If the officers of Mark IX, Ltd. had asked your advice as to the corporate income tax consequences of the dividend what would your advice have been?

Note:

See the Note on Legal Drafting following Problem 3P at page 15.

PROBLEM 38C

Caroline Reid, a fellow associate at your law firm, clipped the following story from the most recent issue of *Money* magazine. She is contemplating investing in one or more of the companies mentioned in the article for the purpose of obtaining discounted vacation travel and would like your opinion of the tax consequences of the related discounts.

Double Dividends

Do you want to more than double your money on an investment in one year? Consider purchasing as little as one share in any number of companies that, in addition to paying their shareholders cash dividends, shower them with discounts, coupons and samples.

For example, Dial Corp. sends a packet of discount coupons along with each quarterly dividend and Wm. Wrigley Jr. Co. annually sends to each shareholder a box of chewing gum (regular or sugar free — your choice) containing twenty packs of gum. "Nice," you say "but that will never double my money." Read on!

Walt Disney Co. provides a 20% discount on the cost of a Magic Kingdom Club Gold Card which entitles holders to a substantial discount on: (1) the admission fee charged at all Disney theme parks; (2) flights on Delta Air Lines; and (3) stays at certain hotels. Not to be outdone, Ralston Purina and Anheuser-Busch offer shareholders discounts at certain hotels, company owned resorts and theme parks such as the Keystone Ski Lodge in Colorado, Busch Gardens and Sea World. It doesn't stop there. CSX Corp. gives shareholders a ten percent discount on stays at its "Life Styles of the Rich and Famous" Greenbrier Resort and Marriott provides its shareholders with discounts at company owned hotels which include not only the well-known Marriott hotels but also its Fairfield and Courtyard holdings.

If discount travel and vacation in the USA is not your cup of tea and you wish to head abroad, you might pick up some Swissair stock before dashing down to see your local travel agent. That friendly airline provides its shareholders with one discount coupon, worth 15 Swiss francs ($13) for each share of Swissair that they own. While you are abroad, if you happen to own 500 shares of Trafalgar House, you can obtain a twenty five percent discount at three of its London hotels (the Ritz, the Stafford or Dukes) or enjoy a fifteen percent discount on most Cunard cruises in the sunny Mediterranean.

Although some companies, such as Swissair and Trafalgar House, tie benefits to the number of shares owned, most provide these "perks" to holders of as little as one share of stock thereby providing for a "payback" which can exceed in the first year alone the purchase price of a single share.

If you are interested in obtaining a list of over one hundred companies providing these and other benefits to shareholders, send a letter requesting the "Double Dividends List" and a self addressed, stamped envelope to: Subscriber Relations Dept.; Money Magazine; 534 6th Ave.; New York, NY 10021.

PROBLEM 39C

John Martinez and Louis Bloom are research chemists who each own 50% of the outstanding stock of Creative Inventions, Inc. (Creative) Both had previously worked for Dupont Chemical Co. and had spent much of their free time experimenting with various chemical compounds. Both John and Lou are extremely capable chemists and were able to develop a number of products which enabled them to terminate their work relationship with Dupont and to set up Creative to exploit their various inventions. At present, Creative holds all the stock in eight subsidiary corporations. Each subsidiary has been formed to exploit one of the new products developed by John and Lou.

Both John and Lou are avid cross-country skiers and that interest prompted their investigation of ways to improve the sport. They have developed and secured a patent on a chemical composition which could be sprayed on the bottom of cross-country skis. This chemical composition performs better than any known wax or composition surface in reacting to temperature and snow conditions thereby providing the optimum surface for any weather condition. The chemical composition needs to be sprayed on skis only once a season. John and Lou call the composition Wax No More. The patent for this product and all related business activities associated with exploiting and selling the product is held by Wax No More, Inc. (WNM), which is one of eight wholly owned subsidiaries of Creative.

The protest letter which follows adequately explains a significant tax problem which arose with respect to Creative's holding and eventual sale of its stock in WNM. The protest was prepared by Christine Pello, an associate in the tax department of the law firm with which you are associated. She believes that this is the best case which can be made for Creative's tax position and asks you to review it for legal accuracy and thoroughness. It is intended that Ms. Pello will handle this issue on her own through the appellate process with the Internal Revenue Service. She would like your assessment of the actual strength of Creative's position so that, in the event it is possible to enter into a compromise with the Internal Revenue Service, she will have the benefit of your thinking as to the strength of Creative's position and so that she will know what she should anticipate as a possible reasonable compromise offer.

Appellate Division of Internal Revenue Service
Denver, Colorado

In the Matter of the Federal Income Tax Liability
of Creative Inventions, Inc.
for the Taxable Year Ended December 31, Year*-2

PROTEST

The undersigned, Creative Inventions, Inc., a Colorado corporation (hereafter "Creative"), hereby respectfully protests against the deficiency in Federal income tax proposed to be assessed against it for the taxable year ended December 31, Year-2, as set forth in the letter addressed to it dated January 16, Year, and signed by the District Director of Internal Revenue, Denver, Colorado.

(a)   The name of the Taxpayer is Creative Inventions, Inc. Its taxpayer identification number is 68-470142. The address of its principal office is 400 Sherman Road, Denver, Colorado 80221.

(b)   The letter advising Creative of the proposed deficiencies with respect to which this Protest is made is dated January 16, Year and is

---

* See explanatory footnote in Introduction, page vii, note 1.

designated by the symbols "CM:T:14E." A report of Revenue Agent Evelyn Louis was attached thereto. By letter dated February 12, Year, signed by the District Director, the time for filing this Protest was extended to April 2, Year.

(c)   The year involved in the Protest, during which the Taxpayer was a calendar year accrual method taxpayer, is the taxable year ended December 31, Year-2. During that period of time, Creative, which owned all the stock of Wax No More, Inc. (WNM), was a member of an affiliated group with WNM but did not file a consolidated return with it.

(d)   The Taxpayer desires a conference in the office of the Appellate Division of the Internal Revenue Service.

(e)   The amount of the adjustments proposed to be made and to which the Taxpayer takes exception is as follows:

Items	Proposed Adjustment
A. Adjustment to Dividends Received Deduction	($4,000,000)
B. Increase in Capital Gains	$4,000,000

(f)   As stated in her report, the agent disallowed the above deduction and made the above inclusion on the following grounds:

> "The distribution from Wax No More, taxpayer's wholly-owned subsidiary, actually represented proceeds from the sale of stock with the result that the corporate dividends received deduction is unavailable and the amount in question should be taxed as a capital gain."

(g)   A statement of the facts and grounds on which the taxpayer relies in connection with the exception taken above is set forth below.

Statement of Facts

Taxpayer, Creative, is a holding company which is the sole stockholder of eight subsidiary corporations, one of which is Wax No More, Inc. (WNM), a Delaware corporation. Creative has held all the stock of WNM from the time of its formation more than eight years ago.

On August 4, Year-2, Creative was approached by Tradewinds, Ltd. (Tradewinds), a partnership, which expressed interest in purchasing WNM for $6,000,000, if mutually acceptable terms could be arranged. At a special meeting of its Board of Directors held August 5, Year-2, Creative turned down Tradewinds' offer but expressed a willingness to explore the issue of a sale at a later date. At the time of the Tradewinds' offer, Creative had an adjusted basis of $100,000 in the WNM stock, and WNM had accumulated earnings and profits of $3,654,520. It was estimated that, by the end of Year-2, WNM would have current earnings and profits of about $400,000.

At a regularly scheduled quarterly meeting of the WNM Board of Directors on September 15, Year-2, the WNM Board unanimously authorized the payment, on September 18, Year-2, of an extraordinary dividend of $4,000,000 to the WNM shareholders of record on September 16, Year-2. On September 18, Year-2, Creative, as the sole shareholder of WNM, received a $4,000,000 distribution consisting of $1,500,000 in cash and a WNM note for $2,500,000. The WNM Board at its September 15 quarterly meeting also authorized WNM management, acting on behalf of WNM shareholders, to explore the prospects for the sale of WNM stock or assets to various potential purchasers. On October 22, Year-2, Judith Dickens, president of WNM, reported to the WNM Board that, after having contacted nine potential buyers of WNM through WNM's investment banker, the best offer that she was able to develop was an offer from Tradewinds to purchase, on favorable terms, all the stock of WNM for $2,100,000. Creative, the then sole shareholder of WNM, accepted Tradewinds' offer and on October 24, Year-2 transferred all the WNM stock to Tradewinds for $2,100,000 in cash. On November 7, Year-2, Tradewinds paid Creative $2,500,000 for WNM's outstanding dividend note. For Year-2 WNM reported current earnings and profits of $454,220. Because WNM's accumulated and current earnings and profits exceeded the $4,000,000 distribution made by it to Creative, the Taxpayer reported the full $4,000,000 as a dividend which qualified for the 100 per cent corporate dividend received deduction under Sec. 243(a)(3) of the Internal Revenue Code of 1986, as amended (the Code). Moreover, Creative reported the $2,000,000 difference between its adjusted basis in the WNM stock ($100,000) and the sales proceeds ($2,100,000) as a long term capital gain.

Presentation of Authorities

Under Sec. 243(a)(3) of the Code, a 100 per cent corporate dividend received deduction is available where the payee owns more than 80 percent of the stock of the payor and both are members of the same affiliated group and do not file a consolidated return.

The Code contains two specific provisions which deny corporate payees the dividend received deduction provided by Sec. 243. First, under Sec. 246(c), the corporate dividend received deduction is denied when the corporate shareholder has held the stock in the payor for 45 days or less. Second, under Sec. 1059, the deduction is denied in the case of an extraordinary dividend when a corporate shareholder has held the stock in the payor for less than two years. Because of Creative's long history of stock ownership in WNM, neither section is applicable to WNM's dividend to

Creative. In addition to the above statutory provisions, the courts have denied the corporate dividend received deduction where a dividend represents a disguised form of sales proceeds. *See, e.g., Waterman Steamship Corp. v. Comm'r*, 430 F.2d 1185 (5th Cir. 1970), *rev'g* 50 T.C. 650 (1968), *cert. denied; Steel Improvement & Forge Co. v. Comm'r*, 314 F.2d 96 (6th Cir. 1963).

Waterman Steamship Corp. v. Comm'r is the leading case recharacterizing a dividend as sales proceeds. In this case, Waterman Steamship Corp., on December 20, 1954, received a written offer from McLean to purchase the stock of two of its subsidiaries (Pan Atlantic and Gulf Florida) for $3,500,000. Waterman promptly declined the offer and counteroffered to sell McLean the stock for $700,000 after the subsidiaries declared a dividend of $2,800,000. McLean promptly accepted the Waterman counteroffer. Since the subsidiaries lacked the cash to pay the dividend it was declared in the form of notes which, after the purchase by McLean, were satisfied with cash borrowed by the subsidiaries from McLean. The Fifth Circuit held that "The so-called dividend and sale were one transaction. Both were part of a pre-arranged plan to sell the stock. We hold that in substance Pan Atlantic [and Gulf Florida] neither declared nor paid a dividend to Waterman, but rather acted as a mere conduit for the payment of the purchase price to Waterman." The Court, nonetheless, observed that "Our decision today should not be interpreted as standing for the proposition that a corporation which is contemplating a sale of its subsidiary's stock could not under any circumstances distribute its subsidiary's profits prior to the sale without having such distribution deemed part of the purchase price."

When, rather than being part of the sale, a dividend is merely paid preparatory to a possible sale, the courts have been unwilling to recharacterize it as sales proceeds and thereby deny a corporate shareholder the Sec. 243 dividend received deduction. The leading case on this front is *Litton Industries, Inc. v. Comm'r*, 89 T.C. 1086 (1987). In the fall of 1967, Litton acquired all the stock of Stouffer. During the summer of 1972, the Litton Board of Directors began to explore the possibility of selling Stouffer and on August 23, 1972, as part of a prospective sales strategy, Stouffer declared a $30 million dividend in the form of a negotiable note for $30 million, such amount was less than Stouffer's accumulated earnings and profits. Two weeks later, Litton management announced Stouffer's availability to a purchaser willing to pay an appropriate price. On March 1, 1973, the Nestle corporation paid Litton almost $75 million in cash for its stock in Stouffer and $30 million in cash for the Stouffer note which Litton held. The Tax Court held that the $30 million dividend could not be recharacterized as sales proceeds since the dividend to Litton, unlike the dividend in *Waterman*, could not be deemed to be a prearranged part of the sale to Nestle.   Critical to the Tax Court's decision was the fact that a considerable period of time had elapsed between the dividend and the purchase by Nestle and the fact that at the time of the dividend Litton was searching for the best possible offer and was not obligated to sell to any particular party.

It is submitted that the facts of Taxpayer's case are virtually identical to those involved in *Litton* and that Taxpayer, therefore, is privileged to take advantage of the Sec. 243 corporate dividend received deduction.   Creative turned down the original Tradewinds' offer.   Therefore, the subsequently declared dividend cannot be viewed as part of the eventual sales proceeds. Subsequent to the rejection of the Tradewinds' offer, the WNM Board of Directors decided to declare a dividend in preparation for an eventual sale of WNM.   Acting pursuant to directions from its Board, WNM management sought to develop favorable offers from other parties, contacted nine such parties and eventually settled on an improved financial offer from Tradewinds as the best possible offer.   It is therefore submitted that the facts in Taxpayer's case closely parallel the facts in *Litton* and are at sharp variance with the facts in *Waterman Steamship*.

For the foregoing reasons, the Taxpayer respectfully protests against the proposed assessment of a Federal income tax deficiency for the taxable year ending December 31, Year-2.

The Taxpayer certifies under penalties of perjury, that the statements of fact contained herein are true to the best of its knowledge, information and belief.

Respectfully submitted,
John Martinez

John Martinez
President, Creative Inventions, Inc.

I declare under penalties of perjury that I, acting as attorney for Taxpayer, have prepared this Protest, and that while I do not know of my own knowledge that the information contained herein is true, on the basis of a review of documents and statements made by agents of the Taxpayer, I believe such information to be true.

Christine M. Pello
Christine M. Pello

Note:

Protest Letters

A taxpayer generally has the opportunity, before commencing litigation or paying a disputed tax, to obtain administrative resolution of a disagreement with the Internal Revenue Service at the Appellate Division Conference level. The taxpayer, of course, may waive the administrative conference and commence litigation or pay the disputed tax.

The protest letter is filed in response to a "30-day letter," issued by the Internal Revenue Service to the taxpayer, which gives him 30 days to appeal a proposed determination. A written protest is required for any Appellate Division Conference.

Many protests are simply letters; no particular form is required. Specific instructions concerning contents are given in an IRS Publication which accompanies the 30-day letter. The protest should include:

(1)   Jurisdictional facts — the taxpayer's name and address, the date and symbols contained in the 30-day letter, the taxable year involved, and the findings the taxpayer disputes;

(2)   A statement of facts, sufficiently detailed for an understanding of the context of each contested issue;

(3)   A clear and concise argument discussing the applicable authorities in a context favorable to the taxpayer and highlighting favorable rulings and cases, particularly those in which the Commissioner has acquiesced;

(4)   A request for a hearing; and

(5)   If prepared by counsel, a statement that it was so prepared and whether counsel knows of his own knowledge that the information contained therein is true.

The protest must be signed by the taxpayer, and he must state that he has examined the protest and that, to the best of his knowledge, it is true, correct and complete. The protest should be prepared with extreme care, since it is signed under oath, and can be used against the taxpayer in the event of litigation.

A protest is essentially a brief, and should be written and researched with the care normally used in the preparation of a brief. It should include a complete discussion of the facts and the taxpayer's arguments. It is frequently desirable to present all possible issues, some of which may be conceded at conference without too great a loss. In drafting, try for short, clear arguments and precise written expression. Often the conferee, although extremely knowledgeable of tax law, may not be a lawyer; a protest should be drafted with this fact in mind.

PROBLEM 40C

Isabel Marion, the general counsel of Southwest Petroleum, Inc. (Southwest), seeks your opinion on the feasibility of a divestiture proposal which she received from Edward Cortes, Southwest's vice-president for financial planning. Southwest is a holding company whose subsidiaries are principally involved in the production, refining and sale of petroleum products. For your convenience, Ms. Marion has sent you a copy of Mr. Cortes' memorandum to her in which he sets forth his divestiture plan.

TO: Isabel W. Marion
             General Counsel
FROM: Edward Cortes
             Vice-President for Financial Planning
RE: Possible Divestment of Lobo Oil, Inc.
DATE: October 4, Year*

Lobo Oil, Inc. (Lobo) is a wholly owned subsidiary of Southwest. At one time Lobo, which holds land and mineral rights in eastern New Mexico, was an extremely profitable company due to the large amounts of very accessible high-quality crude oil located on property owned by Lobo. Within the last few years these oil deposits have become substantially exhausted. The land on which they are located, however, has appreciated significantly because of its agricultural and development potential.

Since Lobo's petroleum-producing capacity is close to exhaustion and since Southwest does not wish to enter into the business of farming or real estate development, Lobo is a suitable candidate for divestment. Lobo's stock, which originally cost $3,000,000 when purchased fourteen years ago, is now worth approximately $20,000,000.

The balance sheet of Lobo, at the close of its most recent fiscal year, is set forth below:

* See explanatory footnote in the Introduction, page vii, note 1.

LOBO OIL, INC.

	Assets			Liabilities	
	Book or Basis	Fair Market Value			Book
	(000's)	(000's)			(000's)
Cash	$ 500	$ 500	Acc. Payable		$ 500
Acc. Rec.	500	500	Capital		
CD's	1,000	1,000	Stated		
Marketable			Capital		3,000
Securities	4,000	7,500	Retained		
Land	3,000	11,000	Earnings		5,500
	$9,000	$20,500			$9,000

I have been informed by the accounting department that Lobo has accumulated earnings and profits of approximately $5,500,000. After speaking with one of our new tax attorneys, Winfield Scott, it is my impression that, since we have made the Section 243(b) election, there is a 100% corporate dividends received deduction available on all dividends received by Southwest from Lobo. Mr. Scott suggested that rather than selling Lobo for $20,000,000, its fair market value, and reporting a long-term capital gain of $17,000,000, we pay out a dividend of $5,500,000 in cash, certificates of deposit and securities which will absorb all of Lobo's accumulated earnings and profits and will be free of tax to Southwest. He proposes that Lobo then be sold for $14,500,000 with resulting capital gain of only $11,500,000.

Mr. Scott has indicated that the only problems that he foresees with his proposal would arise if Southwest had held its stock in Lobo for less than either forty-five days or two years. Under Sec. 243(c) the corporate received dividend deduction is denied where the corporate shareholder has held stock in the payor for less than forty-five days. Under Sec. 1059, if stock has been held by a corporate shareholder for less than two years, some or all of an extraordinary dividend distribution is taxed as capital gain. However, since Southwest has held the Lobo stock for fourteen years, Mr. Scott states that there is no danger of either Sec. 243(c) or Sec. 1059 applying to the transaction. Therefore, the full $5,500,000 distributed by Lobo under Mr. Scott's plan should pass to Southwest free of any tax.

I must confess that Mr. Scott's plan has some appeal to me. First, I appreciate the tax savings. Second, we do not have any purchaser lined up for Lobo, and, as you can imagine, this may take quite some time. One thing which troubles me about Mr. Scott's plan is that I would prefer that Southwest only receive cash and certificates of deposit as a dividend. I do not want the gain on the marketable securities shifted to us. Therefore, I would like your reaction to a proposal that Lobo borrow $4,000,000, secured by its assets, and pay as a dividend to Southwest this cash plus the $1,000,000 in certificates of deposit and $500,000 in existing cash. Since Lobo's net worth would be reduced to $14,500,000, my task of locating a buyer would be facilitated. Moreover, since the $14,500,000 price tag may still prove quite a barrier, I have considered further reducing the price by having Lobo borrow as much as an additional $4,500,000, secured by the land and marketable securities. The additional borrowed cash also would be distributed to Southwest as a dividend. This, I believe, would be free of tax and would reduce the purchase price to $10,000,000, thereby further facilitating a rapid sale of the Lobo stock. I believe that, with a price tag of about $10,000,000, we might be able to sell Lobo within a year or so, assuming that the right buyer could be located.

I would appreciate getting your reaction to the foregoing as soon as possible.

b. Stock Dividends

PROBLEM 41C

F & T Machine Shop, Inc., which you previously represented in Problems 19C and 24C, is now a profitable closely held C corporation. It has 1,000 shares of no par common stock authorized and outstanding. The stock is equally owned by the Rose and Heyden families. Tom Heyden and his son, James, are active in the business. Frank Rose, as he has grown older, has become less active, and no member of his family is presently interested in being active in the business. The Heyden family would like to increase its ownership of the equity in the business. The Rose family, while desiring to preserve some voice in the business, is interested in receiving larger cash dividends.

The families have consulted a partner of yours. She has suggested that the stock be split into 2,000 shares of no par, common stock with 1,000 shares entitled to a cumulative, mandatory if earned, annual dividend of $10 per share. The corporation also will be authorized to issue an additional 4,000 shares of no par common without the $10 dividend feature. The holders of the $10 dividend stock will agree that each time a cash dividend is paid to them, a stock dividend of, in the aggregate, equal value must be paid, from the 4,000 newly authorized shares, on the stock without the $10 dividend feature.

After the stock split, the Rose family will exchange their original 500 shares without the $10 dividend feature for the 500 shares of $10 dividend stock received by the Heyden family. Your partner proposes to have F & T Machine Shop, Inc., in implementing the stock split, send the following letter.

To Our Shareholders: May 15, Year*

The enclosed stock certificates represent the additional shares to which you are entitled under the two-for-one stock split approved at the annual meeting on February 1, Year and effective April 15, Year. Each certificate represents one share of no par, common stock that has a cumulative, mandatory if earned, annual dividend of $10 for each share of common stock held of record at the close of business on April 15th.

You should keep your old stock certificates which represent the same number of shares as they did before. Do not return them to the Corporation.

The stock split does not change your proportionate interest in the Corporation or the aggregate amounts of the Corporation's capital and surplus accounts. In the opinion of Counsel for the Corporation, under the Internal Revenue Code of 1986, as amended, shareholders will not recognize any gain or loss for federal income tax purposes as a result of: (1) the stock split; or (2) a subsequent exchange of some or all of the shares so received for other shares of the common stock of the Corporation, despite differences in dividend rights.

* See explanatory footnote in Introduction, page vii, note 1.

> If the address on the enclosed certificates is incorrect, your ownership of the shares will not be affected. Do not return the certificates, but please notify us so that the corporate records will reflect your correct address.
>
> F. & T. Machine Shop, Inc.
>
> *Frank Rose*
>
> by Frank Rose
> President

Your partner has asked you, as the tax partner in the firm, whether the letter is correct and whether you have any alternative suggestions which might be less costly from an income tax standpoint while still achieving the goals of your clients.

Note:

See the Note on Legal Drafting following Problem 3P at page 15.

PROBLEM 42C

Office Tempo, Inc. (OT) is involved principally in the business of providing temporary office help in the five-county area in which your firm practices. Karen Scott, the president and one of the founders of OT, seeks your advice with respect to the tax consequences of the following. OT at present has three classes of stock: (1) Class A common stock which is voting stock and all 30,000 shares of which are held in equal amounts by Karen and her two co-founders, Daniel Smith and Carmen Vega; (2) Class B common stock which is similar to the Class A stock except that it does not have voting rights and the entire 30,000 shares of this stock is owned by a group of forty-seven local investors; and (3) $8.00 preferred stock which does not have voting rights, but is preferred, entitled to an annual, cumulative dividend of $8.00 per share and to a liquidation preference of $50.00 per share (plus unpaid dividends). All 1000 shares of the outstanding preferred stock are owned by Equity Financing, Inc., a local investment banking firm.

OT has experienced some financial difficulties in recent months and would like to suspend payment of its normal $1.00 per share quarterly dividend on its common stock. Since this would cause severe dissatisfaction

[handwritten margin note: wants to suspend $1.00 div. on stock]

among the Class B common stockholders, Equity, which is also OT's investment banker, proposed that OT declare a stock dividend in lieu of the normal cash dividend. Under Equity's proposal, each OT Class A common stockholder would receive one new share of OT Class A common stock for every ten shares of OT Class A common stock which the stockholder owns. Similarly, each OT Class B common stockholder would receive one new share of OT Class B common stock for every ten shares of OT Class B common stock which the stockholder owns. When Ms. Scott reported that this would not sit well with a number of the Class B stockholders, Equity proposed several other alternatives. First, it proposed that the stock dividend be declared only on the Class A common stock and that the regular cash dividend be declared on the Class B common stock. If this proved unacceptable, Equity suggested alternatively that the Class B stockholders might be more amenable to a stock dividend if they received preferred stock rather than common stock as a stock dividend. Furthermore, in order to minimize the financial drain on the corporation, the Class A stockholders would receive a common stock rather than a preferred stock dividend. It was suggested that this result also could be attained by distributing convertible preferred stock to all common stockholders and by having the Class A, and any of the willing Class B, stockholders convert their new preferred into common stock at an acceptable ratio. Lastly, if all the above proposals proved unacceptable, Equity suggested that OT carry out the stock dividend which it originally proposed. The corporation, however, would inform stockholders that, within a period of sixty days following the stock dividend, it would redeem all tendered stock dividends for an amount equal to their fair market values.

Equity also suggested that, rather than paying Equity in cash for its advice, OT declare a stock dividend of preferred stock on Equity's preferred stock holdings. The dividend would be equal in value to Equity's proposed fee, $20,000, and would be in addition to the normal cash dividend on the preferred.

PROBLEM 43C

Sunrise Chemicals, Inc., throughout its history, has never failed to pay a yearly dividend to its stockholders. This year, however, because of a temporary decline in sales coupled with high interest rates, the officers would like to retain the corporation's cash for working capital purposes and, in fact, raise additional cash from the public without upsetting its present stockholders. The officers propose to distribute to stockholders, as a dividend, an option agreement which permits the stockholder to buy stock of Sunrise Chemicals, Inc. or to require Sunrise Chemicals, Inc. to purchase the option from the stockholder. The officers of Sunrise Chemicals, Inc. would like your advice with respect to the income tax treatment of the stockholders upon receipt of this option and upon its exercise to purchase stock or to have it redeemed. The officers have given you a copy of the option agreement as presently drafted.

Option

December 26, Year*

To the Stockholders of Sunrise Chemicals, Inc.:

This instrument embodies a non-assignable and non-transferable Option to purchase Sunrise Chemicals, Inc. common stock from the corporation at a purchase price per share equal to the fair market value per share, as determined by the market price per share at the close of trading on the date indicated in the upper right-hand corner of this letter.

The number of shares which you may purchase from Sunrise Chemicals, Inc. pursuant to this Option is equal to the number of shares of Sunrise Chemicals, Inc. which you own on the date indicated in the upper right-hand corner of this letter.

At your election, which must be made in writing and delivered to the office of the Shareholder Relations Division of Sunrise Chemicals, Inc. at the address shown below prior to the expiration date of this Option, Sunrise Chemicals, Inc. will purchase this Option from you for an amount equal to 3% of the fair market value, as defined above, of the total number of shares which this Option entitles you to purchase.

* See explanatory footnote in Introduction, page vii, note 1.

This Option will expire at 5:00 p.m., Mountain Standard Time, two years from the date shown in the upper right-hand corner and will be valueless thereafter. Accordingly, you are urged to act promptly.

Very truly yours,

Carol Margolis

Carol Margolis, Manager
Shareholder Relations Division
Sunrise Chemicals, Inc.
1824 King Street
Laramie, Wyoming 80270

If, while the options were outstanding, the comptroller of Sunrise told you that it planned a one-for-one common stock dividend, would you have any concerns with regard to the tax-free nature of the common stock dividend?

Note:

See the Note on Legal Drafting following Problem 3P at page 15.

2. REDEMPTIONS AND PARTIAL LIQUIDATIONS

a. Redemptions

PROBLEM 44C

Square One, Inc. is a Florida corporation with capital stock consisting of 100 shares of voting stock, ten shares of which are owned by each of the following ten persons or entities:

1. Alvin Kelly;
2. Bruce Kelly, the son of Alvin;
3. Clarissa Kelly, the daughter of Alvin;
4. Denise Kelly, the daughter of Alvin;
5. Eunice Kelly, the wife of Bruce;

6.   Frederick Kelly, the son of Bruce and Eunice;

7.   Golden Harbor, Inc., a holding company, the stock of which is owned 30% by Alvin and 70% by Bruce; ~ son of Alvin

8.   Hargrove Enterprises, a partnership in which Frederick has a 30% interest and Ignatius Summers has a 70% interest;

9.   Ignatius Summers, whose connection with the Kelly family rests entirely on his ownership interests in Square One and Hargrove Enterprises; and

10.   Jill Summers, the wife of Ignatius, whose connection with the Kelly family rests entirely on her ownership interest in Square One.

The following lineal chart of the Kelly family accurately conveys the nature of their relationships with the first initial of each member being substituted for his or her name.

Square One's principal business activity is the leasing and management of a moderate size shopping center on the outskirts of Tampa, Florida.   250,000 ÷ N = 25,000

Each party who owns stock in Square One acquired that stock five years ago for $250,000 from Burger Construction, Inc., a large developer of shopping centers. Square One has prospered, and each share of its stock is now worth approximately $50,000. Clarissa and Denise Kelly both have complained of the heavy-handed control of Square One by the Kelly men (Alvin, Bruce and Frederick) and have suggested that part of the corporation's $2,000,000 in retained earnings and profits be used to redeem some of the shares of the Kelly men. Since the Summers have long been pushing for a diminution in Kelly family control, it has been proposed that a corporate restructuring suitable to the Summers, Clarissa and Denise could be produced by redeeming, for $50,000 per share, (1) 5 shares held by Alvin; (2) 5 shares held by Bruce; and (3) all 10 shares held by Frederick.   Total to be redeemed 20

Alvin, Bruce and Frederick Kelly are anxious to avoid having any funds that they receive treated as a dividend and would like to have the benefit of your analysis of the proposal.   Want it treated as a sale?

PROBLEM 45C

The Gallo Family Trust owns 200 of the 1,000 outstanding shares of stock of Speedy Transport, Inc. (Speedy), a local trucking company. Speedy stock is worth $1,000 per share. Paula Gallo, widow of Franco Gallo, a co-founder of Speedy, owns 100 shares of Speedy stock. Franco's son, Lorenzo, owns 100 shares of Speedy stock, and Franco's brother, Antonio (Nino), owns the remaining 600 shares. Under the terms of the trust, income is to be paid to Franco's son, Lorenzo, for his life and at his death the trust is to terminate with the corpus being distributed to Lorenzo's son, Daniel, or his estate.

The actuarially determined value of Lorenzo's life interest is 60% of the total trust assets, and the remainder interest held by Daniel and his estate is 40% of the total trust assets.

Nino is the only Gallo family member who is an operating officer of Speedy. He would like to increase his control of the company and proposes that Speedy redeem all 100 shares directly held by Lorenzo and 50 of the shares held by Paula. Speedy, which has $500,000 in accumulated earnings and profits, would accomplish this by distributing $1,000 per share to the affected shareholders. The Speedy stock held by Paula, Lorenzo and the Gallo Family Trust recently passed through Franco's estate and has a basis of $900 per share in the hands of each of these parties.

The Gallo family seeks your advice as to how the redemption of the stock held by Paula and Lorenzo would be taxed.

PROBLEM 46C

In Problem 41C, you considered a plan which would enable the Heyden family to increase its ownership share in F & T Machine Shop, Inc. (F & T) and the Rose family, while preserving some voice in the corporation, to increase its cash dividends. After receiving your advice as to the possible adverse tax consequences of the plan proposed in Problem 41C, the Rose family reconsidered its objectives and expressed willingness to sell out over a term of years.

Accordingly, your partner has devised a plan which is permissible under state law. Before presenting it to the clients, she seeks your advice as to its income tax implications.

The proposal is that F & T purchase the Rose family stock by giving them a note (F & T note), secured by a pledge of the stock, payable in ten equal annual installments and bearing interest at a rate per annum equal to two percentage points over the Bank of America's prime rate. At the time of purchase, the repurchased stock and the Heyden family stock will be placed in escrow with Seventh National Bank. Subject to the qualifications hereafter stated, the escrow agent will be given an irrevocable power of attorney to vote all stock held in escrow for the term of the escrow agreement. As long as there is no default on the F & T note, the escrow agent must vote the Heyden family stock as directed by the Heyden family. Until the F & T note is fully paid, however, the F & T board of directors must always contain at least one member of the Rose family. Upon its purchase by F & T, state law requires that the Rose family stock, which is placed in escrow, be treated as treasury stock. Consequently, it is not entitled to voting or dividend privileges. As each annual payment is made, one-tenth of the stock originally purchased from the Rose family is to be delivered by the escrow agent to the corporation for cancellation.

In the event of a default by the corporation, the escrow agent must vote the Heyden stock as jointly agreed by the Rose and Heyden families until the default is cured. If a default is not cured within two years and the Rose family so elects, the agent will deliver the Rose stock then remaining in escrow to the Rose family, deliver an equal number of shares of the Heyden stock to the Heyden family, and continue to vote the Heyden stock remaining in escrow as jointly agreed by the two families. The escrow agreement will terminate upon the cancellation by the corporation of all of the Rose stock or twenty-one years from the date of the execution of the agreement, whichever shall first occur, at which time the Heyden stock will be returned to the Heyden family.

Advise your partner of any income tax problems presented by this proposal. Can you suggest any alternatives which might present fewer income tax problems but still accomplish the desires of the clients?

PROBLEM 47C *Indirect Redemptions*
S 304

Marilyn Carson owns 90% (90 shares) of the stock of two corporations, Carson Chrysler-Plymouth, Inc. (CCP) and Tidewater Auto Parts, Inc. (TAP). Marilyn's only child, Norma, owns the remaining 10% of the stock in CCP and TAP. CCP sells new cars in Perth Amboy, New Jersey

mother = 90% ⎤ of CCP
Daughter = 10% ⎦ +
*   TAP*

and through its wholly owned subsidiary, Carson Used Cars, Inc. (UC), sells used cars in Perth Amboy. TAP operates three auto parts stores in the Perth Amboy area. All three companies have been very successful and have substantial accumulated and current earnings and profits. *TAP has 3 auto parts stores*

CCP has $800,000 of retained earnings and a net worth (including the UC stock) of approximately $2,000,000. TAP has $1,000,000 of retained earnings and a net worth of approximately $2,000,000. UC has retained earnings of $400,000 and has a net worth of approximately $800,000.

Mrs. Carson has asked you to investigate various ways in which she or Norma, or both, could, in effect, withdraw earnings and profits from CCP, TAP or UC at capital gains rates by selling all or some of their stock in one of the companies to one of the other companies.

You should consider the tax effect of Marilyn or Norma selling, for $100,000, 5 shares of the following stock to the designated purchasers:

     (a) CCP stock to TAP;   *→ 304(a)(1)*   *brother sister*

     (b) TAP stock to CCP;   *→ brother sister*   *304(a)(1)*

     (c) TAP stock to UC; or

     (d) CCP stock to UC.   *→ 304(a)(2) parent-subsidiary*

Marilyn also asks you to consider the following additional possibilities: (1) forming a new corporation, owned by Marilyn, which will borrow $100,000, with which it would purchase 5 shares of CCP or TAP which the new corporation would retain, using any dividends received to meet interest payments on the $100,000; (2) contribution by her of 5 shares of TAP stock to CCP, in a transaction described in Section 351, in exchange for 1 share of CCP stock and $80,000 of cash; (3) Marilyn's selling to CCP or UC for $200,000 either of the following assets in which she has an adjusted basis of $40,000: (a) a tract of vacant land which Marilyn presently leases to UC as a car lot, or (b) an apartment house which Marilyn wishes to retain directly or indirectly as an investment; (4) completely redeeming all of Norma's interest in TAP or CCP for $200,000; or (5) Norma's selling all her interest in one of the companies to another of the companies for $200,000.

new corp = new co.

PROBLEM 48C

Bootstrap Sales of Stock

This morning's mail contained the following letter to one of your partners from Morris B. Levi, a longtime client of your firm and a highly successful entrepreneur. You and your partner have a conference with him scheduled for tomorrow. Prepare to discuss with him, at length, the issues raised by the letter.

Closely held corp

MORRIS B. LEVI
301 East 56th Street
New York, N.Y. 10017

October 28, Year*

Dear Fran:

I wish your advice about the best method, from a tax standpoint, to acquire all the stock of a corporation which I am interested in purchasing. The company is Bullock Properties, Inc. (Bullock), a New York corporation, whose assets consist solely of several export shops located at Kennedy and Dulles Airports. The shops sell perfume, tobacco and alcohol to tourists leaving the United States. Because sales by these shops are exempt from Federal and State excise and sales taxes, Bullock does a brisk and profitable business. The principal assets of Bullock, which has no liabilities other than $200,000 in wage claims and other accounts payable, consist of: (1) 2 shops including leaseholds and fixtures valued at $1,800,000; (2) inventory valued at $600,000; (3) $1,800,000 in cash and certificates of deposit; and (4) goodwill valued at $800,000. Bullock has $2,200,000 in accumulated earnings and profits arising from operation of the business. The sole shareholder of Bullock, Dorothy Messic, approached me last month about purchasing all her interest in Bullock. After several meetings we agreed to assign the foregoing values to Bullock's assets and concluded that Mrs. Messic's stock is worth $4,800,000.

Since I am only able to raise between $3,000,000 and $4,000,000 to effect the acquisition, I considered purchasing the shops, inventory and goodwill from Bullock for $3,200,000, their agreed value. Anti-assignment clauses in Bullock's favorable leases at Kennedy and Dulles Airports, however, dictated that I purchase the stock of Bullock.

I proposed to Mrs. Messic that, to reduce Bullock's fair market value to my purchasing range, she should cause Bullock to pay a dividend of $1,600,000. Mrs. Messic strongly resisted this suggestion since she wishes to recognize only capital gains on the sale. We then signed an agreement in principle, a copy of which is attached to this letter, that I would purchase

She did not want a Dividend!

---

* See explanatory footnote in Introduction, page vii, note 1.

1,800,000
600,000
800,000
3,200,000   *This excludes the cash figure of 1.8 million*

Purchase price

Mrs. Bullock's stock from her for $4,800,000, contingent on my being able to raise the full purchase price.

Subsequent contacts with Emma Sommerville at Citibank have led me to conclude that I shall only be able to raise $3,600,000. Therefore, I would like your advice about the feasibility of using all or part of Bullock's retained earnings for the purpose of acquiring Bullock's stock from Mrs. Messic.

He's 1.2 million short of purchase price

Wants to use part of Bullock's R.E. to acquire Bullock's stock from Messic!

Very truly yours,

Morris

Morris B. Levi

AGREEMENT IN PRINCIPLE

- it's a binding K under US v Corey - it's an obligation satisfied by Corp - you're dead it's a constructive dividend

This memorandum reflects the agreement in principle between Morris B. Levi (transferee) and Dorothy S. Messic (transferor) as to the method of acquisition of Bullock Properties, Inc. (Bullock) by transferee.

1. Transferor will warrant that the 1,000 shares of Bullock common stock owned by transferor constitute all of the issued stock of Bullock, that such stock is subject to no liens or liabilities and that there exists no warrant, option or right to acquire any of the authorized stock of Bullock.

2. Transferor will warrant that none of the assets of Bullock is subject to any liens or liabilities other than $200,000 in wage claims and other accounts payable.

3. Transferor and transferee agree that the value of the 1,000 shares of Bullock stock owned by transferor is $4,800,000. *4,800 per share*

4. Transferee agrees that, conditioned on his ability to obtain necessary financing on terms acceptable to transferee, transferee shall acquire such stock from transferor for $4,800,000.

5. On or before December 31, Year, transferor and transferee shall enter into a definitive purchase agreement effectuating the above transactions.

6. This memorandum is evidence only of an agreement in principle and understanding between transferor and transferee and of their intention to cooperate in the effectuation of the transactions mentioned above. It is subject to the drafting, negotiation and execution of the above-mentioned

definitive purchase agreement. Until the execution of such purchase agreement, there shall be no legal obligation between the two parties with respect to the transactions contemplated by this memorandum.

On the above basis, the undersigned have approved this agreement in principle as of this 27 day of October, Year.

Morris B. Levi
Morris B. Levi

Dorothy S. Messic
Dorothy S. Messic

Note:

See the Note on Interviewing and Client Counseling following Problem 1P at page 4 and the Note on Legal Drafting following Problem 3P at page 15.

PROBLEM 49C

Mr. C.K. Ching, an old client of your firm, has recently approached you for advice. Twenty-five years ago, Mr. Ching formed Ace Auto Parts, Inc. to engage in the retail auto parts business. Ace has prospered and now operates a chain of twenty-two retail auto parts stores. When Ace was originally formed, Mr. Ching owned 90% of the Ace stock, for which he contributed $9,000, and Claude Paul owned 10% of the Ace stock, for which he contributed $1,000. Paul was brought into the company because of his expertise in the auto parts business. As the company prospered, in order to retain the allegiance of Mr. Paul, Mr. Ching transferred stock to him so that Mr. Paul now owns 30% of the Ace stock (300 shares) and Mr. Ching owns the balance (700 shares).

The discovery that Mr. Ching is suffering from chronic kidney disease has prompted planning for his retirement sometime in the next three years. Mr. Ching and Mr. Paul agree that Ace stock is worth $4,000 per share and that when Mr. Paul assumes complete management of Ace upon Mr. Ching's retirement, it is desirable that he own at least 50% of the Ace stock. Mr. Paul estimates that he will only be able to raise $400,000, or enough to purchase from Mr. Ching one-half of the 200 shares necessary to raise his ownership to

50%. At present, Ace has $2,400,000 in retained earnings and profits, but only $600,000 in such highly liquid assets as cash and certificates of deposit. Mr. Ching and Mr. Paul ask whether there is anything you can suggest to help Mr. Paul increase his ownership to 50%. Although the subject was never directly mentioned, it is apparent that both men are aware of Mr. Ching's delicate state of health. Therefore, your planning should include suggestions that will allow, in the event of Mr. Ching's death prior to his retirement, Mr. Paul to obtain ownership of 50% of the company in exchange for full and adequate consideration.

Note:

See the Note on Interviewing and Client Counseling following Problem 1P at page 4.

PROBLEM 50C

Patrick Phillips, a new associate in your office, has prepared the following memorandum for your review. Although you normally check the work of all new associates with a high degree of care, your interest in the work done by Mr. Phillips is heightened by the fact that you were principally responsible for hiring him.

MEMORANDUM
Estate of Sobel—Section 303 Redemption

P.T. Phillips   November 14 Year*

On June 13, Year, our client, Peter Sobel, died. Mr. Sobel, who was a widower, left his entire estate to be divided equally between his son Simon and his daughter Amanda. Mr. Sobel died possessed of the following assets.

* See explanatory footnote in Introduction, page vii, note 1.

Home	$ 250,000
Tangible Personalty	140,000
Cash	10,000
Securities	
ITB	800,000
Sobel, Inc.	100,000
Acme, Inc.	180,000
Ladycourt, Inc.	400,000
S & P Trucking, Inc.	300,000
Delf Mfg. Inc.	220,000
	$2,400,000

The above values were the values at the date of death and the values which will be used on Mr. Sobel's estate tax return.

The following items will be claimed as deductions in computing Mr. Sobel's taxable estate:

Executor Fees	$ 40,000
Attorneys' Fees	35,000
Funeral Expenses	15,000
Unpaid Medical Expenses	60,000
Loan from City Federal Bank	250,000
	$400,000

I have been able to gather the following information about the stock Mr. Sobel owned at his death. Mr. Sobel's estate owns one percent of the ITB stock which is publicly traded on the Pacific Stock Exchange. It owns one hundred percent of the stock in Sobel Inc., an S corporation, and eighteen percent of the stock in Acme. The balance of Acme's stock is divided between Ladycourt, Inc. and the Sobel Family Trust. Ladycourt, in which the estate owns fifty percent of the stock and Amanda owns the balance, owns eight percent of the stock of Acme. The Sobel Family Trust, which has Simon and Amanda as its sole beneficiaries, owns the remaining seventy-four percent of the stock of Acme. The estate also owns twenty-five percent of the stock of S & P Trucking, Inc. (with Simon owning the balance) and twelve percent of the stock of Delf Manufacturing, Inc.

In addition to the $400,000 in liabilities mentioned above, the estate will also be liable for the following amounts: (1) $525,000 in federal estate tax and $25,000 in interest on such taxes; and (2) $95,000 in state death taxes and $5,000 in interest on such taxes.

In order to fund the payment of these liabilities which amount to $1,050,000 in total, I propose that the estate fully exploit the special exemption provided to estates by Section 303 of the Code.

Section 302, in general, provides that, if any one of four different criteria is satisfied, any property received in redemption of stock is treated as a distribution in part or full payment in exchange for the redeemed stock with the result that any amounts representing recovery of one's basis in redeemed stock will not be taxed, and in most cases any gain or loss which is realized will be treated as capital gain or loss. Proceeds from redemptions not meeting any of the four criteria set forth in Section 302(b) are, to the extent of earnings and profits, treated as a dividend and therefore subject to tax as ordinary income. The four types of redemptions which qualify for favorable treatment are: (1) redemptions not essentially equivalent to a dividend; (2) substantially disproportionate redemptions; (3) complete redemptions of a shareholder's entire interest; and (4) certain redemptions involving partial liquidations. In order to determine ownership of stock for most of the above transactions, stock owned by related persons and entities is attributed under Section 318 to the redeemed shareholder.

Section 303 of the Code, which is entitled "Distributions in Redemption of Stock to Pay Death Taxes," established a special exception for redemptions providing funds with which to pay the federal estate tax, state death taxes, and funeral and administration expenses, including debts of the deceased. If, as is here the case, the redeemed stock is a capital asset, the value of any property received in the redemption, in excess of the adjusted basis of the stock redeemed, will be accorded capital gain treatment to the extent the amount distributed does not exceed the sum of:

(1)   the estate, inheritance, legacy, and succession taxes (including any interest collected as part of such taxes) imposed because of such decedent's death, and

(2)   the amount of funeral and administration expenses allowable as deductions to the estate under Section 2053. * * *

Section 303(b) imposes several limitations on Section 303 redemptions. First, the redemption must take place within certain time limitations not relevant to the present situation. Second, the value of the stock held by the estate (or distributees) in redeeming corporations must exceed 35% of the gross estate less losses deductible under Section 2054 of the Code and claims, funeral and administration expenses, and debts deductible under Section 2053 of the Code. Under Section 303(b), if the estate owns more than twenty percent of the stock of any corporation, all such stock may be aggregated for the purpose of satisfying the 35% test.

Since the value of Mr. Sobel's gross estate, less amounts deductible under Sections 2053 and 2054, will equal $2,000,000, any stock holdings which exceed $700,000 will qualify for redemption under Section 303. Using this test, the ITB stock ($800,000) will qualify, as will the aggregate stock of Sobel, Inc. ($100,000), Acme ($180,000), S & P Trucking ($300,000), and Ladycourt ($400,000). It should be noted that the Acme stock only qualifies for Section 303 treatment after application of the Section 318 attribution rules. I have contacted all of the corporations except Sobel, Inc., and management of each corporation indicated a willingness to redeem some, or all, of the stock held by the estate. They also reported that the following amounts would be available, either from the corporate treasury or as a result of borrowing funds, to meet any possible redemptions:

ITB	$800,000
Acme	180,000
S & P	300,000
Ladycourt	250,000

Other facts worthy of note with respect to the estate's stock holdings include the following items. Since Sobel Inc. is an S corporation for which there is no Section 303 benefit, it was excluded in making the above determinations. ITB is most anxious to engage in such a redemption because Harriet Fleming, its principal shareholder, wants ITB to use its earnings to increase her portion of outstanding shares whenever possible. All corporations have sufficient retained earnings and profits to cover the amounts available for redemption listed above. Lastly, the present fair market value of the stock of all the corporations closely approximates the value used in preparing the Federal estate tax return.

Since such a tax-free clean-out of earnings and profits is a once-in-a-lifetime opportunity, I suggest we first employ it with respect to the Acme, S & P and Ladycourt stock, up to the aggregate amount of $730,000, thereby substantially diminishing the earnings and profits of these family-controlled corporations. I suggest that we ask the Sobel children if they wish to continue holding ITB stock and if we receive a negative reply we should also seek to have the balance of the ITB holdings redeemed from the estate. Although only $320,000 of a redemption then conducted by ITB would qualify for Section 303 treatment because of the $1,050,000 limit on Sobel estate holdings which qualify for Section 303 treatment, such a step will save brokerage fees to the estate or the children if either were to wish to liquidate the balance by a sale in the near future.

Note:

See the Note on Memoranda following Problem 35C at page 177.

b. Partial Liquidations

PROBLEM 51C

After considering the distribution of a dividend as mentioned in Problem 36C, your client Speculation Corporation (Speculation) canceled those plans. An intra-city express mail service similar to the service which it was running in one city, became available for purchase in another city and Speculation decided to purchase that business with the funds which would have been used to fund the contemplated dividend.

Your client now seeks your assistance in connection with another matter. Speculation's directors have determined that it is in the corporation's best interest to terminate its real estate holdings and concentrate on the express delivery service. The board proposes that, with shareholder approval, the apartment houses be distributed to the shareholders in partial liquidation. Since there are several prospective buyers for the apartment houses, the shareholders anticipate that they should be able to sell them to a purchaser or purchasers within several months.

Janice Carillo, the chief executive officer of Speculation, has asked that your firm provide a letter of opinion outlining the tax consequences of a partial liquidation to Speculation and its four shareholders (Janice, Ruth, Thomas and Wise). Jessica Cohen, a new associate in your law firm, prepared the following draft of an opinion letter for your signature. You should review it for accuracy before signing it and sending it off to Ms. Carillo.

[Draft -- 10/2/Year* - JC]

Speculation Corporation

Proposed Partial Liquidation

Dear Ms. Carillo:

You have asked for our opinion as to the tax consequences to Speculation Corporation (Speculation) and its shareholders of a proposed partial liquidation of Speculation.

---

* See explanatory footnote in Introduction, page vii, note 1.

It is our understanding that Speculation is owned by four shareholders, Janice Carillo, Ruth Schlinger, Thomas Glynn and Wise Investments, Inc. (Wise). Ms. Carillo and Mrs. Schlinger, who acquired their stock thirteen years ago, each own 30 percent (30 shares) of Speculation's common stock, which is its only authorized and issued stock. Ms. Carillo and Mrs. Schlinger have an adjusted basis of $180,000 and $240,000 respectively in their stock. Mr. Glynn, who acquired his stock seven years ago, owns 5 percent or 5 shares of Speculation stock and has an adjusted basis of $100,000 in his stock. Wise, which also acquired its stock seven years ago, owns 35 percent or 35 shares of Speculation stock and has an adjusted basis of $700,000 in its stock.

Speculation, which has a net worth of about $8,000,000, conducts two distinct lines of business, an intra city, express mail delivery service which it operates in Salt Lake City and Logan, Utah and a rental real estate business. Speculation has operated the Salt Lake City express mail delivery service for seven years. The Logan operation was purchased by it for about $1,200,000 three years ago. The fair market value of these two enterprises is about $5,500,000. Speculation also holds about $500,000 in cash and two pieces of rental realty, Regency Park and Lindell Manor, which are each worth about $1,000,000 and which comprise its rental real estate operations.

Regency Park, until four years ago, had been operated as a conventional residential apartment complex in which Speculation merely collected rent, provided basic maintenance and let vacant apartments to new tenants. Four years ago, Speculation cleared it of its residential tenants and rented it to Geriatrics, Inc. on a net lease basis. Geriatrics operates Regency Park as a senior citizens' residential complex in which it, in addition to providing residential rental units, conducts numerous activities for its tenants. Among other things, Geriatrics provides staffed recreation activities, a staffed reading room and a modest nurses' station at which tenants can receive basic low level medical attention (e.g. blood pressure monitoring, over-the-counter drugs, etc.).

Lindell Manor opened eleven years ago as a luxury apartment complex. Speculation continuously has provided Lindell Manor tenants with a variety of services such as a 24-hour doorman, a 12 hour a day reception service, package pick up services and access, through Speculation selected independent contractors, to commercial housekeeping, dry cleaning and laundry services. Lindell Manor also has a staffed, modest fitness facility which is available only to tenants for a total of sixty hours per week. Although Lindell Manor had commenced operation as a residential complex, Speculation management concluded, four years ago, that units could be more profitably rented to commercial tenants. Speculation began to switch units over to commercial tenants whenever possible. At present, 75 percent of the units have been converted to commercial use and they account for 85 percent of the gross rent from Lindell Manor. Since the commercial tenants, most of whom are professionals, were in part attracted by the high level of services available at Lindell Manor, Speculation has continued to provide the same level of services to commercial as well as residential tenants. Each of the rental complexes have an adjusted basis of about $60,000 and a fair market value of $1,000,000.

Speculation, which has accumulated earnings and profits of $1,600,000 and current earnings and profits of $400,000, wishes to dispose of its real estate holdings and concentrate its efforts on its intra-city express mail services. The Speculation Board of Directors is contemplating achieving the disposition by adopting a plan of partial liquidation. Pursuant to that plan, and within the same taxable year, Speculation would distribute the rental realty to its shareholders by having each shareholder surrender 25 percent of his, her or its stock in exchange for an interest in Regency Park and Lindell Manor which is in proportion to the shareholders' respective stock holdings in Speculation.

Under Sec. 302(a) and 302(b)(4), proceeds of a corporate redemption which constitutes a partial liquidation are treated as a distribution in exchange for the redeemed stock. If the distribution of the realty qualifies as a partial liquidation, this will result in any gains from such redemption being taxed to all shareholders as a long term capital gain.

Under Sec. 302(e)(1), a distribution is treated as a partial liquidation if it is not essentially equivalent to a dividend, it takes place pursuant to a plan of liquidation, and it occurs within the same taxable year as the adoption of the plan or the next succeeding taxable year. Under Sec. 302(e)(2), a distribution will be deemed not to be essentially equivalent to a dividend if the distribution consists of the assets of a qualified trade or business and the distributing corporation itself is actively engaged in a trade or business. Under Sec. 302(e)(3), a business will be deemed a qualified trade or business if it was actively conducted for five years prior to the redemption and was not within that period acquired in a transaction in which gain or loss was recognized.

Although the Internal Revenue Code does not indicate how to determine the basis of property received in a distribution described in Sec. 302, it is widely agreed that such property will have a basis equal to its fair market value and a new holding period commences for the shareholders. *See,* BITTKER & EUSTICE, FEDERAL INCOME TAXATION OF CORPORATIONS AND SHAREHOLDERS (6th ed.) ¶9.21 [5].

Based solely on the above information which you have supplied to us, we are of the opinion that the contemplated redemption will constitute a partial liquidation which will result in all shareholders receiving long term capital gain on the difference between the fair market value of the interest in the real estate distributed to them and their adjusted basis in the stock redeemed. All shareholders will take an adjusted basis in their distributed interests equal in value to the fair market value of the real estate and will commence a new holding period.

Very truly yours,

Maris, Ruth and Klein

Note:

See the Note on Opinion Letters following Problem 4P at page 22.

PROBLEM 52C

Acutech, Inc. (Acutech), a manufacturer of computer peripheral devices, was founded ten years ago. Norma Blumstein and Jack Wolper each originally owned forty percent of its common stock, and Metro Electric, Inc. (Metro) originally owned the balance of the stock. Norma and Jack received their stock in exchange for several patents and patent applications for computer peripheral equipment. Metro received its stock in exchange for various essential tangible assets and a substantial sum of money. The company has prospered beyond the dreams of its founders. Several years ago, Metro, which was pressed for cash, sold one-quarter of its stock to Macon Mohammed for a 300% profit on its investment. The present adjusted basis of each party in his or her stock holding is as follows: Norma ($10,000), Jack ($10,000), Metro ($300,000) and Macon ($400,000).

Acutech historically has conducted most of its manufacturing, assembly and sales activities from a location in Miami, Florida. About three years after it commenced operations, the participants determined that rather than purchasing key platinum-plated components, Acutech should produce these items itself. To this end, the corporation purchased a jewelry-plating operation in Boca Raton, Florida where it produced all essential platinum-plated components. Since Acutech could not use the full productive capacity of the jewelry-plating plant, it continued the plating of jewelry on a contract basis. Acutech annually used from forty to fifty percent of the plating capacity of the Boca Raton facility and dedicated the balance to contract jewelry production.

Due to advances in alloy manufacturing processes made in France, Acutech recently has determined that it can dispose of its electroplating operation and purchase needed substitute parts from foreign suppliers at a fraction of their former cost. Jack has proposed that Acutech dispose of the electroplating operation by distributing all the assets of that operation to the four shareholders on a pro rata basis. He proposes that they could either: (1) liquidate the rare metals inventory, plating equipment and securities and turn the Boca Raton facility, which is located in a good commercial area, into a rental office building which would be run by the four former shareholders as a partnership; or (2) retain all distributed assets, expand the contract jewelry-plating operation to take up the slack created by Acutech's changed operations and continue operating the business as a partnership with Norma, Jack, Macon and Metro as partners. In the latter case, he proposes use of a partnership since he believes it to be questionable whether the venture could be run at a profit in the first year or two of transition and would like to be able to personally utilize any resulting operating losses.

The assets which Acutech proposes to distribute to its shareholders are listed below:

Asset	Adjusted Basis	Fair Market Value
Cash	$ 100,000	$ 100,000
Platinum Inventory	300,000	500,000
Securities	150,000	200,000
Land	300,000	600,000
Building	400,000	800,000
Plating Equipment	450,000	300,000
	$1,700,000	$2,500,000

The above assets constitute twenty-five percent of the net worth of Acutech. The amount of cash and securities to be distributed were determined by assigning a proportional share of those assets to the plating operation. Since the receivables and payables from the plating operation are virtually equal, Acutech has decided to retain both items. Because of its very impressive profitability, Acutech has no liabilities other than standard industry payables which one would expect for a company of its size.

Please advise Acutech, Metro, Jack, Norma and Macon of the tax consequences of Jack's proposed partial liquidation. Feel free to make any suggestions as to how the tax consequences of Jack's proposal could possibly be improved.

PROBLEM 53C

James P. Cobb, the president of Dixie Loan Co., Inc., a Georgia corporation (Dixie), asks your advice as to the contemplated partial liquidation of Dixie. Dixie makes consumer and mortgage loans. Its mortgage loan operations are conducted at locations in Atlanta, Savannah, Charleston and Columbia. The twenty-three employees in the mortgage loan operations make loans secured by mortgages on single-family and multiple residences. The sources of the loaned funds are Dixie's retained earnings as well as funds borrowed by Dixie from commercial sources. Dixie's consumer loan business employs eighty-four persons and operates out of twenty-seven locations in Georgia and South Carolina. The consumer loans, which are made from the same sources as the mortgage loans, are incurred by individuals to purchase consumer durables which are pledged to secure repayment.

Dixie was founded thirty-two years ago by Mr. Cobb, his brother Horace and a cousin, Garrett Parker. Initially, each paid $80,000 for 1,000 shares of common stock. The business has been well-run, and its profits have exceeded the wildest expectations of its founders. Several years ago, James Cobb sold 400 shares of his stock to Peachtree Securities, Inc. for $1,000 per share. At about the same time, Mr. Parker gave 100 of his shares to his son William, who is employed by Dixie as a branch manager. At present, the stock is estimated to be worth about $1,200 per share with 3,000 shares of stock outstanding in the hands of the above-mentioned shareholders.

The business originally made only consumer loans and began making mortgage loans six years ago. At the end of the first business year in which mortgage loans were made, they accounted in dollar amount for only one and one-half percent of all outstanding loans. At present they account for approximately twenty-five percent. The shareholders, however, feel that, due to the inability to adjust the interest rates on mortgage loans, they will retain more effective financial control over Dixie if it confines its activities to relatively short term consumer loans where, due to rapid turnover of such loans, Dixie is less likely to be caught in a credit crunch whenever there is an increase in the interest rate on the funds Dixie borrows. The shareholders, who are considering going public with Dixie, also believe that they would obtain a higher total return on their stock if Dixie's activities were so confined.

Mr. Parker has suggested that Dixie get out of the mortgage loan business by doing either of two things: (1) closing its four mortgage loan offices and distributing its mortgage loans to shareholders in a partial liquidation; or (2) continuing the mortgage loan operation on a limited, more conservative basis after it is distributed to the existing shareholders in a partial liquidation. If the latter step is taken, Mr. Parker indicated that it might be desirable to have the business operate as a partnership so that any losses could be passed through to the partners. He suggested that the new business would be called Dixie Mortgage, Ltd. He assumed that it would not be necessary to consider any of Dixie's existing goodwill as being distributed since the name Dixie is common on southern commercial enterprises. He noted that he was relatively unconcerned about the loss of limited liability since Dixie's lenders frequently require its shareholders to co-sign its notes in order to obtain the lowest possible interest rate.

If alternative (1) above is undertaken, each shareholder will receive approximately $200 in mortgage notes per share of Dixie stock held; if alternative (2) above is undertaken, the following would be distributed by Dixie to its shareholders:

Assets			Liabilities	
	Fair Market Value	Adjusted Basis		
Accts. Receivable	$1,800,000	$1,700,000	Notes Payable	$440,000
Office Furniture	30,000	45,000		
Leasehold (premium due to favorable terms)	60,000	0		

The listed assets represent all the assets used by Dixie in the mortgage loan business. The liabilities assigned to the mortgage business were determined on an arbitrary basis by selecting from among Dixie's long term, low interest borrowings, and represent approximately 10% of Dixie's liabilities. Dixie has accumulated earnings and profits of $2,300,000 and anticipates that, by year end, when the proposed distribution would take place, it would have current earnings and profits of $300,000 from its normal business operations.

The Dixie shareholders would like your advice with respect to the tax consequences of the above transactions. They are also curious to know whether, if the existing shareholders continue to operate the business as a partnership, any value should be assigned to goodwill for the purpose of computing gain on the transaction.

Note:

See the Note on Interviewing and Client Counseling following Problem 1P at Page 4.

3. PREFERRED STOCK BAIL-OUTS

PROBLEM 54C

Associated Enterprises, Inc., (Associated) is owned by ten shareholders who each own 1000 shares of the common stock. Until Year*-4, Associated had only one class of stock. On November 15, Year-4, the board of directors of Associated voted to declare a dividend of 1 share of newly created preferred stock for every 10 shares of Associated common then held by Associated shareholders. The preferred is entitled to an annual dividend of $4.50 per share and a liquidation preference of $60, plus accrued and unpaid dividends, per share. The preferred was appraised as being worth $60 per share on distribution, and the common was appraised as being worth $100 per share after the distribution. Although Associated had no current earnings and profits in Year-4, it did have accumulated earnings and profits of $40,000.

---

* See explanatory footnote in Introduction, page vii, note 1.

Last year, when Associated had current earnings and profits of $20,000 and (exclusive of such sum) accumulated earnings and profits of $40,000, one shareholder, Horace Biggers, who originally had an adjusted basis of $6,000 in his Associated common stock, sold his one hundred shares of preferred to another shareholder for $80 per share. Also last year, shortly after Horace Biggers' sale, Marilyn Hall, another Associated shareholder, who originally had an adjusted basis of $6,000 in her Associated common, requested that Associated redeem her preferred. Associated's directors were happy to comply with this request. Early in October of last year, Ms. Hall received $8,000 for her 100 shares which Associated then canceled.

Advise Mr. Biggers, Ms. Hall and Associated of the tax consequences of the above transactions.

Would your analysis be any different if you discovered that the original preferred stock distribution was not a distribution of stock only and that four shareholders had received a cash dividend in lieu of the preferred received by the other six shareholders?

PROBLEM 55C

Four years ago, Barbara Stano, Clark Watt and Jane Jordan-Verplant, the sole and equal stockholders of Hydraulics, Inc., consulted you with regard to various ways of putting them in a position to "cash out" some of their investment in the corporation. After obtaining your advice, they opted for a preferred stock dividend because the initial transaction would not be taxable.

Each of them received 100 shares of non-voting preferred having a par value of $250 per share; a cumulative, mandatory if earned, annual cash dividend of 8%; and upon liquidation: (1) preference of par plus accumulated and unpaid dividends and (2) a right to participate on an equal basis with the common stock after the common had received an amount equal to the preference of the preferred stock.

Immediately prior to the dividend, the corporation had $70,000 in accumulated earnings and profits. At the time of the stock dividend, an experienced appraiser, employed by your clients, valued the preferred stock received by each shareholder at $15,000. He reduced the value of the preferred stock below par value because of the closely held nature of the corporation, because the stock was non-voting and because of the low current dividend rate, particularly for a corporation which represented a high investment risk.

Barbara, Clark and Jane have retained ownership of the common and preferred stock over the intervening four years, during which the corporation has been more profitable than in the years prior to the stock dividend. Its accumulated earnings and profits are presently $550,000.

Jane, who seeks your advice, recently suffered a serious physical injury and has been advised that she requires an operation which may cost about $20,000. Although she has always received a substantial salary from the corporation and has other income as a beneficiary under a trust set up by her grandfather, she has never saved a great deal of money. Her income for this year will probably subject her to the highest marginal rate for income tax purposes. She has been subject to this rate for the last five years. Jane believes that next year, after she recovers from the operation, she will receive enough income to be subject to the highest marginal tax rate.

Jane feels that the best way to raise the cash she needs for the operation is to sell her preferred stock. She has a number of possibilities for such a sale and has asked your advice as to which of the following alternatives is preferable: (1) Gerald Shine, a long-time employee of Hydraulics, Inc., in order to obtain an equity interest in the corporation, has offered to purchase all Jane's preferred stock for $25,000; (2) Barbara and Clark are prepared to vote, as directors, to authorize Hydraulics, Inc. to redeem all Jane's preferred for $27,500; and (3) Barbara and Clark each are personally prepared to purchase one-quarter of Jane's preferred for $7,500 if Jane also will sell each 26% of her common for an additional $7,500.

Prepare yourself to advise Jane on the tax consequences of the foregoing.

PROBLEM 56C

William Andrews, an associate in your firm's trusts and estates department, just dropped by your office to tell you that tomorrow Anamaria Vidal, the firm's principal trusts and estates partner, would like to discuss with you the potential Section 306 stock problems raised by several commonly used estate planning devices employed by your firm which involve the creation of preferred stock. He left with you the following memo which describes the techniques to be considered. Prepare yourself for your meeting with Ms. Vidal.

Dehavilan & Redwing

Intra-Office Memorandum

Sept. 3, Year*

TO: Tax Attorneys

FROM: Anamaria Vidal, Principal, Trusts and Estates   *AV*

RE: Possible Code Section 306 Problems with Various Estate Planning Techniques

The following memorandum describes some of the estate planning techniques which are commonly used by our firm. We are concerned whether Section 306 of the Internal Revenue Code of 1986, as amended, has a negative impact on those techniques. For example, if a client of the firm owns all, or a substantial portion of, the stock of a corporation which is of significant worth and is likely to increase in value, the firm often suggests that preferred stock with a fixed cumulative dividend be created and distributed to the client shareholder. This is achieved either as a result of a stock dividend on the common stock or a recapitalization of the corporation under which new preferred stock is issued in exchange for some of the existing common stock pursuant to a tax-free reorganization of the corporation. The purpose of creating the preferred is to create an equity interest which, barring changes in interest rates, will be frozen in value. All increases in value of the corporation attributable to the subsequent growth of the underlying business or appreciation in its assets consequently will be realized by the holders of the common stock. The firm then typically follows two strategies described in the two following paragraphs with respect to the client shareholder.

First, in some cases, voting preferred (which typically has most or all of the voting power) is held by the client who, through inter vivos gifts, distributes the common stock to his or her children or grandchildren thereby transferring all subsequent appreciation in value to more remote generations who, it is hoped, will not confront estate taxes for several decades. The holder of the preferred can: (1) hold it as an income producing asset and transfer it at death to a surviving spouse or other heirs; (2) annually give portions of it to younger generations using the annual gift tax exclusion; (3)

---

* See explanatory footnote in Introduction, page vii, note 1.

ask the corporation to redeem all or a portion of the stock; or (4) sell it to a third party. Because of the voting power often attached to such stock, it is seldom sold and, if sales are made, they most often are made to relatives in whom the client is willing to vest a significant voice in corporate affairs.

Second, in other cases where the size of the estate does not warrant significant inter vivos transfers, preferred stock with a fixed cumulative dividend is created, as was done in the above case. However, in such cases the stock often does not have voting control and in some cases is not entitled to a vote. The client, who in these cases often has an estate which, absent the value of the newly created preferred stock, will not, if properly managed, be subject to estate tax, will typically transfer the preferred stock to his or her spouse (either inter vivos or by will) using the unlimited marital deduction. The common stock then will be allowed to pass to the children, sheltered by the unified estate and gift tax credit, at the death of the client. The purpose of this device is to provide the donee spouse with an income-producing asset which is frozen in value. This will typically be retained by the spouse under a Q-Tip marital trust for life and then be passed to the children, often sheltered by the donee spouse's unified credit. Where this is not done, the donee spouse may dispose of the stock in any of the four fashions described in the first alternative.

I realize that the estate freezes as outlined above will produce some estate and gift tax issues. The trusts and estates department will address those concerns. Please confine your analysis to the Section 306 or other income tax issues raised by the estate freezes.

4. COMPLETE LIQUIDATIONS

PROBLEM 57C

Wally Swenson, an old friend of yours from high school days, has approached you for legal advice. Wally and Monica Lee, a close friend of his who, like Wally, recently inherited a considerable fortune, are considering going into the real estate investment business together. Wally and Monica, acting together, have developed a computer program which they believe is helpful in locating areas of the country which are likely to experience significant economic growth driven by high-technology development. They believe that unimproved real estate in these areas will appreciate at a rate considerably in excess of normal interest rates and the general rate of appreciation for unimproved realty.

Wally has indicated that, because of concerns with potential Super Fund liability arising from toxic materials which might be present on any realty which they could purchase as an investment, they have given some consideration to forming a separate corporation to hold each investment and funding the corporation with cash held or borrowed by Wally or Monica. When the underlying realty was ripe for sale, they would sell the stock of the corporation holding that realty to the party interested in acquiring the realty.

After the purchase of the stock, the purchaser could either continue to hold the stock or could liquidate the acquired corporation to obtain direct ownership of the realty. For example, Wally said if Monica and he were to find a tract of land available for $100,000 which they believed was a good investment, they would form a corporation by contributing to it sufficient funds to enable it to purchase the land and satisfy any additional carrying costs. Assuming that the land increased in value to $250,000 after five years of ownership by the corporation, Wally and Monica would sell the stock in the corporation to those who wished to purchase the land for $250,000. The purchasers then could obtain direct ownership of the land by liquidating the corporation. Wally added that, if these purchasers were comfortable with continued ownership of the land by the corporation, they, of course, need not liquidate the corporation.

Since Wally and Monica are ignorant of corporate and tax law, they seek your reaction to the above and your advice as to various possible alternatives.

PROBLEM 58C

Graphic Impressions, Inc. (Graphic) had operated a contract photo-offset printing business for the last fourteen years. Lawrence and Mildred Fitzgerald, who are husband and wife, and their friend, Norbert Torres, each own 100 of the 300 shares of Graphic common stock, which is the only stock Graphic has issued. Norbert has an adjusted basis of $125,000 in his stock and each of the Fitzgeralds have an adjusted basis of $107,500 in their stock. Due to competition from several larger enterprises, Lawrence, Mildred and Norbert, who are all employed by Graphic, have decided that it is time to call it a day for Graphic and to liquidate the corporation. They caused Graphic to sell all the lesser assets (furniture, cleaning appliances, etc.) used in the business and are considering liquidating Graphic by distributing the following assets to its shareholders in exchange for cancellation of their shares.

Assets	Fair Market Value	Adjusted Basis
Cash	$130,000	$130,000
Acct. Rec.	30,000	35,000
Tenneco Stock	60,000	70,000
United Services Stock	90,000	115,000
US Treasury Bonds	110,000	100,000
Building	200,000	30,000
Land	300,000	40,000
Press	10,000	50,000
Delivery Van	3,000	6,000

Graphic has paid off all its creditors with the exception of the following. It owes $4,000 to Nationsbank on its van. The loan is secured by a lien on the van. It also owes Citibank $50,000, which is secured by a mortgage on the land and building where the printing operation has been conducted. Graphic is personally liable on both loans and they are due on liquidation. Both Citibank and Nationsbank, however, have indicated that they would waive that requirement if the shareholders receiving the property were to become personally liable on the loans. The building was depreciated using the straight-line method and the van and press were depreciated using accelerated methods.

The land and building, which were originally owned by the Fitzgeralds as joint tenants with rights of survivorship, were contributed by them to Graphic at its formation in exchange for the stock held by them. At that time, the building was worth $65,000 and had an adjusted basis of $60,000 and the land was worth $45,000 and had an adjusted basis of $40,000. Mr. Torres obtained his stock in exchange for $55,000 in cash.

Two and one-half years ago, Graphic began to experience financial difficulties. Its three shareholders believed that with a strengthened balance sheet, Graphic would be better able to compete. To this end, Norbert contributed the Tenneco stock now held by Graphic and the Fitzgeralds contributed the United Services stock now held by Graphic. At that time, the Tenneco stock, which had a basis of $70,000 in the hands of Norbert, was worth $50,000 and the United Services stock, which had a basis of $115,000 in the hands of the Fitzgeralds, had a fair market value of $100,000. Two months after this infusion of new capital and before the stock could be sold to enable Graphic to upgrade its equipment, two new competitors entered the local market causing the revitalization plans to be abandoned. Graphic then adopted a very conservative approach toward any new business and investments. Both the Fitzgeralds and Mr. Torres have told you that they then realized that, barring a dramatic and unexpected change in local business conditions, Graphic would have to wrap up operations. The Treasury bonds held by Graphic represent accumulated earnings realized by Graphic in better days. The van, a delivery vehicle, was purchased by Graphic three years ago. It has declined rapidly in value due to extraordinary wear and tear.

The three shareholders seek your advice as to how they should go about liquidating Graphic. They are considering at least three different alternatives. First, they could allow Graphic to sell all assets held by it and distribute all after tax proceeds to the three shareholders in equal amounts. Second, Graphic could liquidate, distributing to each shareholder a pro rata 1/3 share in each of the assets mentioned above. Third, Graphic, which has a net worth of $879,000, could distribute to the Fitzgeralds $586,000 in value consisting of the land and building ($500,000 in gross value subject to the $50,000 debt for a net of $450,000), the United Services stock ($90,000) and $46,000 in cash. All remaining assets, worth $293,000, would be distributed to Norbert in liquidation of his interest.

The three Graphic shareholders would like your advice as to the tax consequences of each of the above. They also ask your advice with respect to the steps which might be taken, consistent with liquidating Graphic, to reduce the impact of taxes on the corporation and its shareholders.

PROBLEM 59C

Your friend, Georgia Masters, consults you about the tax consequences of the liquidation of a corporation, Perfect Images, Inc. (Perfect), which she formed eight years ago and of which she is the sole shareholder. Georgia is the developer of, and the holder of a patent on, a device called a "phantom" which is used for testing the accuracy of magnetic resonance imaging equipment employed in the diagnosis of various medical conditions. After obtaining the patent on the phantom, Georgia, who originally started manufacturing and selling phantoms as an unincorporated sole proprietor, decided that she could most safely exploit its potential by forming Perfect and having it manufacture and sell phantoms to providers of medical services. She eventually settled on a corporation to carry out these tasks because of concerns about personal liability arising from defectively manufactured phantoms. Perfect has operated successfully for a number of years. Georgia was recently diagnosed as having a serious medical condition. Because of the condition, Georgia has decided to liquidate the corporation but retain the patent and license others to manufacture phantoms under the patent. She is not concerned about personal liability in connection with a mere licensing business and, therefore, is willing to hold personally the patent and license others to use it without the benefit of corporate protection.

Georgia has asked your law firm to provide her with a letter of advice outlining the tax consequences to Perfect and Georgia arising from liquidation of Perfect. You assigned to your new associate, Ira Brown-Hidalgo, the task of gathering the relevant material and preparing a draft of the letter for your signature. He has provided you with the following document which you are to review for legal accuracy.

[Draft - 10/18/Year* IB-H]

<u>Perfect Image, Inc.</u>
<u>Complete Liquidation</u>

Dear Ms. Masters:

You have asked for our advice as to the tax consequences to Perfect Image, Inc. (Perfect) and you, as its sole shareholder, of a complete liquidation of Perfect.

Perfect was formed by you eight years ago. In exchange for 100 shares of Perfect, you contributed to the corporation the following assets used by it in its business.

---

* See explanatory footnote in Introduction, page vii, note 1.

Asset	Time of Incorporation		Present	
	Fair Market Value (000 omitted)	Adjusted Basis (000 omitted)	Fair Market Value (000 omitted)	Adjusted Basis (000 omitted)
Patent	100	20	200	12
Land	85	80	60	80
Building	75	70	65	62
Tools	20	18	16	10

The 100 shares of stock were issued to you with an adjusted basis of $188,000. You have had no further capital transactions with Perfect and, at present, still have an adjusted basis in the stock of $188,000.

In addition to the assets mentioned above, Perfect also holds the following assets which it acquired in the past eight years after formation.

Asset	Adjusted Basis (000 omitted)	Fair Market Value (000 omitted)
Cash	203	203
Van	6	8
Computer	3	1
Acct. Rec.	20	18

The land and building have been used by Perfect to conduct its manufacturing and sales operations. The patent and building were depreciated using straight line depreciation. All other assets were depreciated under the most accelerated methods available.

In designating items to be distributed, I have not considered goodwill or going concern value as available for distribution by Perfect since the company will be terminating business and you, the sole shareholder, do not intend to continue similar operations.

Perfect has only two debts, a $40,000 mortgage secured by the land and building and $3,000 in accounts payable. It is your intention to use $3,000 of cash to retire the payables and to use $40,000 of cash to retire the mortgage, which by its terms must be paid on liquidation of Perfect. You then intend to cause Perfect to be liquidated and all its assets to be distributed to you. You will sell all the assets other than the cash, patent and accounts receivable. You intend to license others to use the patent and to collect the accounts receivable or, if that does not prove possible, to sell the uncollected receivables to a dealer in such assets.

Under Sec. 336(a) of the Internal Revenue Code of 1986, as amended, (the Code), a distributing corporation in a complete liquidation is required to recognize gain or loss on the distribution of its assets as if those assets were sold to the distributee at their fair market value. Section 336(d) of the Code limits the recognition of losses to corporate distributors under several circumstances, none of which are relevant to the circumstances under consideration. Under the facts as outlined above, liquidation of Perfect will give rise to the following gains and losses:

Asset	Gain	Loss	Character
Patent	188		Sec. 1231
Land		20	capital
Building	3		capital
Tools	6		Sec. 1231
Van	2		Sec. 1231
Computer		2	Sec. 1231
Acct. Rec.		2	capital

Perfect will be obligated to pay federal and state income tax on the above which, for purposes of illustration only, I estimate will be approximately $50,000. After providing for that liability and payment of the $40,000 mortgage and $3,000 accounts payable, a total of $478,000 in assets will be available for distribution to you. Under Sec. 331, you will recognize a long-term capital gain on the difference between this amount and your basis of $188,000 in the Perfect stock, thus resulting in a long-term capital gain to you of $290,000, which, of course, will be subject to both federal and state income taxes.

I trust that this will be of some help to you as you wrap up Perfect's business and plan your future financial affairs. If you have any questions regarding this, please do not hesitate to call me on my direct line listed on the letterhead.

Very truly yours,

Note:

See the Note on Opinion Letters following Problem 4P at page 22.

PROBLEM 60C

Horace Blount, the general counsel of Argus Properties, Inc. (Argus), would like your advice with respect to several proposed transactions. Argus, a Delaware corporation, is a holding company which owns stock in: (1) Baxter Apartments, Inc.; (2) Cascade Properties, Inc.; (3) Dorton Land, Inc.; and (4) Edgewater Arms, Inc. Argus' 1,000 shares of Baxter common stock (all Baxter's authorized and issued stock) were purchased by Argus three years ago for $10,000,000 and are worth an estimated $7,200,000 ($7,200 per share). The Cascade stock, all of which is owned by Argus, is worth an estimated $7,600,000 and was purchased by Argus six years ago for $4,800,000. The Dorton common stock owned by Argus (75% of the authorized and issued Dorton stock) was purchased by Argus four years ago for $1,800,000 and is now worth an estimated $6,000,000. The Edgewater Arms common stock held by Argus (100% of the authorized and issued Edgewater stock) is worth $3,000,000 and has a basis of $1,200,000 in Argus' hands.

Argus recently received an offer of $7,600,000 for its Cascade stock which it would like to accept. In order to avoid paying the capital gains tax on $2,800,000 and possibly some tax on tax preferences, which would otherwise be due, Horace has suggested that the following course of action be pursued. Argus will sell 250 shares of Baxter stock to Edgewater Arms for $1,800,000, thereby resulting in a $700,000 long term capital loss. Edgewater and Argus then will cause Baxter to be liquidated with Argus receiving $5,400,000 in property in exchange for its stock and Edgewater receiving $1,800,000 in property in exchange for its stock. The Baxter liquidation will result in an additional long term capital loss of $2,100,000 for Argus. The total resulting long term capital loss of $2,800,000 then will be used to offset the $2,800,000 long term capital gain. In order to retain control over Baxter's assets, Blount is anxious to use Edgewater as the vehicle for reducing Argus' Baxter shareholdings below 80%.

If, for tax reasons, it is unwise to follow the above plan, Blount, who owns no Argus stock, feels that it may be possible for him to acquire 250 shares of Baxter stock for $1,800,000 on the understanding that these shares will be exchanged for cash in a complete liquidation of Baxter. Baxter's assets consist of two apartment complexes, Biscayne Villa and Breakers Manor. Biscayne Villa has a gross fair market value of $7,200,000, an adjusted basis of $4,800,000 and is subject to a mortgage of $1,800,000. Breakers Manor has a gross fair market value of $2,800,000, an adjusted basis of $5,200,000 and is subject to a mortgage of $1,000,000. Argus has indicated that, if it is necessary that Blount acquire stock, it would be willing to loan Baxter the $1,800,000 needed to redeem his stock if Baxter is unable to obtain those funds by refinancing the apartment complexes.

Mr. Blount is also interested in your considering the liquidation of Dorton. At present, 25% of the Dorton stock is owned by Norma French who has long been a real corporate gadfly. To remove Ms. French from the scene and to simplify Argus' corporate structure, Mr. Blount is interested in liquidating Dorton. The assets of Dorton consist of two tracts of land located in the Florida panhandle. The first is a relatively small tract of beachfront land worth an estimated $2,000,000 with an adjusted basis of $800,000. The second is a large tract of inland property near Tallahassee worth approximately $8,400,000 with an adjusted basis of $3,200,000. Dorton's capital stock structure consists of 1,000 shares of authorized and issued common stock, of which 250 are owned by Ms. French and 750 by Argus. In addition to owning 75% of the Dorton stock, Argus is also its sole creditor, holding a $2,400,000 note secured by the Tallahassee tract.

Ms. French recently indicated that she would be willing to sell her stock to Argus for $2,000,000 or accept the entire beachfront tract as a liquidating distribution on her stock. Mr. Blount is thrilled with the prospect of being free of Ms. French and would like your advice as to whether he should: (1) purchase Ms. French's stock and then liquidate Dorton, conveying all the land holdings to Argus in exchange for its stock and debt holdings in Dorton; (2) merely liquidate Dorton, distribute the beach tract to Ms. French for her stock and distribute the inland tract to Argus in exchange for its stock holdings and the $2,400,000 note; or (3) have Dorton redeem all of Ms. French's stock in return for the beach tract and leave Argus as the sole shareholder of Dorton. Mr. Blount would like your advice as to the timing of distributions and any formal steps which must be undertaken to produce the most advantageous tax results possible.

PROBLEM 61C

You are an attorney assigned to the Corporate Tax Branch of the Internal Revenue Service. The following ruling request is referred to you for disposition. Prepare yourself to determine whether the requested rulings should be issued and whether you should call for further information or clarification prior to issuing or denying the issuance of the requested ruling.

Turner, Vollow & Weil
201 Market Square
Atlanta, Georgia 30321

March 8, Year*

Peachtree Properties, Inc.
Liquidation of Subsidiaries

Dear Sir or Madam:

On behalf of Peachtree Properties, Inc., a Georgia corporation (Peachtree), and two of its subsidiaries, Queen Shipping, Inc., a Georgia corporation (Queen), and Reliance Radio, Inc., a Florida corporation (Reliance), we hereby respectfully request rulings, hereinafter set forth, with respect to the Federal income tax consequences of the proposed liquidations of Queen and Reliance.

Parties to the Transactions

The address of Peachtree's principal office is 401 Market Square, Atlanta, Georgia 30321. It files its Federal income tax returns, prepared using the calendar year and the accrual method, with the Internal Revenue Service Center, Atlanta, Georgia. Its employer identification number is 12-1473741. Peachtree is a holding company which owns more than fifty percent of the common stock of fourteen different corporations. Peachtree's authorized stock consists of 10,000 shares of voting common stock, par value $1 per share, 9,000 of which were issued and outstanding on February 28, Year. Its stock, which is not publicly traded, is held by eighty-four individual investors.

The principal office of Queen is located at 427 Industrial Drive, Atlanta, Georgia 30322. It files its Federal income tax return, prepared using the calendar year and accrual method, with the Internal Revenue Service Center, Atlanta, Georgia. Its employer identification number is 14-7471635. Queen is engaged in the business of operating a fleet of four tank trucks in which toxic substances are shipped. The authorized stock of Queen consists of 100 shares of voting common stock, seventy five of which are held by Peachtree and the balance of which are held by Susan Manning, the general counsel of Peachtree.

The principal office of Reliance is located at 301 Eastway Drive, Tallahassee, Florida 32306. It files its Federal income tax returns, prepared

* See explanatory footnote in Introduction, page vii, note 1.

using the calendar year and accrual method, with the Internal Revenue Service Center, Atlanta, Georgia. Its employer identification number is 13-4789761. Reliance is engaged in the business of operating a radio station in Tallahassee. The authorized stock of Reliance consists of 100 shares of voting common stock, ninety of which are held by Peachtree and the balance of which are held by Newmark, Inc., an unrelated California corporation (Newmark).

Proposed Transactions

Queen's sole assets consist of four tank trucks each of which is worth $32,000 with an adjusted basis of $40,000. Queen intends to sell its trucks to third parties for their fair market values and liquidate pursuant to a plan adopted February 15, Year. Under the plan, Queen's assets, which will then consist solely of cash representing the proceeds of the sales and any available tax refunds arising from the losses incurred by Queen on the sales, will be distributed to its two shareholders by year end. Peachtree, which has a basis of $300,000 in its 75 shares of Queen, acquired that stock four years ago at Queen's incorporation. Ms. Manning, who has an adjusted basis of $32,000 in her twenty-five shares of Queen, purchased them from Peachtree on February 1, Year.

Reliance's assets consist of a license to operate WFSB-FM, a radio broadcast tower and $2,000,000 in cash. Reliance has no liabilities other than a $1,000,000 demand note which bears interest at 3% above prime and is held by Peachtree. Actual operation of WFSB-FM is carried out under contract by Seminole Broadcasting, Inc., a Florida corporation (Seminole), which is wholly owned by Peachtree. To satisfy certain technical Federal Communications Commission objections, Peachtree has decided to cause Reliance to be liquidated. Reliance will distribute cash and the license for WFSB-FM to Peachtree in exchange for its stock and cash to Newmark for its stock. To enable Newmark to continue to have some participation in WFSB-FM, shortly before the liquidation of Reliance, it will sell to Newmark for the present fair market value of $1,000,000 the radio tower, in which Reliance has an adjusted basis of $1,800,000. Seminole, which will continue as the contract operator of WFSB-FM, will enter into an agreement with Newmark to rent or purchase the tower from it.

After the purchase by Newmark of the tower, Reliance's assets will consist of $3,000,000 in cash and the license for WFSB-FM which is estimated to be worth $8,000,000 and which has an adjusted basis of $50,000 in Reliance hands. Reliance also will remain liable on the $1,000,000 note which is held by Peachtree.

On February 21, Year, the Reliance Board of Directors adopted a plan of liquidation under which Reliance will distribute to Newmark $1,000,000 in cash in exchange for the Reliance stock in which Newmark has an adjusted basis of $100,000. Under that plan, Reliance will distribute the license for WFSB-FM and the remaining $2,000,000 in cash to Peachtree as the holder of a note for $1,000,000 and the remaining 90% of the Reliance stock. Peachtree has an adjusted basis of $90,000 in the stock. Since the sale of the tower will result in a loss which will produce a refund of income taxes to Reliance in a yet to be determined amount, Reliance will distribute 90% of the value of the refund claim to Peachtree and the balance will be distributed to Newmark. At the formation of Reliance six year ago, Newmark and Peachtree each acquired their stock in exchange for $100,000 and $900,000 respectively. Pursuant to the plan, this liquidation will be carried out by the end of this calendar year.

Requested Rulings

In connection with the foregoing, we respectfully request rulings to the following effect:

Liquidation of Queen

1.   The sale by Queen of its tank trucks will be taxed under Section 1231 of the Internal Revenue Code of 1986, as amended (the Code).

2.   Under Section 331 of the Code, Peachtree and Manning will be treated as receiving, in exchange for their stock in Queen, the amounts distributed to them on liquidation by Queen.

3.   Since, pursuant to its plan of liquidation, no property other than cash will be distributed by Queen to its shareholders, no gain or loss will be recognized by it under Section 336 of the Code.

Liquidation of Reliance

1.   The sale by Reliance of the tower to Newmark will be taxed under Section 1231 of the Code.

2.   Under Section 332 of the Code, no gain or loss will be recognized by Peachtree on its receipt of the property distributed to it in complete liquidation of Reliance.

3.   Under Section 331 of the Code, Newmark will be treated as receiving, in exchange for its stock in Reliance, the amounts distributed to it on liquidation of Reliance.

4.   Under Section 337(a) of the Code, no gain or loss will be recognized by Reliance on the distribution by it of property in complete liquidation of Reliance.

5.   Under Section 337(b) of the Code, no gain or loss will be recognized by Reliance with respect to the distribution of $1,000,000 in satisfaction of the loan made by Peachtree.

6.   Under Section 334(b) of the Code, the basis in the hands of Peachtree of the property received by it shall be the basis of that property in the hands of Reliance immediately prior to the distribution.

The issues raised by this application for ruling are not now pending before any field office of the Internal Revenue Service.   Enclosed are powers of attorney authorizing the undersigned and others to represent the respective parties in connection with this application.

Under penalties of perjury, we declare that we have examined this request, including accompanying documents, and to the best of our knowledge and belief, the facts presented in support of the requested rulings are true, correct and complete.

If there should be any doubt as to the issuance of any of the rulings requested herein, the privilege of a conference is requested.   If any additional information is needed, please telephone collect the undersigned, Martin Garcia, at (404)741-3280.

Very truly yours,

Martin R. Garcia

Martin R. Garcia

Commissioner of Internal Revenue
Washington, DC 20224
Attention: Income Tax Division
Attention: Corporate Tax Branch

Note:

See the Note on Ruling Requests following Problem 24P at Page 88.

Part C

ACCUMULATED EARNINGS AND UNDISTRIBUTED INCOME

---

1. ACCUMULATED EARNINGS

PROBLEM 62C

Road Construction Corporation (RCC) is engaged in the heavy construction field, primarily in road construction. Its retained earnings have risen steadily throughout the last eight years from $1,000,000 to $2,400,000. Its taxable income this year amounted to $200,000. The corporation has never paid any dividends. During the last eight years it formed or purchased several wholly owned subsidiaries. Each subsidiary's stock was acquired for a minimum amount of cash, not exceeding $2,000 in any case. The operations of all of the subsidiaries have been financed by loans made to them by RCC.

One subsidiary, Heavy Equipment, Inc. (Equipment), has purchased and owns all the heavy construction equipment which RCC uses, leasing it to RCC for each job. Equipment has retained earnings of about $550,000. It plans, however, in the very near future to acquire four or five new pieces of heavy equipment which will cost in the neighborhood of $900,000 to $1,400,000.

Another subsidiary is Trucking Corporation (Trucking) which has purchased, owns and leases to RCC all motor vehicles used by RCC. Trucking has approximately $800,000 in retained earnings. It anticipates the need, however, over the next four years, to acquire a number of new cars and trucks at an estimated cost of $900,000 to $1,000,000.

A third subsidiary is Real Estate Corporation (Real Estate), which has acquired and owns all of the real estate used by RCC, Equipment and

233

Trucking for offices and storage. Real Estate leases the property to RCC, Equipment and Trucking at a fair rental. Each corporation's share of the rent is based on the number of square feet of floor space which that corporation uses. Real Estate has retained earnings of about $630,000. Because of the expansion of RCC's business, Real Estate plans to construct an addition to its present facilities at an estimated cost of $1,000,000 to $1,100,000.

This year the two controlling stockholders of RCC determined that it would be in RCC's best business interests for it to form a new subsidiary called Crushed Aggregate, Inc. (Aggregate). RCC thereupon formed Aggregate and acquired all its stock for $2,000. The purpose of Aggregate is to locate, purchase, develop and operate stone quarries to produce aggregate materials for use by RCC. Aggregate, once in operation, will sell, at reasonable prices, the processed aggregate to RCC. Total acquisition, development and "start-up" costs are estimated to be approximately $2,000,000. As of this date, Aggregate has not embarked upon the venture.

The two controlling stockholders of RCC, who are both subject to the highest marginal income tax rate, approached First State Bank. They explained the prospective financial needs and current financial situation of RCC and all of the subsidiaries described above. The bank loaned RCC $5,500,000, secured by a security interest in all of RCC's assets and a pledge by RCC of all its stock in its various subsidiaries. As a condition of this loan, RCC agreed that no dividends would be paid by it, that its capital account would be increased by transfers from retained earnings, that salaries would not be increased, and that a compensating balance of 20% of the loan would be maintained with the bank.

RCC thereupon invested the $5,500,000 in certificates of deposit, intending to hold the loan proceeds in this manner until the various needs of the subsidiaries, as described above, must be fulfilled. The reason for borrowing at this time, rather than waiting until the money was actually needed, is that the two controlling stockholders were concerned that interest rates would go up in the near future, and felt that RCC should take advantage of the current rate.

The two controlling stockholders of RCC have asked you to: (1) list the arguments which could be used to show that the penalty arising from the unreasonable accumulation of earnings should be imposed on RCC under the foregoing facts; (2) list the contrary arguments; (3) discuss the issue of who bears the burden of proof; and (4) consider whether, if RCC were publicly owned, any of this would be of concern.

PROBLEM 63C

Examine Problem 48C to determine if there is any cautionary advice that you would now extend to Mr. Levi about the proposed acquisition of Bullock.

PROBLEM 64C

You recently have been employed as an attorney in the New York Regional Office of the Chief Counsel of the Internal Revenue Service. The attorney in charge of your division has asked your assistance in determining whether the office should litigate an accumulated earnings tax case or recommend settlement of the case to the appellate conferee who presently has it. To assist you in your analysis of the case, the attorney in charge of your division has given you the following Taxpayer Statement Under I.R.C. Section 534(c).

Taxpayer Statement Under I.R.C. Section 534(c)

This statement is submitted pursuant to Section 534(c) of the Internal Revenue Code of 1986, as amended, in response to your letter dated September 10, Year* (reference AP: CAR: AOS: CDF), notifying the taxpayer that a proposed notice of deficiency includes amounts with respect to the accumulated earnings tax imposed by Section 531, for the taxable year Year-1.

Grounds

The grounds on which the taxpayer relies to establish that the earnings and profits of the taxpayer were not permitted to accumulate beyond the reasonable needs of the business during the year involved in the proposed notice of deficiency are:

1. Expansion of plant, acquisition of equipment and research and development costs necessary to engage in the manufacture and sale of "strong as steel" glass.

2. Payment of the $1,500,000 note of the taxpayer given in redemption of all of the stock of the taxpayer owned by Mrs. Beatrice Larkin.

* See explanatory footnote in Introduction, Page vii, note 1.

---

3. Adequate provision for the working capital needs of the taxpayer for Year-1.

Supporting Facts

The taxpayer, Magovern Glass, Inc., was incorporated in Year-20. At the time of its incorporation, the 1000 authorized and outstanding shares of common stock of the taxpayer were owned, 500 shares each, by Willard Larkin and Samuel Magovern, the founders of the business. The taxpayer engaged and still engages in the development, manufacture and sale of glass products, including various forms of window, plate and protective glass. The taxpayer was and still is very successful.

In Year-10 the authorized stock of the taxpayer was split 10 shares for every one authorized share, and an additional 20,000 shares of common stock were authorized. The additional common stock authorized was publicly offered and sold. After Year-10, out of 30,000 authorized and outstanding shares of stock, Messrs. Larkin and Magovern owned 1/3 or 10,000 shares. Each one owned 1/6 or 5,000 shares. In Year-3 Mr. Larkin died, and his stock was inherited by his wife, Beatrice Larkin. The stock of the taxpayer is traded over-the-counter in the Northeast. Because the policy of the board of directors of the taxpayer has been and is to use the earnings of the taxpayer for expansion and working capital needs, the taxpayer has never paid more than a small dividend in any year of its existence.

1. Manufacture and Sale of "Strong as Steel" Glass.

In Year-3 the taxpayer acquired the United States Letter Patent of Albert Stores No. 4,317,451 issued on December 3, Year-4. Mr. Stores was and is an employee of the taxpayer. In exchange for the patent the taxpayer agreed to pay a royalty to Mr. Stores based on taxpayer's future sales of products manufactured using the patented invention. The patented invention purports to be a means of manufacturing a glass which is shatterproof and bullet-proof and which can be tempered and molded into numerous shapes and configurations. If the manufacture of such glass proves feasible, the taxpayer will have a substantial competitive advantage over companies manufacturing comparable products.

After the acquisition of the patent, engineers and architects employed by the taxpayer prepared preliminary plans for and estimates of the cost of plant expansion and additional equipment for the taxpayer in order to enable it to manufacture and sell the glass produced under the patent. The estimates indicate plant expansion costs of $600,000 and additional equipment costs of $160,000.

Since the acquisition of the patent, the taxpayer has spent about $60,000 a year in research and development of the product to be manufactured under the patent. To date, much of the research has proved disheartening since it appears that the tempering and molding process adversely affects the strength of the glass. However, the taxpayer's employees who are engaged in the research and development process believe that a solution to the problems noted above will be achieved in the next year or so and at that point the taxpayer will be in a position to begin to manufacture glass under the patent.

2. Payment of $1,500,000 Note.

As mentioned above, in Year-3 Willard Larkin, one of the founders of the business, died and his wife, Beatrice, inherited all his stock in the taxpayer. Under the By-laws and Certificate of Incorporation of the taxpayer, the stock interest held by Mrs. Larkin assured her a position on the board of directors of the taxpayer. Mrs. Larkin was much more interested in increasing her current return on the stock of the taxpayer than in seeing the taxpayer grow, develop new products and finance its working capital needs internally. She consistently opposed the development of "strong as steel" glass, and on many occasions she strongly suggested that much more of the current earnings should be distributed as dividends and that working capital needs should be met by using a line of credit which was available from Lincoln National Bank. At many times she was quite disruptive of board meetings and caused a great deal of dissension among members of the board and the officers of the taxpayer.

In order to remedy this situation, Mr. Magovern and the other members of the board determined that it was in the best interest of the taxpayer to redeem the shares of stock owned by Mrs. Larkin. After extended negotiations, Mrs. Larkin, in Year-1, accepted the taxpayer's note for $1,500,000 in redemption of her shares of stock. The note is payable in equal quarterly installments of principal and interest over a period of ten years at a fair market interest rate per annum. The note is secured by a mortgage on the taxpayer's plant.

3. Working Capital Needs.

In Year-1 the annual cost of goods sold by the taxpayer was $2,400,000 and the peak period inventory was $720,000, resulting in a production cycle of .30. The annual sales for the year were $4,800,000 and the peak period accounts receivable were $960,000, resulting in a collection cycle of .20. The annual purchases for the year were $3,200,000 and the peak period accounts payable were $640,000, resulting in a credit cycle of .20. Subtracting the credit cycle of .20 from the combination of the production cycle (.30) and the collection cycle (.20), .50, produces a figure of .30. Multiplying the taxpayer's cost of goods sold ($2,400,000) plus its operating expenses, other than depreciation and income taxes ($1,600,000), for the year Year-1 by .30 yields $1,200,000, which represents the amount of working capital needed to operate the business for a single operating cycle. The net liquid assets of the taxpayer at the beginning of Year-1 were $700,000. At the end of Year-1, the taxpayer's net liquid assets were $900,000. The average of the two figures is $800,000. This figure indicates that the taxpayer could reasonably accumulate $400,000 for working capital needs.

In summary, the reasonable business needs of the taxpayer during Year-1 required it to have and retain accumulated earnings of at least the sum of the following:

1. Manufacture and Sale of "Strong as Steel" Glass	$ 820,000
2. Payment of $1,500,000 Note	1,500,000
3. Working Capital	400,000
	$2,720,000

The taxpayer's accumulated earnings and profits were $1,700,000 at the end of Year-2 and $2,400,000 at the end of Year-1. Both of these were well below the $2,720,000 required to meet $2,400,000, its business needs. Far from having allowed its earnings and profits to accumulate beyond the reasonable needs of its business, the taxpayer was in the position of having business needs which were not adequately covered by its resources.

The taxpayer certifies under penalties of perjury that the statements of fact contained herein are true to the best of its knowledge and belief.

Respectfully submitted,
Magovern Glass, Inc.

Samuel Magovern

by Samuel Magovern, Pres.

December 3, Year

Statement of Attorney

The undersigned, Laura Fischer, assisted in the preparation of the foregoing Taxpayer Statement Under I.R C. Section 534(c). While she does not know of her own knowledge whether the information contained therein is true, on the basis of a review of documents and statements made by officers of the taxpayer, she believes such information to be true.

Laura Fischer
Laura Fischer

Note:

Section 534 Statement

Section 534 of the Internal Revenue Code provides a means, in the Tax Court, of shifting to the Commissioner the burden of proving that an accumulation was not for the reasonable needs of a business.

Prior to the mailing of a notice of deficiency grounded in whole or in part upon a determination that earnings were permitted to accumulate beyond the reasonable needs of the business, the corporation must be notified in writing by the Commissioner that the proposed deficiency includes an accumulated earnings tax. If the corporation is not so notified, then the burden of proving that the earnings were permitted to accumulate beyond the reasonable needs of the business is on the Commissioner. If the corporation is so notified, it may submit a statement within 60 days of the date the Commissioner's notification is mailed containing the following elements: (1) the grounds on which the corporation relies to establish that the accumulation is not beyond the reasonable needs of the business; and (2) facts sufficient to show that the accumulation was for the reasonable needs of the business.

If the corporation's statement is determined to be more than a "mere notice of intent to prove the reasonableness of the accumulation," then the burden of proving the unreasonableness of the accumulation as to the grounds specified in the statement is shifted to the Commissioner. To achieve this shift, the statement must specifically state and describe both the grounds and facts which, if proven, are legally sufficient to support the reasonable business needs justifying the accumulation.

This means that, for the statement to shift the burden of proof, the corporation must "tip its hand." At times, an attorney for the corporation might deem this unwise. In most cases, despite the filing of a Section 534 statement, caution would indicate that, whether or not the burden of proof is shifted to the Commissioner, all evidence bearing on the purpose for, and reasonableness of, the accumulation should be put in the record. In this context the filing of the statement might be said to shift the burden of persuasion but leave the burden of going forward with the evidence on the corporation.

The attorney's concern may be somewhat alleviated by the amendment of Rule 142 of the Rules of Practice of the Tax Court effective January 1, 1974. Rule 142 now provides that the Tax Court will "ordinarily" rule on timely pretrial motions filed pursuant to Section 534. Therefore, a determination whether the corporation's Section 534 Statement has shifted the burden of proof to the Commissioner may be obtained prior to trial. An affirmative determination may result in the asserted deficiency being withdrawn by the Commissioner prior to trial.

2. PERSONAL HOLDING COMPANIES

PROBLEM 65C

In Problem 3C, Herman Stein asked your advice with respect to the formation of "The Stein Family Estate." As you may remember, you were quite concerned about the possibility that "The Stein Family Estate" might be an association taxable as a corporation.

Assuming that "The Stein Family Estate" is an association taxable as a corporation, review its formation and operation as described in Problem 3C and, on the basis of the expertise you have subsequently acquired, advise Herman concerning the possibility that "The Stein Family Estate" will be subject to the personal holding company provisions of the Code.

PROBLEM 66C

As you may remember, in Problem 44C you advised Alvin, Bruce and Frederick Kelly and Square One, Inc. with respect to the redemption by Square One of certain shares of its voting stock then held by Alvin, Bruce and Frederick. After the redemption planned in Problem 44C took place, you asked Clarissa Kelly, who had been elected president of Square One, to keep in touch with the firm. Square One, Inc. had invested a substantial portion of its earnings from the shopping center in various marketable securities, and you were concerned that any significant reduction in its rental income might present personal holding company problems. Today your firm received the following letter, which was referred to you for reply.

Square One, Inc.
430 Tangerine Drive
Tampa, Florida 33637

November 10, Year*

Palmer, Palmer & Best
1807 Brisbane Building
730 Bay Street
Tampa, Florida   33635

To Whom It May Concern:

A few years ago a very capable young associate of yours, whose name presently escapes me, advised us with respect to the redemption of some of the stock in Square One, Inc. then held by my father, brother and nephew. The associate cautioned us to stay in touch since there was some concern that Square One might face personal holding company problems in future years. Recently, our accountants told us that Square One might face these problems this year and urged us to seek your advice. The accountants stated that you would require our income statement for last year and our projected income statement for this year in order to properly advise us. Last year's income statement is as follows:

Square One, Inc.
Income Statement for the
Period Ended Dec. 31, Year-1

Income

Rental Income	$3,800,000
Investment Interest Income	220,000
Dividend Income	160,000
Total Income	$4,180,000

Expenses

Operating Expenses	$1,760,000
Mortgage Interest	500,000
Depreciation	380,000
Real Estate Taxes	240,000
Total Expenses	2,880,000
Net Income	$1,300,000

* See explanatory footnote in Introduction, page vii, note 1.

Toward the end of last year and at the beginning of this year, there were two events which significantly affected our rental income. First, at the end of last year the state highway department condemned a substantial portion of the land and improvements located on the western side of the plaza. The highway department took title to the property early this year and offered us $1,400,000 for the property taken. We contested this, and about a week ago the matter was settled for $1,600,000 plus approximately one year's interest at 9% per annum. This settlement produced interest income of $144,000, capital gain of $300,000 and depreciation recapture of $100,000. Second, at the beginning of this year there was a serious fire in the part of the plaza leased to Montgomery Ward Department Stores, Inc. This caused a substantial diminution in our rental income since we lost the rent from Montgomery Ward as well as that from some nearby tenants who suffered smoke and water damage. We have settled with the fire insurance company and will use the proceeds to repair the part of the plaza damaged by the fire. We have also collected about $600,000 under our valued use and occupancy policy with respect to the loss of the use of the premises involved in the fire, but that does not come close to replacing the rental income lost. Our projected income statement for this year is as follows:

Square One, Inc.
Projected Income Statement
for the Period Ending Dec. 31, Year

Income

Rental Income	$1,400,000
Investment Interest Income	240,000
Dividend Income	180,000
Interest on Condemnation Award *(excluded)*	144,000
Depreciation Recapture on Condemned Improvements	100,000 — *ordinary income*
Capital Gain on Condemned Improvements and Land	300,000
Proceeds of Valued Use and Occupancy Policy	600,000
Total Income	$2,964,000

Ins. - what risk was insured?

Expenses

if its rent it goes into rental calculation

Operating Expenses	$ 800,000
Mortgage Interest	480,000
Depreciation	180,000
Real Estate Taxes	240,000
Total Expenses	1,700,000
Net Income	$1,264,000

Please let us know at your earliest convenience whether, in your opinion, Square One will have any personal holding company problems this year, and if so, what steps we can take to avoid or minimize such problems. For your information, none of the present shareholders of Square One expect to be subject to high marginal rates of income tax this year. In addition, both Golden Harbor, Inc. and Hargrove Enterprises have indicated a willingness to lease some of the presently vacant space in the shopping plaza and this year to prepay two or three years' rent, which could amount to $400,000 to $600,000, if you felt that this course of action was advisable.

Very truly yours,

Clarissa Kelly

Clarissa Kelly

Part D

COLLAPSIBLE CORPORATIONS

PROBLEM 67C

Mike Ratko (Mike), one of your most important clients, has made a substantial amount of money acting as a broker of, and dealer in, various commercial real estate projects such as office buildings and hotels. Every so often, however, he discovers a project which he believes has potential as a long term investment rather than simply an acquisition with a view to a relatively quick sale to a customer in the ordinary course of Mike's business. The former Olds Hotel in the financial district of the city in which you practice was one of these projects.

The Olds Hotel had been the place to stay and the place to meet in your community during the 60's and 70's. It had fallen on hard times in recent years, and Mike found it could be purchased for about $1,300,000. Mike determined that with about $500,000 in renovations, $200,000 in new furnishings, and a new marketing policy for both rooms and banquet facilities, the Olds Hotel might again be a very profitable establishment. After some investigation, Mike found that $1,400,000 of the $2,000,000 in costs could be financed through a 30-year mortgage from Great Eastern Life Insurance Company (Great Eastern). Mike had about $300,000 to invest in this project, and the other $300,000 could be raised by selling interests in the project for about $30,000 each to ten investors. Mike felt the project might be of interest to investors because of the tax benefits and the high potential for substantial cash flow. You advised Mike to use a corporation as the entity to carry out this project because of the high liability risk in operating a hotel. Mike took your advice and formed Olds Hotel, Inc. (the corporation). In order to make the tax benefits available to Mike and the investors, the corporation, with consent of all the investors, elected subchapter S status. Mike owns 150,000 shares, and each of the other investors owns 15,000 shares of the corporation's 300,000 shares of authorized and issued stock.

About seven years ago, the corporation acquired the Olds Hotel, made the renovations, acquired the new furnishings and made the marketing changes. While Mike regards his investment in the stock of the corporation as a long term investment, he has advised you that he would have sold the stock in the period during which the renovations were being made if a buyer had made the right offer. The investment in the Olds Hotel has been as beneficial as Mike had envisioned. Mike and the investors made personal use of the tax benefits in the early years and received substantial tax-free cash flow in later years. At this point in time Mike and the other investors have a zero basis in their stock in the corporation. The balance sheet of the corporation showing the fair market value of its assets is set out below.

Hilton Hotels, Inc. (Hilton) has expressed an interest in acquiring the Olds Hotel. Representatives of Hilton have told Mike that Hilton will pay $800,000 for the stock of the corporation or $2,000,000 for its assets of which $1,200,000 would be paid by assuming the corporation's liabilities. The $800,000 purchase price of the stock or the net $800,000 purchase price of the assets would be paid $400,000 in cash and a ten-year note of Hilton in the principal amount of $400,000 bearing an interest rate three percentage points in excess of the prime rate. The note would be secured by a pledge of the stock if stock is purchased, or a security interest in the assets subordinate to the Great Eastern security interest if assets are purchased. Since the proposed purchase price is greater than the corporation's basis in its assets, Hilton wants the purchase price to be reflected in the basis of the assets after the acquisition.

Mike has consulted all the investors and they are willing to make the sale to Hilton. Mike has now asked for your advice with respect to how the sale should be made and any provisions or conditions with respect to the sale which you suggest the corporation or its shareholders should impose.

Olds Hotel, Inc.
Assets
(000 omitted)

			Adjusted Basis	Fair Market Value
Cash			$ 20	$ 20
Furnishings	Cost	$ 200		
	Dep.	(180)	20	100
Real Estate	Cost	1,200		
Improvements	Dep.	(440)	760	1,080
Real Estate Land			300	700
Total Assets			$1,100	$1,900

| | Liabilities and Capital | |
| | (000 omitted) | |
	Per Book	Fair Market Value
Trade Accounts Payable	$ 20	$ 20
Long Term Liability to Great Eastern	1,080	1,080
Capital		
300,000 shares issued	600	600
Deficit	(600)	200
Total	$1,100	$1,900

PROBLEM 68C

High Meadows Development, Inc. (High Meadows) began development of a substantial mountain residential and recreational project about five years ago. Recently, the corporation received from Evergreen Glen, Inc. (Evergreen) an offer to purchase all its assets and assume all its liabilities. Ms. Jane Christofer, the president of, and a stockholder in, High Meadows, discussed the offer with you and one of the general partners in your firm. The stockholders of High Meadows would like it to accept the offer. One of the concerns discussed at your conference with Ms. Christofer was whether High Meadows might be considered a collapsible corporation and, if this was a possibility, how all the assets and liabilities could be transferred to Evergreen with the least possible risk of collapsible treatment to the stockholders. At the close of the discussion, the general partner told Ms. Christofer that, in order for the firm to advise High Meadows and its stockholders with respect to the collapsible corporation problem, certain information about the corporation and the project must be made available to the firm.

The general partner recently received the following letter from Ms. Christofer which he has forwarded to you together with a note from him asking you to evaluate the risk of the corporation's being considered collapsible and to suggest a method of transferring the assets and liabilities to Evergreen which will minimize the possibility of collapsible treatment. The note also mentions that Evergreen wishes to acquire a basis in High Meadows' assets equal to its cost of acquiring those assets.

High Meadows Development, Inc.
830 Rapid Street
Gunnison, Colorado 81230

April 7, Year*

Robert Sterne, Esq.
Sterne, Nagel & Pierce
420 Main Street
Colorado Springs, Colorado   80911

Dear Bob:

The purpose of this letter is to give you the information that you requested with respect to High Meadows Development, Inc. and the High Meadows project. The corporation was formed about five years ago. It has 100 authorized and issued shares of common stock. The stockholders are as follows:

Jane Christofer	20 shares
William Christofer	30 shares
Frank Christofer	10 shares
William Blake	10 shares
Janice Wright	20 shares
Arthur Anderson	10 shares

All the stockholders except Art Anderson paid $2,000 a share for their stock. As you know, Art is a real estate dealer and developer who specializes in commercial and residential developments. He received his 10 shares in return for options held by him on the land on which the High Meadows project is presently situated. My nephew, Frank Christofer, who is a dentist, had invested in a number of other projects with Art, who told him of his plans for the High Meadows project. Frank thought the project sounded quite exciting and told my father, William Christofer, and me about it. My father and I had never invested in real estate before. We normally invested the earnings from our medical practice in high-quality securities and municipal bonds. However, we thought the project sounded quite exciting. My father interested our accountant, Janice Wright, in investing in the project, and I told my friend William Blake, one of our local architects, about the project. Neither Janice nor Bill had ever invested in real estate before. Although I think Bill has occasionally taken an interest in a project that he has designed in payment of his fees, he has always sold such interests at the earliest feasible date, usually back to the developer. Because most

---

* See explanatory footnote in Introduction, page vii, note 1.

of us had no real experience with real estate development your partner, Jim Nagel, suggested that we use a corporation to avoid personal liability.

The High Meadows project, as originally conceived by Art, involved the development of a quite pretty mountain meadow with a variety of residential and recreational units. A number of the units were to be single-family unattached residences suitable for year-around living (the subdivision). Two multi-unit buildings were to be developed as condominium projects, and two other buildings were to be constructed as apartment buildings with enough flexibility in design so that the units could be rented on a seasonal basis. All the amenities were to be included such as a community clubhouse and lounge, two swimming pools, a nine-hole golf course and a number of tennis courts. Transportation for residents of the project to nearby ski areas was also to be provided.

By Year-3 the units in the subdivision had been completed. At the end of last year about four-fifths of them had been sold. A number were sold by the corporation using installment land contracts. The corporation reports its income from these sales using the installment method. One of the condominium buildings was also completed by Year-3. We decided to wait before beginning construction of the second building to see how the units in the first sold. At the end of last year all but two of the units had been sold. If we were not going to sell to Evergreen, we would this year begin construction of the second condominium building and maybe even convert one or both of the two apartment buildings, which were completed in Year-2, into condominium projects. The apartment buildings have been the only disappointment in the project. It appears that there is not enough seasonal trade to keep them full, and it seems that those people interested in having a vacation unit would rather own the unit than rent. The clubhouse and lounge and one of the swimming pools were completed in Year-2. The tennis courts and golf course were completed early last year, and the second swimming pool was finished late last year. We are still landscaping, and my impression is that, in a way, landscaping may continue forever. We have not made any substantial repairs or renovations to any of the existing structures.

The balance sheet of High Meadows Development, Inc. at the close of last year, with the purchase price which Evergreen will pay for each asset indicated, is enclosed herewith. The retained earnings figure represents all the income the corporation has ever made, since no dividends have been declared. Let me know when you have finished your analysis of the sale to

Evergreen, so that we can get together and begin to make plans to go forward with the sale in the most advantageous tax fashion.

Sincerely yours,

Jane

Jane Christofer

Balance Sheet Of
High Meadows Development, Inc.
as at Dec. 31, Year-1
Assets

		Adjusted Basis (x 1000)	Purchase Price & Fair Market Value (x 1000)
Cash		$ 40	$ 40
Installment Obligations		390	500
Investments-Marketable Securities		50	70
Unsold units and land in Subdivision		160	180
Unsold units and interests in land in Condominium		40	48
Swimming Pool # 1	$ 30		
(Depreciation)	(6)	24	27
Swimming Pool # 2		40	40
Clubhouse & Lounge	100		
(Depreciation)	(10)	90	93
Apartment Building # 1	400		
(Depreciation)	(26)	374	371
Apartment Building # 2	600		
(Depreciation)	(37)	563	548
Tennis Courts	10		
(Depreciation)	(1)	9	9
Golf Course		20	20
Land*		300	454
		$2100	$2400

* Does not include land remaining in subdivision or interest in land under condominium.

Liabilities and Capital

	Per Book (x 1000)	Fair Market Value (x 1000)
Trade Accounts Payable	$ 40	$ 40
Development Mortgage	1700	1700
Land Acquisition Mortgage	260	260
Capital		
100 Shares Issued and Outstanding	100	100
Retained Earnings	0	300
	$2100	$2400

Part E

TAXABLE ACQUISITIONS OF A BUSINESS

----

1. BASIC ASSET ACQUISITIONS

PROBLEM 69C

Harry Gold, who is the president and sole shareholder of Creative Designs Jewelry, Inc. (Creative), has consulted you with respect to the following matter. Creative operates two custom jewelry production and design facilities on the East Coast of the United States, one in Boston and one in Miami. Creative produces hand-crafted jewelry items at these locations and sells them to jewelry stores and gift shops in the Florida and New England areas. Harry recently agreed, in principle, to acquire all of the assets used by Western Jewelry, Inc. (Western) in its custom jewelry operations in Philadelphia. Since Creative does not have a commercial presence in the middle Atlantic states, when the opportunity arose to acquire such a presence at an acceptable price, Harry seized the opportunity.

Western has operated a number of custom jewelry production facilities on the West Coast for a number of years and several years ago decided to start such an operation in the Philadelphia area. It did so through a wholly owned subsidiary called Spectacular Specialties, Inc. (Spectacular). Sally Silver, the president and sole shareholder of Western agreed, in principle, to sell to Creative all of the assets used by Spectacular in its Philadelphia operations. Apparently, Sally has decided that the expansion to the East Coast was not a good idea and desires to confine operations to the West Coast. The agreement between Harry and Sally provides for the sale of all Spectacular's assets, other than cash, to Creative for the average of the fair market value range of those assets as determined by Commercial Appraisals, Inc. (Commercial). Commercial established a value range of $780,000 to

$1,020,000 for the assets, which resulted in an average fair market value of $900,000.

As part of its purchase of the assets, Creative also will be allowed to use the name Spectacular Specialties with respect to the acquired operation in Philadelphia. In addition, since Harry was extremely concerned about the possibility of Western commencing new operations on the East Coast, he insisted that Western provide a covenant not to compete in any states east of the Mississippi for the next eight years. Western was willing to do so for $40,000. The parties also agreed that, in the event Western breached its covenant not to compete, it would pay Creative liquidated damages of $160,000 which sum was to be reduced by $20,000 per year from the date of signing of the final agreement.

Sheila Saunders, your firm's principal corporate partner and the individual for whom you do most of your work, was providing advice to Harry on the proposed acquisition. She has been called to London in connection with a major corporate transaction and has provided Harry with the following memorandum and the suggestion that he contact you about any problems which arise in her absence.

To: Harry Gold

From: Sheila Saunders   *Sheila*

Re: Spectacular Specialties Asset Purchase

Date: November 3, Year*

I have been unexpectedly called to an emergency meeting in London. I was unable to reach you by phone to go over matters with you prior to your meeting with Ms. Silver to discuss the purchase of Spectacular assets. I left word with your secretary that I would be sending you this memo and the name of the associate you should contact in my absence.

I have listed below all of the assets which Creative will purchase from Spectacular, Western's wholly owned subsidiary. Opposite the assets, I have listed (in thousands) the fair market value range set by Commercial. In the next column I have listed (in thousands) the price which I would like to see you allocate to each of those assets. You will note that the total of the figures which I have proposed in the allocation column equals $900,000, the

---

* See explanatory footnote in Introduction, page vii, note 1.

mean between the low ($780,000) and the high ($1,020,000) of the fair market values. This figure matches the $900,000 agreed upon purchase price. In your meeting with Ms. Silver, you should not depart from my proposed allocation figures except for the amounts allocated to trained staff, designs, customer list and goodwill. You may employ any combination of values among these four assets so long as the total does not exceed $300,000 and you do not assign to any asset a purchase price in excess of the appraiser's maximum fair market value. Finally, I understand that you have agreed to pay Western an additional $40,000 for a covenant not to compete. Western has agreed to pay Creative $160,000 in liquidated damages if Western violates that covenant, with a step down of the liquidated damages by $20,000 each year from the date of signing of the final agreement.

Assets	Fair Market Value Range	Purchase Price Allocation
Receivables	$ 45 - 50	$ 50
US Gov't Securities	170 - 170	170
Building	200 - 250	200
Land	100- 150	100
Equipment	30 - 40	40
Inventory	35 - 50	50
Designs	30 - 50	50
Trained Staff	30 - 50	50
Customer List	40 - 60	60
Goodwill	100 - 150	130
	$780 - 1,020	$900

When Harry met Sally to further discuss the purchase of Spectacular's assets, he found her to be reluctant to accept Ms. Saunders' suggestions. Sally indicated to Harry that she would prefer not to make any allocation of the purchase price and instead simply sell all the assets mentioned above for $900,000. In addition, Western would provide Harry with the covenant not to compete containing the $160,000 liquidated damages provision in exchange for $40,000. Harry has consulted you in an effort to understand exactly why Ms. Saunders advised him not to depart from the allocation contained in her memorandum and would like you to explain, as well as you can, the reasons for her suggestions and the reasons why Sally objects to going forward with the transaction in that manner.

2. ACQUISITION OF A CORPORATION

PROBLEM 70C

Benjamin Duffy inherited all of the stock of P&D Machine Shop, Inc. (P&D) four years ago. Ben worked at P&D with his parents for a number of years prior to acquiring ownership of the company and, while he understands the day to day business quite well and has some understanding of commercial law, he has virtually no understanding of corporate and tax law.

Precision Lathe Manufacturing, Inc. (Precision) is a competitor of P&D. Two brothers, Ralph and Steve Lamont, each own one-half of the stock of Precision. The brothers are in their mid-sixties and have concluded that they should sell Precision and retire. Ben is interested in purchasing either all of the stock of Precision or all of its assets, subject to any existing liabilities. Precision has an excellent reputation as a machine shop. In fact, just last year it recovered $40,000 in a product defamation suit. The damages were based on injury to the reputation of the corporation and its products and were not reported as income by the Lamonts, who believed that the recovery was not subject to tax.

After obtaining the assistance of an appraiser, Ben offered to purchase all of the assets of Precision for $620,000 in cash plus assumption of $160,000 of liabilities. The assumed liabilities consist of $6,000 of accounts payable, a $72,000 loan on machinery and equipment and a $82,000 mortgage on plant and land. The Lamonts, who each paid $10,000 for their stock thirty years ago, have indicated that they would prefer to sell their stock to Ben for a total of $620,000.

Ben's sister, Patricia, told him that he should reject the deal offered by the Lamonts. She took one look at the current financial statement of Precision and said, "You know that the stock of this baby is worth less than its assets." Ben told you that he nodded his head and said, "Sure — I'm no dummy." He indicated that he was not about to let his kid sister, who teaches a business course at a local community college, know that he really did not have the foggiest idea what she meant. Ben would like you to explain to him how Precision's assets can be worth more than its stock and, if that is the case, to assist him in determining a dollar amount to use in a counter offer for the Precision stock.

He also has told you that, in examining Precision's financial statement set forth below, there are a few facts which you ought to keep in mind. The corporation uses the accrual method of accounting for income tax purposes. The plant has been depreciated under the most accelerated method available as has the equipment which is, on the average, three years old. Finally, although the Lamonts have assured him that they do not intend to reenter the machine shop business, Ben has told them that he wants them to sign a covenant not to compete within a 200 mile radius during the next eight years. The Lamonts have indicated their willingness to do so. As a demonstration of their good faith on the issue of their intention to retire, they do not ask to be paid anything for the covenant if Ben accepts their proposal that he pay them $620,000 for all the stock in Precision.

Precision Lathe Manufacturing Inc.

Assets
(000 omitted)

	Adjusted Basis	Approximate Fair Market Value
Cash	$ 10	$ 10
Gov. Securities	40	60
Accounts Receivable	34	34
Finished Inventory	70	100
Raw Materials and Work-in-Process	100	106
Machinery and Equipment $160		
(Depreciation) (88)	72	100
Plant 240		
(Depreciation) (140)	100	160
Land	68	110
Goodwill	26*	100
	$520	$780

<u>Liabilities and Capital</u>
(000 omitted)

	Per Books	Approximate Fair Market Value
Accounts Payable	$ 6	$ 6
Machinery and Equipment Loan	72	72
Mortgage on Plant and Land	82	82
Capital		
Stated Capital	20	20
Surplus	340	340
Excess of Fair Market Value over Book	-	260
	$520	$780

*The adjusted basis in goodwill is the cost of securing a trademark developed by the corporation eight years ago. The corporation has not amortized this cost for income tax purposes.

PROBLEM 71C

Claire Consula, a wealthy investor who has been a client of your law firm for a number of years, seeks your advice on the following matter. Claire is interested in purchasing an office condominium unit in the Franklin Square Office complex for use in the management of her financial affairs.

Teleservices, Inc. (Teleservices) has managed quite a few 900 number telephone operations, each of which provided a specialized service aimed at a discrete audience (e.g., personal counseling, instant sport scores, financial information, etc.). To satisfy state telemarketing regulatory requirements, Teleservices decided to incorporate separately, as wholly-owned subsidiaries, each of the 900 number operations. Several months ago, under pressure from the state attorney general and its bankers, Teleservices decided to terminate all operations. To date, the process of termination has left it with three wholly-owned subsidiaries (Sport, Inc., Finances, Inc. and Homeline, Inc.), each of which owns no assets other than an office condominium unit, any one of which would be suitable for Claire's purposes. Teleservices will sell to Claire the stock of any of the three corporations. Since Teleservices has an adjusted basis in the stock of each of these subsidiaries which is substantially above the fair market value of the subsidiary stock, it is insistent on selling its stock in each subsidiary rather than liquidating them and selling the office condominium units outright.

Teleservices has offered to sell Claire the stock of either Sport, Inc. (Sport), Finances, Inc. (Finances) or Homeline, Inc. (Homeline) for $400,000. While the office condominium units held by each subsidiary are physically identical, there are several significant differences between the subsidiaries themselves. Sport and Finances each have an adjusted basis of $300,000 in the condominium units which they own and Homeline has an adjusted basis of $450,000 in its unit. While both Homeline and Sport were financially successful, that was not the case for Finances and it has a net operating loss of $90,000 which is about to expire.

Claire has informed you that she is willing to purchase the stock of any one of the three subsidiaries or to arrange for its purchase by CC Properties, Inc. (CCP), a corporation wholly owned by Claire. She has also informed you that, after she or CCP acquires the stock, it is acceptable to her that the acquired corporation either be liquidated or be allowed to continue in existence. She would like your advice as to the income tax consequences of the various choices that face her.

PROBLEM 72C

Your client Sunrise Chemical, Inc. (Sunrise) is in the process of negotiating with Gloria Martinez, the sole shareholder of Ideal Chemical Corp. (Ideal), regarding the sale of all of her Ideal stock. Robert P. Bello, the general counsel of Sunrise, has informed you that actually Sunrise is interested in acquiring the assets of Ideal but Ms. Flynn is insistent upon the acquisition being conducted as a sale of the stock of Ideal. Sunrise is extremely interested in removing Ideal as a competitor and in acquiring several of its valuable patents as well as the plant, plant site, processing unit and intangible assets related to those patents. As a result, Mr. Bello has informed you that it is likely that Sunrise will go ahead with the proposed acquisition of all of the Ideal stock, assuming that the parties are able to agree upon a reasonable price. The balance sheet for Ideal is set forth below.

Jennifer Taylor, a recent graduate of a prestigious LL.M. in taxation program and a new associate at your law firm, has provided you with the following memorandum regarding the potential purchase of Ideal by Sunrise.

Prepare yourself to discuss the contents of the memorandum in your next strategy meeting with Mr. Bello.

<u>Memorandum to File #3046.0250</u>
<u>Sunrise Chemical, Inc. Acquisition of</u>
<u>Ideal Chemical Corp.</u>

Jennifer Taylor   March 15, Year*

Sunrise Chemicals' management is in the process of negotiating with Ms. Gloria Martinez for the purchase of all of her stock in Ideal Chemical Corp. (Ideal). The latest balance sheet of Ideal, which is in my possession and a copy of which is attached as exhibit A, indicates that the Ideal assets have an aggregate gross fair market value of $7 million. The balance sheet also shows liabilities totaling $1.5 million consisting of an $800,000 mortgage on the plant, $50,000 worth of payables and an unsecured operating loan from Nationsbank of $650,000. The balance sheet also shows in a footnote a potential $3 million environmental cleanup liability with respect to Ideal's land. Over its years of operation, Ideal has polluted its land to a considerable extent. Under state environmental legislation, since the pollution is stable and presents no threat to health at present, there is no immediate obligation to clean up the site. However, state law does require that, in the event of a transfer of the land in a sale, it must be cleaned up, thus resulting in the $3 million clean up cost for the seller. State law also provides that the sale of control through the sale of stock (more than 50% of voting common) of a corporation holding polluted land results in imposition of cleanup responsibilities on the corporation which is sold. Thus, regardless whether Sunrise purchases all of the stock of Ideal or simply buys the assets of Ideal, Ideal will have the obligation to clean up the land, an obligation which is presently estimated to be $3 million. According to my analysis, this added $3 million liability will reduce the net value of the transferred stock to no more than $2.5 million ($7 million - $1.5 million - $3 million).

If Sunrise purchases the stock of Ideal and does not make a Section 338 election with respect to the acquisition, Ideal will be left with its present basis in all of its assets. This means, for example, that Ideal will be left with a basis of zero in patent number # 4,578,142 and that the inventory, for which Sunrise (if the stock price is equal to the sum of the fair market value

---

* See explanatory footnote in Introduction, page vii, note 1.

of the underlying assets minus liabilities) would be paying $100,000, will have an adjusted basis of only $80,000. In the case of depreciable property, such as the patent, this will result in no depreciation being available, and in the case of property such as the inventory it will result in immediate recognition of all built-in gain on the stock's sale. This inherent tax liability, which results from the purchase of stock from Ms. Martinez rather than the assets of Ideal, should be considered in determining the purchase price of the stock of Ideal. I am of the opinion that, given the negative tax implications of a stock purchase without a Section 338 election, Sunrise should insist on a discount of $200,000 and thus should be willing to pay only $2.3 million for the stock of Ideal.

I have several suggestions regarding the proposed acquisition. First, I suggest that, after the purchase, Sunrise make an election to have the acquisition of the stock treated as a Section 338 transaction. It is my opinion that, because of the cleanup charge with respect to the land, the land should be treated as having a fair market value of only $500,000 ($3.5 million - $3 million). This should result in Ideal's having a $2 million loss on the land under Section 338. This loss could be offset against the gain which would result under Section 338 with respect to the plant, patents, inventory, processing unit, goodwill, trained staff, and know how. Since the aggregate gain on these items will be $1,880,000 and thus will be less than the $2 million loss which will result from the land, there will be no tax cost to Ideal as a result of having made the Section 338 election. Moreover, there will be an additional $10,000 loss with respect to the receivables. When this loss and the $2,000,000 loss on the land are offset against the $1,880,000 gain, a net loss of $130,000 will result.

As a result of the Section 338 election, the land, which is a nondepreciable asset, will have an adjusted basis of $500,000, whereas the plant, patents, processing unit, good will, trained staff, know how and the inventory will each receive a basis which is stepped up to their respective fair market values. In the case of the inventory, this step up in basis will mean that its sale by Sunrise will generate no taxable income and in the case of the patents, goodwill, trained staff and know how, it will mean that these assets qualify for write-off over 15 years under Section 197. The plant, with respect to the $200,000 write up in adjusted basis, will be depreciable over 39 years and the processing unit, with respect to the $100,000 write up in adjusted basis, will be depreciable over 5 years. The fact that the basis in the land will be stepped down from $2.5 million to $500,000 will be of no consequence until it is sold. Since it is Sunrise's intention to have Ideal continue its operation of the plant at its present site, the lower adjusted basis in the land will be virtually meaningless to Ideal whereas the increased basis in depreciable assets and inventory will be of considerable tax value.

In addition, Sunrise should be aware that the $3 million in environmental cleanup expenses which are incurred by Ideal as a result of the transfer will be immediately deductible under Rev. Rul. 94-38, 1994-1 CB 35. This $3 million deduction can be used by Ideal to wipe out any income from the present year and then can be carried back as a net operating loss carryback. I estimate that this will result in a refund of federal and state taxes to Ideal of approximately $1.2 million.

If we can obtain the $2.3 million purchase price which I feel is appropriate, and we subtract from this purchase price the $1.2 million in tax refunds which will be available as a result of the clean up operation, the actual net cost to Sunrise of the purchase of Ideal is only $1.1 million. To this one should add the potential tax savings resulting from the write up of the depreciable assets and inventory. This produces a unique opportunity for Sunrise to acquire Ideal at virtually no after tax cost.

Exhibit A
Ideal Chemical Corporation
Balance Sheet
(000's omitted)
Assets

	Book and Adjusted Basis	Fair Market Value
Cash	$ 100	$ 100
Receivables	110	100
Land*	2,500	3,500
Plant	1,000	1,200
Processing Unit	300	400
Inventory	80	100
Patent #4,578,142	0	800
Patent #4,713,471	40	200
Goodwill	0	300
Trained Staff	0	100
Know How	0	200
	$4,130	$7,000

	Liabilities	
Payables	$ 50	$ 50
Mortgage on Plant	800	800
Operating Loan	650	650
Paid-in-Capital	100	100
Earned Surplus	2,530	5,400
	$4,130	$7,000

* In addition to the stated liabilities, there is a clean-up liability of approximately three million dollars in connection with environmental degradation of the land listed as an asset. The fair market value assigned to the land does not reflect this liability.

PROBLEM 73C

Reynolds Products, Inc. (Reynolds), a manufacturer of plastic household supplies, successfully prosecuted a treble damage antitrust suit which left the company with over $200,000,000 in cash after taxes and attorney fees. Since any company which holds substantial liquid assets is the likely target of a hostile takeover bid, the officers and directors of Reynolds are anxious to have Reynolds divest itself of a substantial part of this cash by using it to acquire several privately held companies whose businesses would complement those of Reynolds or provide it with sound investments. Tamara Wilkes, the general counsel of Reynolds, has previously consulted your partner, Simeon Braga, about Reynolds' acquisition plans. In the process of her discussions with Mr. Braga, Wilkes has acquired some initial exposure to the consequences of a Section 338 election and the circumstances under which such an election is desirable. She has sent Mr. Braga the following memorandum outlining several potential acquisition targets and seeks advice with respect to the impact of Section 338 on the three contemplated acquisitions discussed in her memorandum. As Mr. Braga is planning to be out of the country on the business of other clients, he has given you the memorandum and asked you to set up a conference with Ms. Wilkes to consider the matters discussed in the memorandum.

To: Simeon Braga

From: Tamara Wilkes

Re: Proposed Acquisitions

Date: November 1, Year*

Based on our previous discussions, it is my understanding that if Reynolds purchases the stock of a corporation, that corporation, for tax purposes, will be left with the adjusted basis in its assets which it had prior to the acquisition unless the acquisition qualifies for a Section 338 election by virtue of our purchasing at least 80% of the stock of the corporation within 12 months and our timely election of Section 338 treatment. The consequence of any such election will be that the acquired corporation will be deemed to have sold its assets to itself for their fair market value with the result that the acquired corporation will recognize both gain and loss, as the case may be, on such assets and will then have a basis for those assets equal to their fair market value.

I understand that acquiring corporations seldom make Section 338 elections. The reason for this is that, in most such situations, the acquired corporation will recognize gain resulting in current income tax which will exceed in present value terms the tax advantage of the resulting write up in the basis of the acquired corporation's assets. There are three basic circumstances in which this is not the case and a Section 338 election makes economic sense. First, such an election usually makes sense where there are aggregate unrealized losses built into the acquired corporation's assets which will adequately compensate for the gains which will be recognized on a Section 338 election. In evaluating the advantage of an election in such a case, it is also necessary to weigh the effect of a write up and write down in basis of the acquired corporation's assets with considerable care being given to determining the timing of the use by the acquired corporation of its basis in each of its assets. Second, if the acquired corporation has net operating losses which are about to expire, and which are sufficient to absorb all or most of the gain, a Section 338 election would also make economic sense. Finally, a Section 338 election might be feasible if the owners of the acquired corporation are willing to treat the income tax on the net gain recognized as a result of the Section 338 election as a corporate liability thereby reducing the purchase price paid for the stock of the corporation. With these considerations in mind, I have evaluated the

---

* See explanatory footnote in Introduction, page vii, note 1.

following three potential corporate acquisitions with respect to their candidacy for a Section 338 election and would like your reaction to my conclusions.

WRAP, Inc. This corporation (WRAP) owns and operates an FM station WRAP-FM in Durham, NC. As its call letters might lead you to conclude, the station specializes in providing musical offerings (rap, ska, punk, and reggae) which appeal to today's youth. WRAP is a calendar year, accrual method taxpayer which has depreciated its assets under the most accelerated methods available. Although some of the assets held by WRAP, principally its land and building, have declined in value, other assets such as its license and goodwill have appreciated considerably. The assets of WRAP are set forth below:

Assets
(in 000's)

	Adjusted Basis	Fair Market Value
Cash	$ 800	$ 800
Receivables	200	200
Land	13,500	8,000
Building	5,500	3,000
Broadcast Eqpt.	700	900
Tower	1,200	2,200
Recording Collection	400	800
Trained Staff	0	200
License	0	5,000
Goodwill	0	1,000
	$22,300	$22,100

WRAP has the following debt outstanding: (1) $100,000 in payables; (2) a $9,000,000 mortgage on land and building; and (3) a $3,000,000 operating loan from Citibank. The net fair market value of the WRAP assets (assets minus liabilities) is therefore $10,000,000.

WRAP is owned by five investors, each of which owns twenty percent of its common stock which is the only authorized stock of the corporation. While four of the investors are willing to sell all of their stock for $2,000,000 each, a fifth investor, for estate planning reasons, is unwilling to sell at present. It is Reynolds' officers intention to purchase the stock from the four investors for $8,000,000 and to effect a timely Section 338 election. If I understand things correctly, the resulting losses on the land and building will more than wipe out the gains on other assets. While the basis in the land and building will be decreased, the basis in the other assets will be increased. Moreover, since the land is not depreciable, the building is depreciable over a long period of time and the other assets whose bases will be changed are depreciable over shorter periods of time, the net effect of the changes in basis which follow from the election will be advantageous to WRAP and will come at no tax cost since its losses will more than offset its gains.

Please confirm my understanding of the workings of the Section 338 election. I also would appreciate it if you would advise me of the impact of the failure to acquire all the WRAP stock on our Section 338 election and on the treatment of the above mentioned WRAP liabilities under Section 338.

Carson Metals, Inc. (Carson). Carson is a manufacturer of metal kitchen products. Eighty percent of its stock is owned by its founder, Jaume Serra. We propose to acquire all the stock held by Mr. Serra in exchange for $7,000,000. The other twenty percent of the Carson stock was acquired by us through a purchase from Mr. Serra six months ago for $1,000,000.

Carson is a calendar year taxpayer which uses the accrual method of accounting for both financial and tax purposes. Carson's plant has been depreciated using the straight-line method, and all personal property has been depreciated using the most accelerated method of depreciation available. Carson has had a rather checkered financial past and has a $3,200,000 net operating loss which is about to expire. Despite its poor record, Carson has recently turned the corner and we believe it to be an attractive investment opportunity. The most recent financial statement of Carson is set forth below:

Carson Metals, Inc.
Assets
(in 000's)

		Basis or Book	Fair Market Value
Cash		$ 200	$ 200
Securities		100	80
Accounts Receivable		280	280
Inventory (FIFO)		420	500
Raw Materials		250	270
Machinery & Equipment	$ 900		
(Depreciation)	(400)	500	900
Plant	2,600		
(Depreciation)	(300)	2,300	3,400
Land		2,750	570
Goodwill		-0-	3,600
		$6,800	$9,800

Liabilities		
Accounts Payable	$ 200	$ 200
Mortgage on Plant and Land	1,600	1,600
Capital		
Stated Capital	500	500
Earned Surplus	4,500	7,500
	$6,800	$9,800

Although a Section 338 election will result in a substantial gain for Carson, the $3,200,000 net operating loss will more than offset that and the election will provide Carson with a step up in basis in many of its assets. I would appreciate it if you would confirm my analysis, determine the gain which will be recognized on a Section 338 election to see if the $3,200,000 net operating loss is sufficient to cover it, determine the basis of the Carson assets after a Section 338 election and inform me of the steps which must be taken to secure the election, if you deem it desirable.

Northern Technology, Inc. (Northern). Northern formerly produced pharmaceutical products under four patents which it had purchased. Several years ago, Northern decided to terminate all production activities and to continue in existence as a patent licensing company. At present its sole business consists of licensing others to produce pharmaceutical products under its patents. All profits are distributed each quarter to Peter Overton, the sole shareholder of Northern. A copy of the most recent financial statement of Northern is provided below:

Northern Technology Inc.
(in 000's)

Assets

	Book and Adjusted Basis	Fair Market Value
Cash	$ 100	$ 100
Patent #4,714,311	500	2,000
Patent #4,971,884	3,500	7,500
Patent #4,81,739	2,400	8,900
Patent #5,217,446	3,000	1,000
	$9,500	$19,500

	Liabilities	
Paid in Capital	$2,000	$ 2,000
Earned Surplus	7,500	17,500
	$9,500	$19,500

Since the gains on the first three patents listed above greatly exceed the loss on the fourth patent and since Northern does not have a net operating loss, there is no reason for us to make a Section 338 election if we purchase Mr. Overton's stock. As I understand it, the fact that Northern will continue with its existing adjusted basis in each of its assets should have an impact on the price that we should pay Mr. Overton for his stock. Rinaldo Franceschi, our investment banker, told me that we should attempt to close a deal in the $15-16 million purchase price range. Does all this seem reasonable to you?

In closing, I would like to add one other consideration. Assuming that we do negotiate a deal with Mr. Overton at a fair price, the thought has occurred to me that, after acquiring Northern, we could let it take advantage of the $2,000,000 loss attributable to patent #5,217,446 by purchasing that patent from Northern for $1,000,000. The resulting $2,000,000 Section 1231 loss will then be available to be applied against the royalties which Northern will collect on its three remaining patents. Please give me your reaction to this clever little idea of mine!

3. LEVERAGED BUYOUTS

PROBLEM 74C

Your friend, Cherise Chapel, is an investment officer at the pension trust which administers the pension fund for county employees in the county in which you practice and reside. Cherise specializes in publicly traded equity and bond investments and has several independent investment advisors who work closely with her on a fee basis to help make decisions about purchasing and selling publicly traded investments for the pension fund. Sandra Sandoval, another investment officer, is normally in charge of making investment decisions regarding privately placed debt and equity investments for the fund. Sandra was recently involved in a serious automobile accident and will be away from work for the next three to four weeks. Cherise, who has been asked to take over Sandra's duties with respect to non-publicly traded investments, was recently visited by Marcus Perry, a representative of Clio, Ltd. Clio, Ltd. is a group of investors which specializes in taking publicly traded companies private, re-engineering the companies and then selling them, either publicly or privately, at a considerable profit. Clio, Ltd. has focused its attention on Quik Mart, Inc. (Quik Mart) which runs a chain of convenience stores and gasoline stations in the Southwest and Southeast. Mr. Perry has approached Cherise about the possibility of the county pension fund participating with the Clio group in a leveraged buyout of Quik Mart. Cherise is concerned about what Mr. Perry told her, as it all sounds too good to be true, and would like your advice as to the feasibility, from a tax standpoint, of what Clio, Ltd. intends to accomplish.

According to Mr. Perry, Quik Mart presently trades over-the-counter at about $15.00 a share. With 10 million shares outstanding this results in the Quik Mart stock having an aggregate value of approximately $150 million. Since the $.60 per share dividend was last increased five and one-half years ago and Quik Mart's management has not capitalized on the potential for growth which exists in the markets which it serves, the value of the stock has remained dormant for the last four years, during which it has traded in the $13-17 per share range.

According to Mr. Perry, Quik Mart this year will have a before tax income of approximately $19 million on gross receipts of approximately $600 million. After allowing for $8 million in federal, state and local income taxes, Quik Mart will have approximately $11 million of income remaining out of which it can pay dividends which cost it in the aggregate about $6 million. The remaining $5 million can be used to replace existing facilities as they wear out, to expand into new markets or to add to surplus. Perry indicated that it is the intention of Clio, Ltd. to carry out a leveraged buyout of Quik Mart offering its shareholders $20.00 per share. Clio, Ltd. intends to carry out the acquisition of Quik Mart by forming a new corporation, Speedy, Inc. (Speedy), which will borrow the $200 million which is necessary to effect the acquisition. Speedy will then offer to acquire Quik Mart for $20.00 a share in a statutory merger which will result in the transfer to it of all the Quik Mart assets. All the stock of Speedy will be owned by Clio, Ltd.

Mr. Perry has asked Ms. Chapel whether the pension trust would be interested in loaning Speedy up to $10 million to enable it to carry out the acquisition. He indicated that he was in the process of contacting a variety of different sources, such as banks, pension trusts and insurance companies, for the purpose of obtaining the full $200 million in financing which Clio, Ltd. believes is necessary to effect the acquisition. Mr. Perry would like to acquire three different types of financing. First, he is interested in borrowing $10 million at approximately 7% for up to 2 years. Clio, Ltd. intends to pay off this loan within the two year period by liquidating some of Quik Mart's less profitable and money-losing operations and using the proceeds to retire the $10 million short-term debt. Second, Clio, Ltd. is interested in borrowing approximately $90 million at 8% for a period of 20 years, with retirement of this debt commencing in a staged fashion within about 10 years. This debt will be secured by a lien on the Quik Mart real estate, including both the land and the buildings. Third, Clio, Ltd. is interested in borrowing $100 million in a form which Perry refers to as mezzanine debt. He feels that Clio, Ltd. will have to pay approximately 10% per annum in interest on this debt, which will be secured in part by a lien on the inventory and fixtures of Quik Mart. He estimates that the maximum value of these assets is only about $40 million and he therefore believes that this debt, because of its junior status, will have to bear the 10% interest rate. This debt, like the debt secured by the land and building, will also have a 20 year term, but there will be no repayment required on the debt for 15 years, at which point in time the corporation will use an annual lottery for the purpose of determining exactly which of this debt is to be retired in each of the remaining five years during which it will be outstanding.

When Cherise put pencil to paper, she determined that the interest on the three forms of indebtedness will come to about $17.9 million and that, based on Mr. Perry's assumptions, the income of Quik Mart is only $19 million. When she called this to Mr. Perry's attention, he seemed rather nonplused and indicated, "Of course we are going to terminate payment of all dividends for the foreseeable future and the figures that we have worked out give us a little bit more than $1 million in breathing room on the deal, which will expand to almost $2 million once we retire the short-term debt within the first two years of our ownership of Quik Mart." He indicated that through aggressive management of the corporation, Clio, Ltd. felt that it could increase the earnings of Quik Mart by approximately 10% a year for the first few years. Cherise explained to Mr. Perry that dealing with transactions of this sort was not her usual responsibility and that she would like to get back to him with respect to his proposal.

Cherise has contacted you about this transaction. She has asked you whether it will pass muster from a tax standpoint and whether all the interest paid by the corporation on the $200 million of debt will be deductible. Please prepare yourself to advise her on this matter.

PROBLEM 75C

Your client, Caroline Lukens, who recently inherited a substantial fortune, has consulted you about the following matter. Her cousin Oscar, who has an MBA from Stanford, is a pleasant, smart fellow who has never held a job since graduating four years ago. However, he is held in high regard by a number of successful investors and businesses which hire him as a consultant on complex financial matters. Caroline, who concedes that Oscar is a bright fellow, suspects that he often is in over his head with respect to some of these matters. Oscar has recently proposed to Caroline that she allow him to use a large part of her inherited fortune to assist him and a group of other investors in purchasing, in leveraged buyouts, the equity interests in corporations which he believes are undervalued.

As Oscar explained it to Caroline, the group of investors (of which she would be one) will attempt to purchase all of the stock of one or more corporations using a considerable amount of debt. They intend to use the earnings of the acquired corporations to service the debt, thereby acquiring the corporations for almost nothing. According to Oscar, a small group of investors will be organized and will borrow enough cash to purchase the stock of the present shareholders at a significant premium. The acquisition indebtedness, on consummation of the purchase of the corporation, will become acquired corporation debt or debt of a corporation into which the acquired corporation is merged. The surviving corporation, as long as is necessary to service the debt, will cease all dividend payments on its stock, which will be held by the investor group. The earnings, and perhaps the assets, of the acquired corporation will be used to service the debt, with all interest on such debt being deductible for tax purposes. Since virtually all earnings will be dedicated to debt service, the stock of the investor group will have only a modest initial value, but as earnings grow ever so modestly there will be a dramatic increase in the value of the stock held by the investor group.

Caroline was rather dubious about all this and asked Oscar to provide her with a written explanation of just how a leveraged buyout works. Oscar sent Caroline the following letter and she has approached you to ask for your evaluation of its contents.

Oscar L. Burbank
1965 Ramona Avenue
Salt Lake City, UT 84108

Dear Caroline,

You have asked me to explain to you in writing some of the basic principles underlying a leveraged buyout. This letter represents my best attempt to explain to you what normally transpires in such a transaction.

Typically, a group of investors who are interested in acquiring an existing corporate enterprise with very little cash investment will be formed. The investors hope to acquire the corporation under an arrangement whereby they will use assets and earnings of the acquired corporation to service the debt which is issued to accomplish the acquisition.

One of the distinguishing features of a number of corporations which are acquired in leveraged buyouts is the presence of a significant amount of cash, or other assets which can be readily reduced to cash, which can be used in the redemption of some of the stock of existing shareholders. Occasionally, a decision is made to acquire a corporation which has an operating division which is promising but which produces little present revenue. The division is then sold to generate cash which can be used to fund a portion of the buyout. Moreover, I will explain below some of the steps which can be taken with respect to debt that can result in significant tax refunds while providing additional cash to be used in furtherance of the acquisition.

The most significant step in a leveraged buyout involves the transformation of equity into debt by the group of acquiring investors. Typically, the investor group, which makes a tender offer to acquire the stock at a price which represents a substantial premium over its present trading price, will negotiate, in advance, financial backing from a variety of sources. The investors often arrange for banks to commit to indirectly loan to the corporation to be acquired a large portion of the money which will be used to carry out a redemption of the interests of old shareholders. Often this debt will be secured by a lien against the acquired corporation's assets and will bear an interest rate at a relatively conventional level.

The next step involves the commitment on the part of a number of financial institutions to provide a second tier of debt which, because of its junior status, is often referred to as mezzanine debt. Typically, this debt is issued in unsecured form and should bear a high interest rate because of its unsecured nature and junior status. In order to secure tax advantages, however, the debt is often issued at an interest rate which is below the interest rate which would otherwise be expected to prevail under normal market conditions. The result of this is to create what is known as an original issue discount. Debt instruments which are issued at an interest rate which is below that which would be demanded by market conditions trade at a substantial discount from their face amount. For example, if a borrower is unwilling to pay the 12% interest which would be required by the market on a $1,000 bond of the borrower and instead chooses to issue the $1,000 bond at an interest rate of 6% with payment due in twenty years, one could expect that the bond purchasing community would only be willing to pay something on the order of $700 for each $1,000 bond. Holders of the indebtedness would look not only to the $60 of interest which would be payable annually but also to the increase in the value of the bond which would occur each year as the term of the bond approached the ultimate repayment date, when the borrower would be called upon to pay the full $1,000 face amount of the bond.

Under the tax law, corporations which issue original issue discount bonds are entitled to claim a deduction each year which roughly reflects the projected annual increase in value of the bond. Similarly, holders of the indebtedness are required to accrue, as income, the amount allowed to the issuer as an interest deduction. Use of original issue deep discount mezzanine debt will provide the acquired corporation with deductions for interest which do not represent actual out of pocket cash outlays but merely represent the accrued original issue discount. Moreover, if these bonds are issued to tax exempt organizations such as pension trusts or charitable entities, the requirement that income be accrued by the holders turns out to be relatively meaningless. In some cases, the acquiring investors cause the acquired corporation to borrow mezzanine debt at such a deep discount that the accrued interest deduction, when added to other expenses of the corporation, gives rise to a net operating loss which can be carried back against income from prior years, thereby generating a tax refund which provides additional cash which can used to service acquisition indebtedness.

Typically, the acquiring investors are willing to offer a price for the target corporation's stock which reflects a premium over the price at which the corporation's stock was trading or, in the case of a privately held company, its value to investors. The acquiring investors often anticipate dramatically changing the nature of the operations of the acquired corporation with virtually all of its income being used to service the normal bank debt and the mezzanine debt. This dedication of earnings to debt payments means that not all corporations are appropriate targets for leveraged buyout transactions. The ideal candidate for a leveraged buyout is a corporation with a relatively stable stream of income which operates in an industry which is not subject to cyclical economic pressures. For this reason a corporation such as RJR Nabisco was an ideal candidate for a leveraged buyout since the steady stream of income produced by its tobacco and food businesses could be committed to servicing the debt incurred in the takeover without much fear of that debt not being paid during an economic downturn. Another feature of corporations which are ideal candidates for leveraged buyouts is that they conduct their business in areas of the economy in which the stock of such corporations does not trade at a significant price earnings (PE) ratio. The reason for this is that a corporation in an industry with a high PE ratio would not generate sufficient earnings to enable the takeover debt to be serviced. This accounts for the fact that we do not see leveraged buyouts in industries such as the pharmaceutical industry or in the high technology sector. Leveraged buyouts are most prevalent in relatively unexciting but stable industries such as the food and banking industries in which stock trades at a relatively low PE ratio.

There are relatively few tax problems which pose significant concerns when conducting a leveraged buyout. At first blush, one might be concerned about the IRS attempting to reclassify the above-mentioned debt as stock thereby barring an interest deduction for the cash paid as interest and for the original issue discount. Tax lawyers tell us that there is little likelihood of this occurring if the debt is not held by the same parties which hold the stock or, if some is so held, it is not held in the same proportion as such parties hold stock. They also inform us that in avoiding reclassification of acquisition debt as stock it is helpful that the debt not be convertible into stock. Moreover, they indicate that there is scant likelihood of debt being reclassified as equity if the target is a large, publicly held corporation. Tax attorneys also have advised us that although Congress in the late 1960's decided to disallow the interest deductions on certain corporate acquisition indebtedness by enacting Section 279, the basic nature of that section causes it to be, if not a toothless tiger, at least one that is easily declawed. As long as acquisition indebtedness is not made convertible into the stock of the acquired corporation nor part of an investment unit which includes an option to acquire such stock, it is relatively easy to avoid Section 279. Although there are several other ways of avoiding the application of Section 279, not including conversion rights with acquisition indebtedness is totally consistent with the aims of the acquiring investor group and happily provides protection from Section 279.

Ideally, one would like to find a suitable target corporation which is held by a single investor or a small group of private investors who were willing to sell out to the private investor group. This, unfortunately, is seldom the case. Most often the subject of a leveraged buyout is a publicly traded corporation. Since it is impossible to get all the investors in such a corporation to agree to the acquisition, it is often necessary to conduct the leveraged buyout with the assistance of a newly created "dummy" corporation which, in the course of the acquisition, will be merged into the target corporation or which will have the target corporation merged into it. This merger will be conducted under state law which provides dissenting shareholders with an opportunity to exercise appraisal rights. Pursuant to the merger, the old shareholders of the target corporation will be offered either cash or the opportunity to exercise appraisal rights. The actual manner in which such transactions are carried out can vary considerably. The whole process is rather tricky and best left to tax lawyers to structure based upon state law considerations as well as the posture of the individual corporations which are involved.

In addition to confronting resistance from minority shareholders who can be squeezed out in a merger as described above, we often encounter significant resistance to a buyout from the management of the target corporation which sees itself as losing its existing employment under a new regime. To deal with this and to gain the support of this group which can create quite a problem for the acquiring investor group, it is often necessary to provide some members of existing management with what we in the trade refer to as a "golden parachute." This is typically a continuing consulting relationship with the target corporation for several years at a salary which is several times management's present salaries. Since consulting fees are deductible, while money paid to acquire stock is not, one often makes the decision to provide a rich "golden parachute" to management to gain support for a takeover of a corporation at a lower price than that which might be expected were management unwilling to endorse the acquisition.

I know all this is rather complicated so, if you wish to discuss any of the details with me, I am willing to do so. Due to the complicated and tax driven nature of leveraged buyouts I suggest that you might want to consider discussing this whole matter with your tax advisor who I feel will be able to tell you that what I am proposing is basically nothing other than a garden variety leveraged buyout and that this device can provide you with an excellent mechanism for using tax money to conduct an acquisition which will be of great financial benefit to you.

Very truly yours,

scar

Part F

CORPORATE DIVISIONS AND REORGANIZATIONS

---

1. DIVISIONS

PROBLEM 76C

Review Problem 53C and determine whether you might suggest that Dixie Loan enter into a transaction other than a partial liquidation. If the basis of the shareholders in their stock was so large that a partial liquidation would result in a loss, would this affect your advice? Would your advice be affected by whether the shareholders could use the loss? Should the fact that substantial losses may arise in the mortgage loan business influence whether you recommend a corporate division?

PROBLEM 77C

Examine Problems 36C and 51C and consider the feasibility of separately incorporating Speculation's real estate holdings and distributing the stock to Speculation's shareholders in a corporate division. Is this a feasible means of eliminating Speculation's real estate holdings and allowing it to concentrate on its express delivery service?

PROBLEM 78C

In Problem 82C you are advised that Standard Tool Company, Inc. (Standard) would like to effect a tax-free acquisition of Monroe Power Tool, Inc. (Monroe) but does not want to acquire the unincorporated operating division of Monroe known as Monroe Household Products (Household).

Consider whether, in the light of the desires of Standard, Monroe and the shareholders of both corporations that the acquisition be tax-free, a "spin-off" of Household to the shareholders of Monroe prior to Standard's acquisition of Monroe is an acceptable means by which Standard can avoid acquiring the Household division. In analyzing this approach, assume that the shareholders of Monroe, who are in favor of the acquisition of Monroe by Standard, are not interested in retaining the Household division. Instead, these shareholders would like to dispose of Household, in a tax-free transaction, to one of the potential purchasers mentioned in Problem 82C at the same time as, or immediately after, Standard acquires the remainder of Monroe.

PROBLEM 79C

Your client, Abe Burkhart (Abe), has asked your advice regarding the least costly method, in terms of income tax payable, which will allow his young general manager to purchase a substantial interest in the retail clothing business operated by Hi Lite Clothes, Inc. (Hi Lite). Abe presently owns 100% of the stock of Hi Lite. Because of the magnitude of Hi Lite's retained earnings ($1,400,000), the purchase of a substantial stock interest is beyond the manager's financial capability. Abe has proposed the formation of a new corporation to which Hi Lite will transfer all its assets, less $1,300,000 in certificates of deposit, in return for all the new corporation's stock. Since Hi Lite has a substantial basis in all its assets, it then will be liquidated, and Abe will receive the stock of the new corporation and the certificates of deposit. Six months later, the manager will purchase, for cash, enough shares of the new corporation to give him a 49% interest, and Abe will give the manager an option to purchase his 51% interest over a term of years.

Advise Abe of any concerns that you have with respect to the proposed transaction in light of Section 368(a)(1)(D). Is there a way of avoiding its application? Consider whether it would be advisable to transfer to the new corporation some, but not all, of the various retail clothing stores owned by Hi Lite, together with enough retained earnings to operate the transferred stores. Assume, for example, that one out of seven stores plus most of the liquid assets would be kept by Hi Lite and that all the stores have been operated by Hi Lite for at least five years. Hi Lite then will be liquidated, and the manager will buy a 49% stock interest in the new corporation and be given the option to purchase Abe's 51% interest.

Finally, in the context of the alternative suggested in the first paragraph above, consider the feasibility of the following plan. You, as an accommodation to your client Abe, will buy shares of Hi Lite from Abe at fair market value. You will purchase enough shares so that, after the liquidation of Hi Lite and the manager's purchase of 49% of the stock of the new corporation, the new corporation will be owned 49% by the manager, 49% by Abe and 2% by you. Of course, the first shares of the new corporation's stock to be purchased by the manager pursuant to his option will be the shares owned by you. The purchase price of your shares only will be an amount that, together with the share of Hi Lite's liquid assets which you received on the liquidation of Hi Lite, returns to you the purchase price you paid to Abe for the shares of Hi Lite plus fair interest on the purchase price. During the first five years that the option is outstanding, its exercise will be subject to Abe's consent.

Note:

Attorney Participation in a Transaction

Can an attorney ethically offer to purchase some of a client's stock to enable the client to avoid a potential income tax problem? Does the answer depend on whether the attorney has all of the risks of ownership of the stock?

2. REORGANIZATIONS

a. Reorganization Defined

PROBLEM 80C

Your client, H.R. Phillips, Inc., a major producer of pharmaceutical products, is interested in acquiring Norris-Parker Inc., a small producer of several important new drugs. Jerry Newhauser, the treasurer of Phillips, is in charge of the acquisition team and seeks your advice as to the form that the acquisition should take.

Norris-Parker, which is traded on the NASDAQ, has 1,000,000 shares of common stock outstanding. The stock recently closed at $36 per share. Jerry Newhauser reports that sixty-eight percent of the stock is held by mutual funds and tax-exempt organizations such as pension funds and that ten percent is held by Phillips, which acquired it over the course of the last year for $3,000,000. The remainder of the stock is owned almost exclusively by various individual shareholders, most of whom acquired it in the last five years for prices ranging from $24 to $40 per share.

The balance sheet of Norris-Parker, as of the close of its fiscal year two months ago, is as follows:

NORRIS-PARKER, INC.

(000 omitted)

Assets

	Basis & Book Value	Fair Market Value
Cash	$ 400	$ 400
CD's	1,600	1,600
Securities	1,000	1,100
Accounts Receivable	500	500
Patents	300	10,000
Land (plant location)	1,600	4,400
Plant	2,000	16,000
Inventory (LIFO)	600	2,000
Tangible Personalty	2,000	6,000
Goodwill	-0-	4,000
	$10,000	$46,000

Liabilities

	Book Value	Fair Market Value
Current Liabilities	$ 800	$ 800
Mortgage on Plant	5,200	5,200
Paid-in Capital	2,000	2,000
Retained Earnings	2,000	38,000
	$10,000	$46,000

Mr. Newhauser informed you that Phillips' investment banker, Greer, Auchincloss and Richards, estimates that if more than 80 percent of Norris-Parker stock is to be acquired in a tender offer by Phillips for Phillips stock,

Phillips will have to offer to the existing Norris-Parker shareholders Phillips stock worth $40 per share. The investment bankers also noted that if Phillips intended to accomplish this acquisition with a cash tender offer, it could expect to spend $44 per Norris-Parker share. Mr. Newhauser also informed you that Norris-Parker management would be amenable to accepting an offer to sell all its assets in exchange for an assumption by the purchaser of all its liabilities, plus $40,000,000 in value consisting of any combination of Phillips common stock, debt and cash. Please advise Mr. Newhauser on the tax consequences and desirability of the various alternatives.

PROBLEM 81C

The chair of the tax department of the firm with which you are associated recently received the following memorandum from one of the partners in the business and corporate department of the firm. The chair has given you the memorandum and asked that you provide him with your answers to the questions raised in the memorandum.

Scotland, Plaset, DeFo & Tasc
2100 Broadway, Suite 710
Denver, CO   80202

Inter Office Memo

TO: Kenneth Kline
FROM: Suzanne Laughing-Eagle
RE: Acquisition of Lumber Mart Inc. by the Gumble Co., Inc.

Our client, the Gumble Co., Inc. (Gumble), is a corporation whose stock is publicly traded on the New York Stock Exchange. Gumble is a diversified corporation engaged in various retail businesses including the operation of drug stores, convenience department stores, and lumber and building materials suppliers. It recently emerged from a Chapter XI proceeding in bankruptcy as a lean, but quite healthy, concern. The bankruptcy reorganization substantially reduced its debt burden, expanded its stated capital and capital surplus and left it with 3,000,000 authorized but unissued shares of $10 voting preferred. The preferred has a liquidation preference and par value of $10 plus accrued dividends and a cumulative dividend of 14%. It does not, however, participate with common after receiving its dividend or liquidation preference. The issued and outstanding preferred is now trading at about $10 a share. The preferred is entitled to one vote per share. Gumble also has 6,000,000 shares of common stock, par value $1, authorized but unissued. The common stock represents the basic equity in Gumble and is entitled to one vote per share. The issued and outstanding common stock is now trading at about $5 a share.

One of the business strategies which the management of Gumble proposed in the Chapter XI reorganization plan was the acquisition of financially strong, smaller corporations whose businesses complemented that of Gumble. In this manner, Gumble management hoped to build Gumble into a strong, financially healthy concern. The acquisition strategy was the reason that Gumble emerged from the bankruptcy reorganization with the substantial amount of authorized but unissued preferred and common stock. The management of Gumble hoped that this stock could be used to carry out future acquisitions. Recently the management of Gumble has discovered a corporation which appears to be an ideal choice for the first acquisition. The corporation is Lumber Mart, Inc. (Mart). Mart owns and operates a number of drive-through lumber and building materials facilities in Colorado, Arizona, New Mexico and Utah. These are states in which Gumble presently has no lumber and building materials locations.

Mart, while being a small corporation which is about a quarter of the size of Gumble, is very healthy. It has both a class of common stock, par value $1, and a class of preferred stock outstanding. The common stock is the only voting stock and has been trading on the Midwest Stock Exchange at about $15 a share. The preferred stock has a liquidation preference and par value of $30 a share, a cumulative dividend of 5%, does not participate with common after receiving its preference, and has been trading at about $15 a share. Mart has 90,000 shares of common and 10,000 shares of preferred outstanding.

The management of Gumble has approached the management of Mart with a proposal that Gumble acquire Mart. The purchase price proposed by the management of Gumble was $2,000,000, to be paid in either 200,000 shares of Gumble preferred stock or 400,000 shares of Gumble common stock or some combination thereof. The management of Mart felt, assuming the transaction was tax-free, that the proposal, in general, was acceptable. Mart's management, however, was of the opinion that no distinction should be made between its common and preferred in the receipt of the Gumble shares. If Gumble common stock was used and each share of Mart, preferred or common, received four shares of Gumble common or, if Gumble preferred was used and each share of Mart, preferred or common, received two shares of Gumble preferred, the Mart management felt that all of the common stockholders and about 85% of the preferred stockholders would go along with the acquisition. If, however, the

Mart preferred received more Gumble stock per share than the Mart common received, it was doubtful that a majority of the common stockholders would approve the transaction. The Gumble management felt that the approach suggested by the Mart management was acceptable.

The Gumble management has now asked us for our assistance in structuring the acquisition. The Gumble management has informed us of the following goals and objectives to be achieved, if possible, in the acquisition. First, the acquisition must satisfy the desires of the Mart management described above. Second, it must avoid, if possible, giving any Gumble shareholders a vote or appraisal rights with respect to the transaction. The bankruptcy reorganization was recently approved, and Gumble management would prefer to avoid another shareholders' meeting. Third, the transaction should be structured in a manner which would avoid diluting the financial equity of current Gumble shareholders, now or in the future. The net worth of Mart presently equals at least two million dollars. Fourth, the acquisition must avoid, if possible, giving the shareholders of Mart, or at least most of them, voting and appraisal rights with respect to the acquisition. Fifth, if Mart is retained as a subsidiary of Gumble, any continuing minority interest in Mart should be avoided. Sixth, the Black & Decker tool and the Weyerhauser lumber franchises held by Mart, which are not assignable, should not be lost as a result of the acquisition. Seventh, Gumble's present assets should not be subject to any liability resulting from any product warranty given by Mart prior to the acquisition. Mart's express product warranties have a maximum term of two years, and the statute of limitations on implied product warranties runs after two years following the delivery of the product. Finally, since Gumble has an in-house union, the union contract Mart entered into with the local A.F.L.-C.I.O. affiliate, which has two years to run, should not be assumed.

Please advise me and the Gumble management of: (1) the various forms of acquisition which are available; (2) the various ways Mart's desires with respect to its preferred stock can be accomplished; and (3) the best way of structuring the transaction to achieve all, or at least most, of the goals expressed to us by Gumble management while still having the transaction treated as a tax-free reorganization.

PROBLEM 82C

As tax counsel to Standard Tool Company, Inc., a Delaware corporation (Standard), you have been asked to determine the most appropriate method of effecting a proposed acquisition on a tax-free basis. Standard's principal business is the manufacture of hand tools, and it is interested in expanding its operations to include the growing market for power tools and equipment. Therefore, Standard is considering acquiring Monroe Power Tool, Inc., a Michigan corporation (Monroe), the principal business of which is the manufacture and distribution of hand-held power tools and equipment. In addition to its power tool business, Monroe, through an unincorporated operating division, Monroe Household Products (Household), has for the last seven years manufactured and distributed a line of small kitchen appliances.

At a conference with Standard management, you learned of several factors which concern management and which will probably affect the type of acquisition you will recommend. Standard management is not interested in acquiring the Household division since that operation has never been very profitable and since it is believed that the manufacture and marketing of kitchen appliances is inconsistent with the image Standard has developed as a leader in the hardware industry. Although several potential purchasers of the Household division are anxiously waiting in the wings, Standard management is willing to acquire and retain the Household division if that should prove necessary to effect a tax-free reorganization.

Harry Farber, Standard's general counsel, has voiced some concern about acquiring the assets and liabilities of Monroe or entering into a merger with Monroe since both alternatives would expose Standard's assets to claims of plaintiffs in future product liability actions brought against Monroe for products previously sold. Monroe management has informed Standard that at least ninety percent of its shareholders will accede to the acquisition if the terms are fair, but that a small minority (from five to ten percent) will probably object regardless of how reasonable the terms are. Harry Farber has suggested that these persons either be bought out by Standard for cash, be allowed to stay on as a minority or be left to exercise their rights as dissenters under state law.

In the course of your conversations with Mr. Farber, it was mentioned that Mary Ford, one of Standard's directors, would like you to consider: (1) whether it might be possible to use cash or Standard bonds as well as Standard stock to effect the acquisition, thereby keeping dilution of control of Standard's present shareholders to a minimum; and (2) the possibility of Monroe using all or some of its $640,000 in liquid assets to achieve the desired result by redeeming out a number of its shareholders prior to the acquisition.

Farber also indicated that Standard intends to retain Monroe as a subsidiary or as an operating division but that it would like to be in a position which permits it to dispose easily of Monroe's operations if that appears to be necessary from a business standpoint or necessary to avoid any possible antitrust actions which might be brought.

The balance sheets, as of December 31 of the preceding year, for Standard and Monroe, who are both on a calendar year basis, are as follows:

Standard Tool Company, Inc.

(000 omitted)

Assets

	Basis & Book Value	Fair Market Value
Cash	$ 200	$ 200
CD's and US Bonds	3,000	3,100
Accounts Receivable	2,150	2,150
Inventory	3,650	4,550
Plant	8,000	12,000
Goodwill	-0-	2,000
	$17,000	$24,000

Liabilities

	Book Value	Fair Market Value
Current Liabilities	$ 1,450	$ 1,450
Mortgage on Plant	6,350	6,350
Paid-in Capital	500	500
Retained Earnings	8,700	15,700
	$17,000	$24,000

Monroe Power Tool, Inc.*

(000 omitted)

Assets

	Basis & Book Value	Fair Market Value
Cash	$ 40	$ 40
CD's and US Bonds	600	600
Accounts Receivable	1,300	1,300
Inventory	1,060	1,260
Plant	3,000	4,000
Goodwill	-0-	800
	$6,000	$8,000

Liabilities

	Book Value	Fair Market Value
Current Liabilities	$ 750	$ 750
Mortgage on Plant	3,250	3,250
Paid-in Capital	600	600
Retained Earnings	1,400	3,400
	$6,000	$8,000

*This balance sheet consolidates figures for all Monroe operations and includes its Household division.

The assets (exclusive of any allocation to paid-in capital and retained earnings) and liabilities of Monroe's Household division, stated separately, are as follows:

Household Division

(000 omitted)

Assets

	Basis & Book Value	Fair Market Value
Cash	$ 10	$ 10
Accounts Receivable	100	100
Inventory	500	640
Plant	250	750
Goodwill	-0-	100
	$860	$1,600

Liabilities

	Book Value
Current Liabilities	$500
Mortgage on Plant	300
	$800

a. Assuming that the Household division is not "spun off" to the Monroe shareholders as considered in Problem 78C, Mr. Farber, who is aware that no single type of reorganization will satisfy all of Standard's goals, would nonetheless like you to point out the various problems involved in any of the basic types of reorganizations as well as any of the tax-free triangular reorganizations.

b. Assume that you decided, when considering Problem 78C, that the way to handle the Household division was to "spin it off" prior to the acquisition of Monroe by Standard. Would that decision have any impact on your choice among the types of reorganizations which you considered in paragraph a above?

c. What would be your reaction if Mr. Farber informed you that although Standard wishes to control the new combined entity, if you deem it essential to have Monroe acquire Standard in order to realize Standard's business goals, you should consider structuring the acquisition in this manner?   Any such reversal of roles, of course, will leave Standard shareholders in control of the combined entity, and as a condition of the merger agreement, Standard management and directors also will become the dominant management and supervisory groups in the combined entity.

Note:

See Note on Interviewing and Client Counseling following Problem 1P at page 4.

PROBLEM 83C

Eugene Novak, the general counsel of National Forest Products, Inc. (National), a Delaware corporation, seeks your advice as to the tax consequences of a proposed acquisition of Southern Building Supplies, Inc. (Southern), a Georgia corporation. National runs a conventional timber operation consisting of the growing, cutting and processing of timber and the distribution of finished lumber on a nationwide basis. Southern's business is smaller than, but similar to, National's with the exception that it also produces finished concrete products and only operates in a six-state area. National wishes to acquire Southern to increase its overall share of the national market, thereby realizing greater economies of scale. Since National's presence in Southern's existing market area is quite limited, the acquisition also would give National a foothold in an important expanding market. National only produces and distributes wood building materials and is not interested in entering the concrete building materials business. If possible, National would prefer not to acquire Southern's concrete products operation.

Southern has two classes of stock outstanding, no par common stock and non-participating preferred stock which is entitled to a cumulative annual dividend of $6.00 per share and a liquidating preference of $60.00 per share plus accrued and unpaid dividends. The common stock is voting common stock. The preferred stock is non-voting stock unless the preferred dividends are in arrears by more than one year. If the preferred dividends are in arrears, the preferred stock is entitled to vote for one member of the board of directors until the dividends on the preferred stock are current. There are 1,500,000 shares of Southern common and 500,000 shares of Southern preferred outstanding. The preferred is held entirely by Exeter Life Insurance Co. The common stock is owned by various entities and individuals.

At present, National directly owns ten percent of the common stock of Southern, having acquired it by purchase over the last six months. Through its wholly owned subsidiary, Timber Supply, Inc. (Timber), National also indirectly owns another five percent of Southern's common stock. This stock was purchased by Timber almost fourteen months ago when National first contemplated acquiring Southern. Two percent of the common stock of Southern is owned by National's president, Hiram Porter, who purchased it over two years ago. Forty percent of the common stock of Southern is held by various qualified pension funds. Ten percent of the common stock is held by various bank trust departments with one-half of those holdings being held by Mutual Bank and Trust Co., which is National's principal commercial banker. The balance of the Southern common stock is held by individual members of the general public and by mutual funds.

National wishes to acquire Southern either by merger, by acquisition of control of Southern's common stock or by acquisition of Southern's assets and liabilities less, if possible, the assets and liabilities of its concrete products division. National asks you to consider using cash, National stock or debt to effect the acquisition. Mr. Novak has noted that if control of Southern's common stock is sought, National would like to avoid acquiring Southern's preferred stock.

The balance sheet, as of December 31 of the preceding year, of Southern, which is a calendar year and accrual method taxpayer, is as follows:

Southern Building Supplies, Inc.		
(000 omitted)		
Assets		
	Basis & Book Value	Fair Market Value
Cash	$ 3,000	$ 3,000
CD's and US Notes	9,000	9,000
Acct. Rec.	7,800	7,800
Processed Inventory (LIFO)	7,200	11,700
Land	12,000	60,000
Standing Timber	9,000	30,000
Plant	4,500	9,000
Equipment	4,500	6,000
Goodwill	-0-	13,500
	$57,000	$150,000

Liabilities		
	Book Value	Fair Market Value
Acct. Payable	$ 2,100	$ 2,100
Mortgage on Plant	6,000	6,000
Inventory Financing	6,000	6,000
Loan on Equipment	3,900	3,900
Capital		
Paid-in Capital	4,500	4,500
Retained Earnings	34,500	127,500
	$57,000	$150,000

(handwritten: 132 million)

The assets and liabilities (exclusive of any allocation to paid-in capital and retained earnings) of Southern's concrete products division which are included in the above balance sheet are as follows:

Concrete Products Division
(000 omitted)
Assets

	Basis & Book Value	Fair Market Value
Cash	$ 300	$ 300
CD's	3,000	3,000
Acct. Rec.	3,900	3,900
Inventory	3,000	4,500
Land	3,000	12,000
Plant	3,000	6,000
Equipment	1,200	1,800
Goodwill	-0-	6,000
	$17,400	$37,500

Liabilities

	Book Value
Acct. Payable	$ 900
Mortgage on Plant	3,300
Inventory Financing	2,400
Loan on Equipment	900
	$7,500

Please advise National as to the advisability and possibility of structuring its acquisition of Southern as a tax-free, or as a taxable, transaction. Please also advise the corporation of the possible tax consequences to Southern and its shareholders of the proposed means of acquisition of Southern by National.

PROBLEM 84C

When you checked your e-mail this morning, you discovered the following message which was forwarded to you by Raphael Gronder, the partner in charge of the tax department in the firm with which you are associated. The note from Mr. Gronder which was pasted to the message said "Please take a look at this message and let me know of any problems or concerns." Jim Mavrotis, the person who sent the message to Mr. Gronder, is the CEO of Biostat, Inc. (Biostat), a relatively new client of the law firm. Biostat, whose stock is listed on the NASDAQ, was founded eight years ago and quickly became one of the leading companies providing biostatistical services to major pharmaceutical companies.

DATE:	12 Nov. Year* 2:32:44 - 0800 (PST)
FROM:	J. Mavrotis <jmavrotis@email.pkd.msi>
TO:	R. Gronder <rgronder@email.pkd.msi>
SUBJECT:	ASA Merger

Over the course of the last few weeks we have carried on secret merger talks with the management of Acme Statistical Analysis, Inc. (ASA). ASA is owned by three of the founding officers and directors of ASA and a wealthy private investor, Ester Rashad, who owns 70 percent of the ASA common stock. ASA has developed several software programs for biostatistical analysis which are user friendly and far more sophisticated than anything now available. Mrs. Rashad, who seems to call the shots on any sale of ASA, is insistent on the acquisition being conducted as a tax free reorganization at least with respect to her investment in ASA. The three other shareholders in ASA each own 10 percent of the ASA stock and are willing to receive Biostat stock in exchange for their stock.

* See explanatory footnote in Introduction, Page vii, note 1.

We are willing to acquire all the ASA stock for one million shares of Biostat stock which closed last night at $20.00 per share. The problem is that the ASA shareholders believe their company to be worth considerably more based not on current earnings but on the potential for its new software. They believe that $20 million reflects the value of the company to us if we simply incorporate it into our operations, but if we were also to license their software for use by others, they believe that we could realize after tax profits over the course of the next ten years which would justify a value of $25 million for ASA. Because of what we believe to be the limited applicability of the software for use by others, we do not share that view.

I would like to know whether it is possible for us to acquire ASA for 1 million shares of Biostat stock and, in addition, to agree to pay to its shareholders either in cash or in stock of Biostat something like fifty percent of the net after tax profits derived from licensing ASA's software over the next ten years. I personally believe that we will pay them very little, if anything, in addition to the 1 million shares of Biostat under such an arrangement but I am willing to agree to such an arrangement to clinch the deal.

While we are on the subject of contingent payments, I would like you to consider an additional issue. ASA carries on its books $300,000 in receivables; $200,000 of this is from a company, Norwich Health Products, Inc., which is in bankruptcy. We quite honestly believe that little, if any, of this $200,000 will ever be collected and would be willing to overlook this fact were we able to purchase ASA for $20 million (1 million shares of Biostat). If, however, we are going to set this acquisition up as some sort of contingent deal, the thought has occurred to me that, at least as part of a negotiating strategy, we somehow work this into the transaction.

Please excuse me if any of this seems a bit disjointed but I banged it out to you at 2:30 am shortly after our discussions with the ASA representatives hit a snag over the valuation issue. I will call you sometime this afternoon after I have gotten some sleep and you have had an opportunity to discuss this with some of your people.

Best regards,

Jimmie

PROBLEM 85C

Norman Meyers, the general counsel of Chicago Coal and Oil Company, an Illinois corporation (Chicago), which sells and distributes fossil fuels in the Chicago metropolitan area, would like your advice with respect to a proposed recapitalization project which Chicago is considering. Chicago's capital stock consists of 1,000,000 shares of authorized (400,000 outstanding) no par common, which has recently been trading on the American Stock Exchange at about $45 per share and normally pays an annual per share dividend of $5.00. Chicago's indebtedness consists of: (1) $4,000,000 face amount 6% subordinated debentures due Year*+20 which were issued for their face amount; and (2) $3,000,000 in loans from various banks. Robert Foster, Chicago's principal shareholder, is anxious to consolidate his control over Chicago by having Chicago's recapitalization plan include the exchange by some existing Chicago shareholders of their stock for new issues of Chicago: (1) nonvoting redeemable preferred stock; (2) bonds; or (3) nonvoting common stock (class B). Chicago management is interested in this proposal since it will provide an opportunity for neutralizing some troublesome minority shareholders.

Pursuant to the plan, assenting shareholders would be given the opportunity to surrender twenty shares of Chicago common stock in exchange for one $1,000 face amount subordinated debenture of Chicago bearing interest at two percentage points over the prime rate and due Year+20. If this offer does not result in surrender of at least 50,000 shares of Chicago common stock, Chicago management intends to consider offering the shareholders who did not surrender their stock the opportunity to obtain either newly created nonvoting preferred or class B common stock. The holders of Chicago common stock would be allowed to obtain four shares of new class B common stock for every three shares of voting common stock surrendered. With the exception of voting privileges, the class B common stock would be entitled to all rights and privileges of the existing common stock. Holders of common stock who did not wish to exchange their stock for class B common stock would be entitled to surrender their stock on a one for one basis for newly issued nonvoting preferred stock of Chicago. The preferred stock would be entitled to an annual dividend of $8.00 and would be redeemable in Year+14 at $50 per share.

* See explanatory footnote in Introduction, page vii, note 1.

Due to the need to improve its debt-equity ratio in order to meet the demands of creditors and to prevent the newly issued bonds from increasing Chicago's indebtedness beyond what management deems to be a prudent range, Chicago management is considering adopting another recapitalization plan. Under this plan some of Chicago's existing debenture holders would exchange their debentures for any one of the three new securities mentioned above. Due to a rise in interest rates, the outstanding $1,000 face value 6% subordinated debentures are currently trading for $680. By offering to issue seven new debentures having an interest rate equal to two percentage points in excess of the prime rate at the time of issuance and a face amount of $1,000 (it is anticipated that the debentures would trade for their face amount) in exchange for ten 6% subordinated debentures, Chicago could substantially reduce its balance sheet liabilities.

Mr. Meyers has pointed out that a more dramatic reduction in liabilities might be produced by offering existing debenture holders an opportunity to exchange their debentures for the new class B common or the new preferred at attractive ratios. He suggests, for example, if one assumes that the new class B common stock will be worth $40 per share, many holders of existing debt would be responsive to an offer to issue 18 shares of the new class B common stock in exchange for each old $1,000 bond bearing interest at 6%. Since 18 shares of the new class B common stock would be worth $720 or $40 greater than the fair market value of the bonds, it appears that a substantial number of the holders of the debt would respond favorably to such an offer.

Advise Chicago management of the tax consequences of the various exchanges which are being considered under its recapitalization plan.

PROBLEM 86C

You are an attorney assigned to the Reorganization Division of the Internal Revenue Service. The following ruling request has been referred to you for action. Prepare yourself to determine whether the rulings requested should be issued and whether you should call the taxpayer for further information or clarification prior to issuing, or denying issuance of, the requested rulings.

Morris, Beddow & Simons
101 Liberty Plaza
New York, N.Y. 10019

May 8, Year*

<u>Merger of Taft Properties, Inc. with Monument Properties, Inc.</u>

Dear Sir:

On behalf of Taft Properties, Inc., a Pennsylvania corporation (Taft), we hereby respectfully request rulings, hereafter set forth, with respect to the Federal income tax consequences of a proposed merger of Taft with Monument Properties, Inc., a Delaware corporation (Monument), pursuant to an Agreement and Plan of Reorganization dated April 29, Year between Monument, Taft and the shareholders of Taft (the Agreement), a copy of which is enclosed as Exhibit A.

The proposed transaction is scheduled to close on July 31, Year and is conditioned on, among other things, obtaining from the Internal Revenue Service the rulings requested herein.

<u>The Parties to the Proposed Reorganization</u>

1. <u>Taft</u>

The address of Taft's principal office is 301 East 66th Street, New York, N.Y. 10021. It is a calendar year taxpayer which files its Federal income tax returns with the Internal Revenue Service Center, Andover, Massachusetts, and its employer identification number is 28-234197. Taft's sole business consists of the ownership, rental and management of two office buildings located in New York City.

The authorized stock of Taft consists of 1,000 shares of voting common stock, par value $1 per share, all of which were issued and outstanding on May 7, Year. The stock is held by thirty-two individuals, with no one holder owning more than five percent of the stock. A copy of Taft's most recent balance sheet and financial statement is attached as Exhibit B.

2. <u>Monument</u>

The principal office of Monument is located at 301 East 66th St., New York, N.Y. 10021 . Monument was incorporated on April 2, Year for the purpose of carrying out the transaction described below. It will prepare its

---

* See explanatory footnote in Introduction, page vii, note 1.

tax returns on the basis of the calendar year, and they will be filed with the Internal Revenue Service Center in Andover, Massachusetts. It has filed an application for an employer identification number and has been issued temporary number TY-14784. Monument's sole asset consists of $10. After the proposed reorganization has been carried out, its business will consist of the ownership, rental and management of the two office buildings presently held by Taft.

The authorized stock of Monument consists of 1,000 shares of voting common stock, par value $1 per share, of which one share was issued and outstanding on May 7, Year.

The Proposed Reorganization

Taft is a Pennsylvania corporation. The laws of that state do not permit formation of a so-called "close corporation." The laws of the state of Delaware provide for the formation of a "close corporation." The shareholders and management of Taft are of the opinion that close corporation status would be advantageous since it would simplify and improve: (1) existing management of the corporation; and (2) shareholder-management relations. Among other things it allows for shareholder agreements restricting discretion of directors and provides for participation by shareholders in the management of the corporation. *See* 8 Del. Code Ann. section 350 et. seq. This is the business reason for the proposed reorganization.

Under Delaware law, a close corporation can have no more than 30 shareholders. *See* 8 Del. Code Ann. section 342(a)(1). It is proposed that the transformation of Taft into a close corporation take place by merging it with Monument under Delaware law, with Monument emerging as the surviving entity. To comply with the 30 shareholder requirement, it is proposed that, immediately prior to the merger, Taft redeem for cash the stock owned by two of the Taft shareholders, Morris D. Klein and Palmer L. Thayer, who own an aggregate of 10 percent of the stock of Taft and who are unrelated to the other Taft shareholders. Pursuant to the Agreement, the amount of cash to be given to these individuals will be equal to ten percent of the net worth of the corporation. The single outstanding share of Monument is owned by its incorporator, the undersigned. Pursuant to the Agreement, on the merger of Taft into Monument, this share will be canceled. Each of the remaining thirty Taft shareholders, under the Agreement, will be issued one share of Monument stock in exchange for each share of Taft stock. On the merger, Taft will cease to exist, and all its assets will be transferred to Monument. The name change effected by the merger was necessary since there presently exists a Delaware corporation called Taft Properties, Inc.

None of the Taft shareholders, who shall be issued Monument stock, have any present intent to sell or otherwise dispose of the Monument stock.

Requested Ruling

In connection with the foregoing, rulings are respectfully requested to the following effect:

1) Under Section 302 of the Internal Revenue Code of 1986, as amended (the Code), the proposed redemption of the Taft stock held by Messrs. Klein and Thayer will be considered a distribution in full payment in exchange for their surrendered stock.

2) The proposed merger of Taft into Monument will be considered a reorganization within the meaning of Section 368(a)(1)(F) of the Code and Taft and Monument will each qualify as a party to a reorganization under Section 368(b).

3) Under Section 1032(a) of the Code, no gain or loss will be recognized by Monument on receipt of the Taft assets in exchange for Monument stock.

4) Under Sections 361(a) and 357(a) of the Code, no gain or loss will be recognized to Taft on the transfer of its assets to Monument.

5) Under Section 362(b) of the Code, the basis of the assets of Taft acquired by Monument will be the same as the basis of those assets in the hands of Taft immediately before the merger.

6) Under Section 1223(2) of the Code, the holding period of the assets of Taft acquired by Monument will include the period during which those assets were held by Taft.

7) Under Section 354(a)(1) of the Code, no gain or loss will be recognized by the shareholders of Taft on the exchange of their shares of Taft for shares of Monument.

8) Under Section 358(a)(1) of the Code, the basis of the Monument stock acquired by the former shareholders of Taft will be the same as the basis of the Taft stock surrendered in the exchange, and under Section 1223(1), the holding period of those shares will include the holding period of the Taft stock surrendered therefor, provided that such Taft stock was held as a capital asset on the date of the exchange.

To the best knowledge of the taxpayer, the issues raised by this application for ruling are not now pending before any field office of the Internal Revenue Service in connection with an active examination or audit of a tax return already filed, nor are such issues being considered by a branch office of the Appellate Division. Enclosed is a power of attorney and declaration authorizing the undersigned and others to represent the taxpayer in connection with this application.

Under penalties of perjury, I declare that I have examined this request, including accompanying documents, and to the best of my knowledge and belief, the facts presented in support of the requested rulings are true, correct and complete.

If you have any doubt as to the issuance of the requested rulings, the privilege of a conference is requested. If any additional information is needed, please do not hesitate to call the undersigned collect at (212) 731-1400.

Very truly yours,

Paula R. Martinkofsky

Paula R. Martinkofsky

Commissioner of Internal Revenue
Washington, D.C. 20224
Attention of Income Tax Division
Attention of Reorganization Division

Note:

See Note on Ruling Requests following Problem 24P at page 88.

b. Treatment of Parties to a Reorganization

PROBLEM 87C

As a new member of the Reorganization Branch of the Income Tax Division of the Treasury, the following ruling request has been referred to you for disposition. Consider whether you should issue the requested rulings or should first request more information or clarification with respect to certain matters.

Friday, Riordan & Ford   Martin, Barton & Fish
107 Professional Building   1409 U.S. Steel Building
Philadelphia, PA   19104   Pittsburgh, PA   15220

                                                January 4, Year*

Acquisition by Vickers Publishing Co., Inc. of the
Stock of Erie School Products, Inc.

Dear Madam or Sir:

On behalf of Vickers Publishing Co., Inc., a Delaware corporation (Vickers), and Erie School Products, Inc., a Pennsylvania corporation (Erie), we hereby respectfully request rulings, hereinafter set forth, with respect to the Federal income tax consequences of a proposed acquisition by Vickers of the stock of Erie solely in exchange for part of Vickers' voting stock pursuant to an Agreement and Plan of Reorganization dated as of December 22, Year-1 between Vickers and the shareholders of Erie (the Agreement), a copy of which is enclosed as Exhibit A.

The proposed transaction is scheduled to close on April 1, Year, or two days after the effective date of registration with the Securities and Exchange Commission of the Vickers Common Stock to be issued to exchanging Erie Shareholders, whichever is later (but not after August 31, Year), and is conditioned on, among other things, obtaining from the Internal Revenue Service the rulings requested herein.

The Parties to the Proposed Reorganization

1. Vickers

The address of Vickers' principal office is 714 Garrison Avenue, Princeton, N.J. 08540. It files its Federal income tax returns, prepared on the basis of a fiscal year ending April 31, with the Internal Revenue Service Center, Andover, Massachusetts, and its employer identification number is 13-1427415. Vickers and its subsidiaries are engaged in the publication and supply of primary and secondary school instructional materials and the production and distribution of audiovisual educational materials and equipment.

The authorized stock of Vickers consists of 3,000,000 shares of voting common stock, par value $1 per share, of which 1,809,710 shares were issued and outstanding on November 30, Year-1, and 14,150 were reserved for issuance under an employee stock purchase plan.   The

---

* See explanatory footnote in Introduction, page vii, note 1.

common stock is publicly held by approximately 1,800 shareholders of record and is traded on the American Stock Exchange. The Vickers stock is entitled to one vote per share. Enclosed herewith as Exhibit B is a copy of the most recent Annual Report of Vickers.

2. Erie

The principal office of Erie is located at 14 River Road, Pittsburgh, Pennsylvania 15219. It files its Federal income tax returns, prepared on the basis of a fiscal year ending November 30, with the Internal Revenue Service Center, Andover, Massachusetts, and its employer identification number is 08-1422935. Erie is engaged in the manufacture and distribution of school office equipment and playground equipment.

The authorized stock of Erie consists of 1,000,000 shares of common stock, par value $1 per share, of which 450,000 shares were issued and outstanding on November 30, Year-1. At November 30, Year-1 there were outstanding in the hands of two of Erie's shareholders warrants to purchase 1,000 shares of Erie stock at $24 per share. The Erie stock is entitled to one vote per share. The outstanding stock of Erie is presently held by a total of 62 shareholders of record.

A copy of the most recent consolidated balance sheet of Erie is enclosed as Exhibit C.

Business Reasons for the Proposed Reorganization

The principal business of Vickers and its subsidiaries is the publication and distribution of instructional materials and the production and distribution of educational materials and equipment. In recent years, Vickers has been expanding its activities in the educational market, which management believes has a strong growth potential. The acquisition of Erie will represent a further step in this direction. Erie is an established and well-respected business operating in sectors of the educational market in which Vickers is not presently very active. After the proposed reorganization, the combined enterprise will be able to offer a more complete line of products and services in this market, and it is believed that the combination of the experience and resources of Vickers and Erie will lead to more effective development of the businesses and properties of the two companies.

Transactions To Be Effected Prior to the Proposed Reorganization

The proposed reorganization will not become effective until Vickers, at its own expense, has secured the registration with the Securities and Exchange Commission of its common stock to be issued to the exchanging Erie shareholders. Vickers, at its own expense, will also apply to the New York Stock Exchange for the listing of its stock and will endeavor to qualify the stock to be issued for offering and sale under state blue sky laws.

Prior to the effective date of the reorganization, Erie will declare a dividend of $1.00 per share on its outstanding stock (an aggregate amount of $450,000), payable on March 31, Year. Such dividend will represent the normal annual dividend of $.40 per share and a special dividend of $.60 per share. On Erie's books, retained earnings will be reduced by the entire amount of the dividend. No other dividends will be paid on Erie stock prior to the reorganization.

Prior to the effective date of the reorganization, Erie will acquire, for $20,000 in cash, the warrants to purchase Erie stock held by two of its shareholders.

Erie plans to enter into long term employment contracts with two of Erie's employees who are also principal shareholders of Erie. The compensation to be paid to these individuals pursuant to such contracts is not substantially greater than the compensation they could expect to receive if Erie were to continue to operate as an independent entity.

The Proposed Reorganization

Pursuant to the Agreement, the Erie shareholders will deliver their Erie stock to Vickers on the closing date and will receive in exchange therefor 1.25 shares of Vickers stock for each share of Erie stock surrendered.

The Agreement provides that fractional shares of Vickers common stock will not be issued to Erie shareholders and that any party entitled to receive a fractional share will, in lieu thereof, receive from Vickers cash equal to the value at the closing date of the fractional share of Vickers stock which the Erie shareholder otherwise would have received.

Vickers and the shareholders of Erie will each bear their own expenses incurred in connection with the acquisition, including any counsel fees, and none of such expenses shall be paid by or charged to Erie. So far as is known by the management of Vickers and Erie, persons who will own at least 50% in value of the minimum amount of Vickers stock to be received by the Erie shareholders have no concerted plan to sell, distribute or otherwise dispose of such stock.

Vickers has no present intention of selling or otherwise disposing of the Erie stock to be acquired pursuant to the proposed reorganization, or of liquidating Erie, and intends to allow Erie, after the acquisition, to carry on its business as a subsidiary of Vickers. Vickers does not presently own any stock of Erie, and Erie does not own any stock of Vickers.

Pursuant to the agreement, subsequent to the consummation of the proposed acquisition, Vickers will assist Erie in obtaining, through Vickers' normal financing channels, one or more bank lines of credit in the aggregate principal amount of $2,000,000, which will be used by Erie for working capital and capital expenditure purposes. In the event that Erie is unable to obtain such line or lines of credit, Vickers will loan to Erie, at a rate of interest of one-half of 1% over the prime commercial rate, a principal amount sufficient to give Erie an aggregate line of credit equal to $2,000,000.

Requested Rulings

In connection with the foregoing, we respectfully request rulings to the following effect:

1. The proposed acquisition by Vickers of Erie stock will constitute a reorganization within the meaning of Section 368(a)(1)(B) of the Internal Revenue Code of 1986, as amended (the Code), and Vickers and Erie will each qualify as a party to a reorganization under Section 368(b).

2. Under Section 1032(a) of the Code, no gain or loss will be recognized by Vickers on the issuance of its stock in exchange for Erie stock.

3. Under Section 358(a) of the Code, the basis of Erie stock acquired by Vickers in exchange for Vickers stock will be the same as the basis of the Vickers stock exchanged therefor plus any amounts paid for fractional shares.

4. Under Section 1223(2) of the Code, the holding period of Vickers for the Erie stock acquired by it will include the periods for which such stock was held by the exchanging Erie shareholders.

5. Under Section 354(a)(1) of the Code, no gain or loss will be recognized by the shareholders of Erie upon the exchange of their Erie stock solely for Vickers stock.

6. Under Section 358(a) of the Code, the basis of the Vickers stock received by the shareholders of Erie in exchange for their Erie stock will be the same as the basis of their shares of Erie stock exchanged therefor.

7. Under Section 1223(1) of the Code, the holding period of the Vickers stock received by the Erie shareholders will include the holding period of the Erie stock surrendered therefor, provided that such Erie stock is held as a capital asset on the date of the exchange.

8. Under Section 1223(1) of the Code, the holding period of the Erie stock received by Vickers will include the period for which Vickers has held in its treasury the Vickers stock exchanged for the Erie stock.

The issues raised by this application for a ruling are not now pending before any field office of the Internal Revenue Service. Enclosed are powers of attorney authorizing the undersigned and others to represent the respective parties in connection with this application.

Under penalties of perjury, we declare that we have examined this request, including accompanying documents, and to the best of our knowledge and belief, the facts presented in support of the requested rulings are true, correct and complete.

If there should be any doubt as to the issuance of any of the rulings requested herein, the privilege of a conference is requested. If any additional information is needed, please telephone collect the undersigned, Peter L. Roberts at (215) 479-7900, as to questions concerning Vickers, and the undersigned, Margaret A. Skorpac, as to questions concerning Erie, at (412) 641-1422.

Very truly yours,

Peter L. Roberts
Peter L. Roberts

Margaret A. Skorpac
Margaret A. Skorpac

Commissioner of Internal Revenue,
Washington, D.C. 20224
Attention of Income Tax Division
    Reorganization Branch,
    T:PS:T.
Encls.

Note:

See Note on Ruling Requests following Problem 24P at page 88.

PROBLEM 88C

Processor Corporation (Processor) is a client of the firm with which you are associated. Processor makes computer hardware which, as the name implies, processes information fed into a computer. Processor has done very well over the years. Its processing hardware is regarded as the "top-of-the-line" in the industry. The hardware is well covered by patents issued to Processor. Processor has contracts with a number of major computer manufacturers to supply the manufacturers with the processing hardware. While the patents for the processing hardware are carried on Processor's books at cost, its management estimates that the patents' value is somewhere between ten and sixteen million dollars. Since Processor has been very successful, it has built up liquid assets such as certificates of deposit in amounts totaling $6 million.

Recently, a publicly held corporation, IBC Corporation (IBC), which manufactures a line of computer hardware, proposed that it acquire Processor. In the acquisition, the shareholders of Processor will receive four shares of IBC, which have been registered with the Securities and Exchange Commission and listed on the New York Stock Exchange, for every one share of Processor owned by a shareholder. This four to one exchange places a value on Processor's patents of about $10 million. IBC, however, has agreed to value the patents using the receipts from the sales of processing hardware by Processor in each year of the six years following the closing of the acquisition. If the value of the patents determined over the six-year period exceeds $10 million, each former shareholder of Processor will receive an additional share of IBC with respect to each 24 shares of Processor formerly held for every $1,000,000 by which the value of the patents during the six years exceeds $10 million.

Processor Corporation has outstanding four classes of stock, Class A voting common, Class B non-voting common, Series A preferred stock and Series B preferred stock. It also has outstanding various options (issued under employee stock purchase and incentive stock option plans) and warrants for the purchase of its Class A common stock. Prior to the closing of the acquisition, all stock options and warrants issued by Processor which can be exercised, will be exercised. IBC will assume those options and warrants which cannot be exercised prior to the closing. In addition, prior to the closing, the Class B common stock, the Series A preferred and the Series B preferred stock of Processor will be converted into Class A common voting stock of Processor.

The management of Processor anticipates that 10 to 15 percent of its shareholders will dissent from the transaction, and their shares will have to be acquired by Processor for cash. This should not present a serious economic problem since Processor, as mentioned above, has substantial liquid assets. IBC will not issue fractional shares to the shareholders of Processor, but instead will pay cash to the shareholders of Processor in lieu of fractional shares.

Finally, IBC will put in escrow, with an independent escrow agent, enough shares of its common stock so that the escrow agent can distribute to the shareholders of Processor the additional shares of IBC stock to which they will be entitled if the value of the patents exceeds $10 million. The Processor shareholders' rights to the escrowed stock will be assignable only to members of a shareholder's immediate family and on the death of a shareholder.

The merger agreement provides that the firm with which you are associated will render an opinion to Processor. The opinion must thoroughly deal with the income tax effects of the transaction between Processor and IBC on Processor and the shareholders of Processor. The firm requires that any legal opinion given by the firm be thoroughly reviewed by at least two attorneys. The firm's opinion with respect to this matter has been prepared by Jennifer Goldsmith, a senior associate in the firm. The chair of the tax department of the firm has asked that you review the opinion and has delivered to you the opinion as set out below. Consider whether you should approve the opinion or suggest that changes be made to it before it is issued.

Halle, Edwards, Blaine & Vargas
1400 Liberty Bank Building
372 Apricot
Santa Monica, California   90401

December 6, Year*

Processor Corporation
6352 Interlocken Drive
Santa Monica, CA   90403

Ladies and Gentlemen:

This opinion is being delivered to you in connection with the Agreement and Plan of Merger, dated as of August 13, Year (the "Agreement"), among IBC Corporation ("Acquiror"), IBC Merger Corporation, a wholly-owned subsidiary of Acquiror ("Sub"), and Processor Corporation ("Target"). Sub will merge with and into Target (the "Merger") pursuant to the Agreement.

Except as otherwise provided, capitalized terms not defined herein have the meanings set forth in the Agreement. All section references, unless otherwise indicated, are to the Internal Revenue Code of 1986, as amended (the "Code").

We have acted as counsel to Target in connection with the Merger. As such and for the purpose of rendering this opinion, we have examined originals, certified copies or copies otherwise identified to our satisfaction as being true copies of the originals of the following documents (including all exhibits and schedules attached thereto):

(A)   the Agreement;

(B)   Certificates from Acquiror and Target containing certain representations of Acquiror, Sub and Target (the "Certificates of Representation");

(C)   Affiliate Agreements from each of Target's affiliates (the "Affiliate Agreements");

(D)   Investment Letters from certain Target shareholders ("Investment Letters");

(E)   the Consent Solicitation/Prospectus (the "Consent Solicitation/ Prospectus") included within Amendment No. 1 to the Registration

* See explanatory footnote in Introduction, page vii, note 1.

Statement on Form S-4 (33-63993) filed on September 18, Year with the Securities and Exchange Commission;

(F)   An Escrow Agreement among Acquiror, Target and California National Bank (the "Escrow Agreement");

(G)   such other instruments and documents related to the formation, organization and operation of Acquiror, Sub and Target and related to the consummation of the Merger and the transactions contemplated thereby as we have deemed necessary or appropriate.

In connection with rendering this opinion, we have assumed (without any independent investigation or review thereof) that:

1.   Original documents (including signatures) are authentic, documents submitted to us as copies conform to the original documents, and there is (or will be prior to the Closing) due execution and delivery of all documents where due execution and delivery are a prerequisite to the effectiveness thereof;

2.   All representations, warranties and statements made or agreed to by Acquiror, Sub and Target, their managements, employees, officers, directors and shareholders in connection with the Merger, including but not limited to those set forth in the Agreement (including the exhibits), the Certificates of Representation, the Investment Letters, the Affiliate Agreements, the Consent/Solicitation Prospectus and the Escrow Agreement, will be true and accurate at all relevant times, and all covenants contained in such agreements will be performed without waiver or breach of any material provision thereof; and

3.   The Merger will be effective under the applicable state law.

Based on our examination of the foregoing items and subject to the limitations, qualifications, assumptions and caveats set forth herein, we are of the opinion that, if the Merger is consummated in accordance with the provisions of the Agreement and the exhibits thereto, for federal income tax purposes:

The Merger will constitute a reorganization within the meaning of Section 368(a) of the Code and accordingly: (1) no gain or loss will be recognized by Acquiror, Sub or Target as a result of the Merger; (2) no gain or loss will be recognized by the shareholders of Target upon the exchange of their Target Class A common stock solely for shares of Acquiror common stock pursuant to the Merger; (3) the aggregate tax basis of the shares of Acquiror common stock received in exchange for Target Class A common stock pursuant to the Merger (including fractional shares of Acquiror common stock for which cash is received) will be the same as the aggregate value of the Target Class A common stock exchanged therefor; (4) the holding period for the Acquiror common stock received in exchange for Target Class A common stock pursuant to the Merger will include the holding period of the Target Class A common stock exchanged therefor, provided such Target Class A common stock was held as a capital asset at the time of the Closing; and (5) a Target shareholder who receives cash proceeds in lieu of a fractional share of Acquiror common stock or a holder which exercises its appraisal rights will recognize gain or loss equal to the difference, if any, between such shareholder's tax basis allocated to the fractional share or to a dissenting shareholder's Target Class A common stock, as the case may be, and the amount of cash received, and such gain or loss will constitute capital gain or loss.

The foregoing consequences also will apply to holders of Target Class A common stock who receive such stock upon the exchange of their Target Series A preferred stock, Series B preferred stock or Class B common stock (collectively, the "Exchanged Stock"). In the exchange, (1) no gain or loss will be recognized to the shareholders of Target upon the exchange of their Exchanged Stock solely for Target Class A common stock, (2) the aggregate tax basis of the shares of Target Class A common stock received will be the same as the value of the Target Exchanged Stock exchanged therefor, and (3) the holding period for the Target Class A common stock received in exchange for the Exchanged Stock will include the holding period of the Exchanged Stock exchanged therefor, provided such Exchanged Stock was held as a capital asset as of the time of the exchange.

This opinion does not address the various state, local or foreign tax consequences that may result from the Merger. In addition, no opinion is expressed as to any federal income tax consequences of the Merger except as specifically set forth herein and this opinion may not be relied upon except with respect to the consequences specifically discussed herein.

This opinion only represents our best judgment as to the federal income tax treatment of the Merger and is not binding on the Internal Revenue Service or the courts. The conclusions are based on the Code, existing judicial decisions, administrative regulations and published rulings. No assurance can be given that future legislative, judicial or administrative changes will not adversely affect the accuracy of the conclusions stated herein. Nevertheless, by rendering this opinion, we undertake no responsibility to advise you of any new developments in the application or interpretation of the federal income tax laws.

This opinion is being delivered in connection with the Agreement. It is intended for the benefit of Target and its shareholders. It may not be relied upon or utilized for any other purpose or by any other person or entity and may not be made available to any other person or entity without our prior written consent.

Very truly yours,

Jennifer Goldsmith

Jennifer Goldsmith for
Halle, Edwards, Blaine & Vargas

Certificate of Representations

December 1, Year*

Halle, Edwards, Blaine & Vargas
1400 Liberty Bank Building
372 Apricot
Santa Monica, California   90401

Dear Counsel:

    The undersigned officer of Processor Corporation ("Target"), in connection with the opinion to be delivered by you pursuant to Section 9.3(d) of the Agreement and Plan of Merger dated as of August 13, Year (the "Merger Agreement"), among IBC Corporation ("Acquiror"), IBC Merger Corporation, a wholly-owned subsidiary of Acquiror ("Sub"), and Target , and recognizing that you will rely on this certificate in delivering your opinion, hereby certifies that, to the best knowledge and belief of the undersigned, after due inquiry and investigation, the facts relating to the contemplated merger (the "Merger") of Sub with and into Target pursuant to the Merger Agreement, which facts are described in the Consent Solicitation/Prospectus which is included in Amendment No. 1 to the Registration Statement on Form S-4 (33-63993) (the "Registration Statement") filed on September 18, Year with the Securities and Exchange Commission under the Securities Act of 1933, as amended, and the certifications stated below, insofar as such facts and certifications pertain to Target, are, true, correct and complete in all material respects and, insofar, as such facts and certifications pertain to Acquiror and Sub, the undersigned has reason to believe that such facts and certifications are true, correct and complete in all material respects.

---

* See explanatory footnote in Introduction, page vii, note 1.

1.   The Conversion of the Class B common stock and the Series A and B preferred stock of Target into the Class A common stock of Target ("Conversion"), and the Merger will be consummated in compliance with the material terms of the Agreement and the Registration Statement, and none of the material terms and conditions therein have been waived or modified in any respect.

2.   The fair market value of the Target Class A common stock received by each Target shareholder pursuant to the Conversion will be approximately equal to the fair market value of the Target Class B common stock, Series A preferred stock and Series B preferred stock plus accrued and unpaid dividends thereon surrendered in exchange therefor.

3.   None of the Target Class A common stock received by any shareholder of Target pursuant to the Conversion will be consideration for services rendered or with respect to accrued interest and all of such shares shall be issued solely in exchange for shares plus accrued and unpaid dividends of Target previously held by such shareholder.

4.   There is no plan or intention by the shareholders of Target who own 5 percent or more of the Target stock, and to the best of the knowledge of the management of Target, there is no plan or intention on the part of the remaining shareholders of Target to sell, exchange or otherwise dispose of any of the shares of Target Class A common stock received pursuant to the Conversion except pursuant to the Merger.

5.   No shareholder-employee of Target has exercised an incentive stock option through the transfer of statutory option stock (as defined in Section 424(c)(3)(B) of the Code).

6.   The fair market value of the Acquiror common stock and other consideration received by each Target shareholder in the Merger will be approximately equal to the fair market value of the Target Class A common stock surrendered in the exchange.

7.   There is no plan or intention by the shareholders of Target who own 5 percent or more of the Target stock, and to the best of the knowledge of the management of Target, there is no plan or intention on the part of the remaining shareholders of Target to sell, exchange or otherwise dispose of a number of shares of Acquiror common stock received in the transaction that would reduce the Target shareholders' ownership of Acquiror common stock to a number of shares having a value, as of the date of the transaction, of less than 40 percent of the value of all of the formerly outstanding stock of Target as of the same date. For purposes of this representation, shares of Target Class A common stock exchanged for cash or other property, surrendered by dissenters, exchanged for cash in lieu of fractional shares of

Acquiror common stock or subject to options or warrants assumed by Acquiror will be treated as outstanding Target stock on the date of the transaction. Moreover, shares of Target stock and shares of Acquiror stock held by Target shareholders and otherwise sold, redeemed or disposed of prior or subsequent to the Conversion or the Merger are considered in making this representation.

8.   Following the merger of Sub into Target ("the transaction"), Target will hold at least 70 percent of the fair market value of its net assets and at least 50 percent of the fair market value of its gross assets and at least 90 percent of the fair market value of Sub's net assets and at least 70 percent of the fair market value of the Sub's gross assets held immediately prior to the transaction. For purposes of this representation, amounts paid by Target or Sub to dissenters, amounts paid by Target or Sub to shareholders who receive cash or other property, amounts used by Target or Sub to pay reorganization expenses, and all redemptions and distributions (except for regular, normal dividends) made by Target will be included as assets of Target or Sub, respectively, immediately prior to the transaction.

9.   Prior to the transaction, Acquiror will be in control of Sub within the meaning of Section 368(c) of the Code.

10.   Target will not issue additional shares of its stock that would result in Acquiror losing control of Target within the meaning of Section 368(c) of the Code.

11.   Acquiror has no plan or intention to reacquire any of its stock issued in the transaction.

12.   Acquiror has no plan or intention to liquidate Target; to merge Target with or into another corporation; to sell or otherwise dispose of the stock of Target except for transfers of stock to corporations controlled by Acquiror; or to cause Target to sell or otherwise dispose of any of its assets or of any of the assets acquired from Sub, except for dispositions made in the ordinary course of business, transfers of assets to a corporation controlled by Target and cash dividends paid to Acquiror which shall not exceed the amount of liquid assets owned by Target.

13.   Sub will have no liabilities assumed by Target and will not transfer to Target any assets subject to liabilities in the transaction.

14.   Following the transaction, Target will continue its historic business or use at least 60 percent of its historic business assets in a business.

15.   Acquiror, Sub, Target, and the shareholders of Target will pay their respective expenses, if any, incurred in connection with the transaction.

16.   There is no intercorporate indebtedness existing between Acquiror and Target or between Sub and Target that was issued, acquired, or will be settled at a discount.

17.   In the transaction, shares of Target Class A common stock representing control of Target, as defined in Section 368(c) of the Code, will be exchanged solely for voting stock of Acquiror.   For purposes of this representation, shares of Target Class A common stock exchanged for cash or other property originating with Acquiror and shares of Target stock subject to options or warrants assumed by Acquiror will be treated as outstanding Target Class A common stock on the date of the transaction.

18.   At the time of the transaction, Target will not have outstanding any warrants, options, convertible securities, or any other type of right, including previously issued options and warrants for Target stock which will be assumed by Acquiror in the Merger, pursuant to which any person could acquire stock in Target that, if exercised or converted, would prevent Acquiror's acquisition or retention of control of Target, as defined in Section 368(c) of the Code.

19.   Neither Acquiror, Sub nor any direct or indirect subsidiary of Acquiror owns, nor has it owned during the past five years, any shares of the stock of Target. Acquiror's President, Yassor Nefatir, and a member of Acquiror's Board of Directors, Madiline Koch, neither of whom owns more than 4 percent of the stock of Acquiror, each owns 3 percent of the Class A common stock of Target.

20.   Acquiror, Target and Sub are not investment companies as defined in Section 368(a)(2)(F)(iii) and (iv) of the Code.

21.   On the date of the transaction, the fair market value of the assets of Target will exceed the sum of its liabilities, plus the amount of liabilities, if any, to which the assets are subject.

22.   Target is not under the jurisdiction of a court in a Title 11 or similar case within the meaning of Section 368(a)(3)(A) of the Code.

23.   None of the compensation received by any shareholder-employee of Target will be separate consideration provided in exchange for any of the shareholder-employee's shares of stock of Target. Compensation paid to any shareholder-employee will be for services actually rendered and will be commensurate with amounts that would be paid to third parties bargaining at arm's-length for similar services.

24. Payment of cash in lieu of fractional shares of Acquiror common stock is solely for the purpose of avoiding the expense and inconvenience to Acquiror of issuing fractional shares and does not represent separately bargained for consideration.

25. There is no outstanding capital stock of Target which is subject to any forfeiture restriction under Section 83 of the Code.

26. Acquiror will place $5 million of its common stock in escrow pursuant to an Escrow Agreement. The stock may be periodically distributed to Target shareholders during the six-year term of the Escrow Agreement or may be returned to Acquiror at the end of the term, pursuant to Section 14 of the Merger Agreement ("contingent stock pay-out provision") and Section 7 of the Escrow Agreement. A Target shareholder cannot assign the shareholder's rights under the Escrow Agreement, except to members of the shareholder's immediate family or on the shareholder's death, without the consent of California National Bank, the Escrow Agent. The consent of the Escrow Agent will not be unreasonably withheld. If Acquiror is required by the terms of the contingent stock pay-out provision to pay more than $5 million of its common stock to the Target shareholders, it will take all actions necessary or appropriate to create and issue such additional stock.

We will promptly and timely notify Halle, Edwards, Blaine & Vargas if we discover that any of the above representations cease to be true, correct or complete.

Very truly yours,

Processor Corporation

By: _Yassor Nefatir_
          Sign Name

By: _Yassor Nefatir_
          Print Name

President

Note:

See Note on Opinion Letters following Problem 4P at page 22.

Certificate of Representations

In Problem 88C the opinion letter is based on the factual representations made in the Certificate of Representations. This is in contrast with the more typical opinion letter which will contain a statement of the relevant facts. See the opinion letter in Problem 4P at page 22. The advantage of using a Certificate of Representations is that the facts on which the opinion letter is based are set forth in a separate document or documents signed by the parties to the transaction. This helps to avoid a later assertion by the recipient of the opinion letter that the facts were not as set forth in the opinion letter. In Problem 88C the opinion letter is being rendered to the attorneys' client. The attorneys also prepared the Certificate of Representations. Do the attorneys face any conflicts in preparing the Certificate?

PROBLEM 89C

You are a new tax attorney on the general counsel's staff at The House of Pauline, Inc. (Pauline) which is the latest run away sensation in the franchised food industry and is listed on the NASDAQ. The Pauline line of food has a distinct New Orleans touch (poor boys, gumbo, etouffé, andouille, jambalaya, etc.) and has been greeted with enthusiasm by an American public tired of fried chicken, hamburgers and pizza. Although Pauline principally franchises others to operate restaurants bearing the "House of Pauline" name, it occasionally operates a restaurant either directly or as a wholly owned subsidiary.

Pauline management is confident that the value of Pauline franchises, which have substantially appreciated in the last few years, will continue to appreciate, and it has recently begun to reacquire franchises and to purchase the stock of companies holding franchises. These buy backs take the form of both taxable cash purchases and tax free reorganizations. Sarah Chang, the general counsel of Pauline, has asked you to explain the tax consequences to Pauline of three contemplated buybacks which are to be structured as reorganizations. She has also asked you, as an accommodation to investors who will be selling back their franchises, to explain the tax consequences of these transactions to the investors.

Acme Resources, Inc. All the stock (100 shares) of Acme is owned by Charles Young who has a basis of $200,000 in his stock. Mr. Young at present owns no Pauline stock. Mr. Young formed Acme two years ago by contributing $200,000 to it in exchange for all of its stock. Acme used $100,000 to purchase from Pauline the franchise for Bergen County, New Jersey. It used $80,000 to purchase a site for what Mr. Young intended to be the location of his first restaurant and placed the remaining $20,000 in a checking account. Health problems caused Mr. Young to call a halt to any further development. Pauline is anxious to establish a presence in the large consumer market covered by the franchise held by Acme. Pauline's management and Mr. Young have agreed that his stock is worth $300,000. Although Mr. Young would like the sale of his stock to be as tax free as possible, he is also in need of some cash and has agreed to allow Acme to be merged into Pauline in exchange for $20,000 in cash and 2,800 shares of Pauline which are currently trading for $100 per share. After the merger Mr. Young will own .47% of the Pauline stock. The balance sheet of Acme is set forth below:

Acme Resources, Inc. (in 000's) Assets		
	Book & Adjusted Basis	Fair Market Value
Cash	$ 20	$ 20
Land	80	80
Franchise	100	200
	$200	$300
Liabilities		
	Book & Adjusted Basis	Fair Market Value
Paid In Capital	$200	$200
Surplus		100
	$200	$300

Billings Investment, Inc. Billings owns a Pauline franchise for the city of Savannah. Irene Fitzgerald, who owns all 100 shares of Billings stock and has held it for the last six years, has an adjusted basis of $60,000 in that stock. Ms. Fitzgerald, who has reached the golden years of life, wishes to step away from the day to day operation of a restaurant, and Pauline has arranged to acquire her 100 shares of stock in exchange for 5,000 shares of Pauline stock which is worth $100 per share. Pauline intends to hold the stock of Billings and to operate it as a wholly owned subsidiary. The balance sheet of Billings is set forth below:

Billings Investment, Inc.
(in 000's)

Assets

	Book & Adjusted Basis	Fair Market Value
Cash	$ 50	$ 50
Building	60	100
Land	40	120
Furniture & Fixtures	20	30
Inventory	30	35
Franchise	30	150
Goodwill	0	50
	$230	$535

Liabilities

	Book & Adjusted Basis	Fair Market Value
Mortgage on Land	$ 35	$ 35
Paid in Capital	60	60
Retained Earnings	135	440
	$230	$535

Capital Properties, Inc. Capital owns the Pauline franchise for Denver where it owns and operates a single restaurant. The outstanding stock of Capital consists solely of 100 shares of common stock, 90 of which are owned by Ricky Rashid and ten of which are owned by Sandra Sanchez. Mr. Rashid has an adjusted basis of $90,000 in his 90 shares which he acquired at original issue 5 years ago. Ms. Sanchez has an adjusted basis of $50,000 in her 10 shares which she acquired by purchase from Mr. Rashid four months ago. The Capital operation has recently suffered from mismanagement and Pauline, which is anxious to provide new ownership for the franchise, has agreed to acquire all Capital's assets and to assume its $200,000 bank loan in exchange for 4,000 shares of Pauline stock. Ms. Chang has indicated that she prefers to carry out the acquisition in this fashion since she would like to avoid Pauline's exposure to potential claims from parties which have done business with Capital in the past. After the exchange Capital will be liquidated with Mr. Rashid receiving 3,600 shares of Pauline stock and Ms. Sanchez receiving 400 shares of Pauline stock.

Ms. Chang has indicated that it is likely that Ms. Sanchez will object to the transaction as proposed and threaten to exercise her dissenter's rights under state law. If Ms. Sanchez's acquiescence to the transaction, structured as described above, cannot be obtained in advance, Ms. Chang has decided that the transaction should be structured in the following manner, which she believes, under state law, will come closest to accomplishing Pauline's goals. First, Pauline will create a new wholly-owned subsidiary called New Pauline Inc. (Newco). All the Newco stock will be issued to Pauline in exchange for $10. Capital will be merged into Newco in exchange for 3,600 shares of Pauline stock and $40,000 in cash, which Ms. Chang is certain is all that will be required to be paid to Ms. Sanchez as a dissenter. After obtaining approval of the appropriate state court, 3,600 shares of Pauline common worth $100 per share will be issued to Mr. Rashid in exchange for his stock and the $40,000 cash will be issued to Ms. Sanchez in exchange for her stock. The most recent balance sheet of Capital is set forth below:

Capital Properties, Inc.
(in 000's)
Assets

	Book & Adjusted Basis	Fair Market Value
Cash	$ 80	$ 80
Land	110	130
Building	50	80
Furniture & Fixtures	15	10
Inventory	15	20
Franchise	50	140
Goodwill	0	140
	$320	$600

Liabilities

	Book & Adjusted Basis	Fair Market Value
Mortgage	$200	$200
Paid in Capital	100	100
Retained Earnings	20	300
	$320	$600

c. Liquidation—Reincorporation Doctrine and Incidental
  Concerns in Reorganizations

PROBLEM 90C

In Problem 28C, you were asked by Barbara Carter to consider the tax consequences of a one-shot election of S corporation status coupled with the sale by her corporation, Boutique, Inc. (Boutique), of the land and building it owned. Her brother has now completed his tax course and proposes that Barbara liquidate Boutique, retain the cash and securities and personally sell the land and building for $280,000. He further proposes that she pay off the $40,000 loan and contribute the remaining assets, worth about $320,000, as well as the $80,000 in payables to a new corporation, Barbara's World, Inc., which would operate a business similar to Boutique's out of rented quarters in a nearby suburban shopping mall. Barbara seeks your advice with respect to the tax consequences of following Paul's recent suggestion.

PROBLEM 91C

In Problem 79C your firm's client, Abe Burkhart, consulted the firm with which you are associated about the possibility of selling a portion of his interest in Hi Lite Clothes, Inc. (Hi Lite) to the young store manager employed by the corporation. As you will recall, Hi Lite has substantial retained earnings primarily in the form of liquid assets and, unless these assets are distributed prior to a sale, the young manager, Robert Humphries, will not be financially able to purchase the stock interest which both Robert and Abe feel is desirable. The general partner in charge of the tax department of the firm with which you are associated assigned Walker Rucker, a new associate in the firm, to the matter. The partner has asked that you review the memorandum prepared by Mr. Rucker for her.

MEMORANDUM FOR MS. VALLECILLO

Abe Burkhart—Hi Lite, Inc.

Proposed Sale and Liquidation

W. Rucker   February 3, Year*

     Abe Burkhart is the sole shareholder of Hi Lite Clothes, Inc. (Hi Lite), a local chain of men's clothing stores. The current net worth of the corporation is approximately $2,900,000, of which $1,300,000 is in the form of highly liquid assets such as cash or certificates of deposit. The retained earnings of Hi Lite are approximately $1,400,000. None of Mr. Burkhart's children are interested in participating in or owning the business. Over the course of the last few years, Mr. Burkhart has relied extensively on the assistance of Robert Humphries, a trusted young employee in operating the stores. Mr. Humphries is interested in purchasing the business from Mr. Burkhart. Both men agree that it is desirable that Mr. Humphries initially acquire at least forty-nine percent of the ownership of Hi Lite, that Mr. Burkhart retain control of the business for the next few years, and that thereafter Mr. Humphries have the option of acquiring the balance of the stock from Mr. Burkhart for its fair market value. Mr. Humphries recently inherited $400,000 at the death of his mother. Putting this amount together with $164,000 of savings and $220,000 which he is able to borrow means that Mr. Humphries is able to raise no more than $784,000 to carry out the purchase.

     To reduce the net worth of Hi Lite so that Mr. Humphries is able to purchase forty-nine percent of the Hi Lite stock, Mr. Burkhart has proposed either of two strategies. First, that Hi Lite be liquidated, that he retain $1,300,000 of liquid assets and that he contribute the remaining assets (inventory, some cash, leaseholds, fixtures, accounts receivable, etc.) to a newly formed corporation (Newco) in exchange for one hundred percent of the Newco common stock. Mr. Humphries then will purchase from Mr. Burkhart forty-nine percent of the Newco common stock and will be given an option allowing him to purchase the balance from Mr. Burkhart over a term of years. Second, if this strategy proves unworkable, Mr. Burkhart proposes that a new corporation be formed which will acquire, in exchange for its

---

* See explanatory footnote in Introduction, Page vii, note 1.

stock, all of the assets of Hi Lite other than $1,300,000 in liquid assets. Hi Lite would then hold all of the stock of the new corporation and $1,300,000 in liquid assets. Next, Hi Lite would be liquidated leaving Mr. Burkhart holding the $1,300,000 in liquid assets and all of the stock of the new corporation. He then would sell forty-nine percent of the stock to Mr. Humphries for $784,000 and also offer Mr. Humphries the same option to acquire the balance of the stock over a term of years. Since Mr. Burkhart has an adjusted basis of $1,400,000 in his stock in Hi Lite, it is his hope that either of the above strategies will result in his realizing a long term capital gain of $1,500,000 on the liquidation of Hi Lite. He hopes that he will be in possession of $1,300,000 of cash or certificates of deposit with a basis equal to their fair market value and stock in a newly formed corporation with a basis of $1,600,000. Because of this "stepped-up" basis in the stock of the new corporation, a considerably smaller gain, if any, than would otherwise be the case, will be realized by Mr. Burkhart on his subsequent sales of stock to Mr. Humphries.

Section 301 of the Code treats as a dividend, and consequently as ordinary income, all nonliquidating distributions by a corporation to a shareholder to the extent that the corporation has either current or accumulated earnings and profits equal to the amount of the distribution. Mr. Burkhart hopes that by liquidating Hi Lite he can cause the distribution to be treated as a complete liquidation under Section 331 of the Code. If he is successful, the result will be that to the extent the fair market value of the distributed property exceeds his adjusted basis in the Hi Lite stock, it will be treated as a capital gain rather than as ordinary income.

Unfortunately for Mr. Burkhart, the Internal Revenue Service has been successful in using the liquidation-reincorporation doctrine to challenge transactions such as he proposes. The application of this doctrine results in the characterization as a dividend of the distribution of the assets kept out of corporate solution. This occurs when a reincorporation of the principal operating assets follows the liquidation, and the reincorporated entity has a meaningful commonality of ownership with the liquidated corporation. Typically, the Service has followed two different strategies in such situations. On some occasions it has attempted to label the transactions as a sham and characterize the distributions as dividends. *See Telephone Answering Service Co.,* 63 T.C. 423, *aff'd,* 546 F.2d 423 (4th Cir. 1976), *cert. den.,* 431 U.S. 914 (1977); Rev. Rul., 76-429, 1976-2 Cum. Bul. 97. More commonly, however, it attempts to characterize the distribution of the liquid assets retained by the shareholders as a dividend and to recharacterize the Section 351 transfer of the operating assets as a reorganization of the old corporation which took place as part of a step transaction. *See, e.g., Smothers v. U.S.,* 642 F.2d 894 (5th Cir. 1981); *Reef Corp. v. Comm.,* 368

F.2d 125 (5th Cir. 1966); *Comm. v. Berghash*, 361 F.2d 257 (2d Cir. 1966); and *James Armour, Inc.*, 43 T.C. 295 (1964).

Most of the litigated cases involving purported liquidation-reincorporations involve use by the Service of the latter doctrine. The fact that the Service is reluctant to rely extensively on the sham doctrine may be indicative of the fact that it has less than total confidence in it. *Cf. Smothers v. United States*, 642 F.2d 894, 898 at fn. 9. The fact that an extensive change of ownership will occur along with the liquidation serves to distinguish Mr. Burkhart's proposed transactions from those involved in the cases which sustain the use of the sham doctrine. Nonetheless, we should be extremely reluctant to counsel Mr. Burkhart that he can proceed with confidence that the Service will not be able to treat as dividends the retained corporate assets under the sham doctrine.

Under the classic liquidation-reincorporation doctrine, the principal legal burden which the Service must shoulder is the characterization of the formation of the new corporation as a reorganization. Since a statutory merger is not involved, the proposed transaction cannot be deemed an "A" type reorganization. Since there is no resulting parent subsidiary relationship, a "B" type reorganization is not involved. Moreover, since consideration other than voting stock is present, a "C" reorganization is not present. Lastly, since there are two corporations involved and a mere reshuffling of the corporate capital structure is not involved, there is no "E" type reorganization. Therefore, in order to employ the liquidation-reincorporation doctrine, it will be necessary to classify the shift from old Hi Lite to new Hi Lite as a "D" or an "F" type reorganization.

In *Smothers v. United States, supra,* the Court at p. 898 indicated that

"In general, reincorporation transactions are most easily assimilated in § 368(a)(1)(D) ("D reorganization"), as the IRS attempted to do in this case. A transaction qualifies as a D reorganization only if it meets six statutory requirements:

(1) There must be a transfer by a corporation (§ 368(a)(1)(D));

(2) of substantially all of its assets (§ 354(b)(1)(A));

(3) to a corporation controlled by the shareholders of the transferor corporation or by the transferor corporation itself (§ 368(a)(1)(D));

(4) in exchange for stock or securities of the transferee corporation (§ 354(a)(1));

(5) followed by a distribution of the stock or securities of the transferee corporation to the transferor's shareholders (§ 354(b)(1)(B));

(6) pursuant to a plan of reorganization (§ 368(a)(1)(D))."

Requirements (2) and (3) above provide the two principal ways in which taxpayers attempt to avoid the imposition of the liquidation-reincorporation doctrine. Numerous cases have held that the "substantially all the assets" test of Section 354(b)(1)(A) is not a simple mathematical test and should be applied to the operating assets of the business. *See, e.g., James Armour Inc., supra*, and *Smothers v. United States, supra*. Under Section 368(a)(2)(H), the control requirement for a D reorganization involved in a liquidation-reincorporation (as well as several other transactions) is the same as the Section 304(c) control requirement (50% of the combined voting power of all classes of voting stock or 50% of the total value of all stock).

In applying the above tests, as articulated in *Smothers*, to Mr. Burkhart's proposed transactions, it is apparent that both transactions will be branded as classic liquidation-reincorporations resulting in dividend treatment of the $1,300,000 in liquid assets which are being distributed. Moreover, since the transactions will be caught under the D reorganization theory, full discussion of the F reorganization is unnecessary. Two matters should be noted with respect to applying the F reorganization to the liquidation-reincorporation area. First, the Service has been reluctant in recent years to advance the doctrine because it does not want the F reorganization applied in an expansive fashion. *See Smothers v. United States, supra* at 898 fn. 9. Second, although the F reorganization traditionally has been seen as allowing only minimal changes in ownership, the courts have allowed transactions involving significant changes in ownership to qualify as F reorganizations where necessary for application of the liquidation-reincorporation doctrine. *See Reef Corp. v. Comm.*, 368 F.2d 125 (5th Cir. 1966) (redemption of 48% of the stock of the reincorporated corporation does not prevent F reorganization treatment).

In conclusion, I suggest that we recommend two alternative means of accomplishing Mr. Burkhart's goals. First, to avoid classification as a D reorganization, I suggest that Mr. Burkhart structure the transaction so that he retains only 49% of the stock. Mr. Humphries could purchase 49% as proposed. The remaining 2% of the stock could be transferred by Mr. Burkhart to us or to his wife. With our cooperation or that of his wife, Mr. Burkhart could retain control of Hi Lite until Mr. Humphries is able to exercise the option which would eventually enable him to acquire Hi Lite as originally planned. Second, if this proves unacceptable, I propose that, on its liquidation, Hi Lite be reconstituted as Mr. Burkhart proposed with the single exception that it be reconstituted as a limited liability company in which Mr. Humphries purchases from Mr. Burkhart 49% of the membership interests for $784,000 and in which Mr. Burkhart retains 51% of the membership interests. I propose that a limited liability company be used since it will provide both participants the limited liability accorded them by a corporation. I propose that both Mr. Burkhart and Mr. Humphries be constituted manager-members of the limited liability company and that voting be by membership interests. Mr. Humphries would be given options, as originally planned, to enable him to purchase the balance of the membership interests over a period of time.

Note:

See Note on Memoranda following Problem 35C at page 177, Note on Limited Liability Companies following Problem 4P at page 22, and Note on Attorney Participation in a Transaction following Problem 79C at page 277.

PROBLEM 92C

Road Construction Corporation (RCC), which you will remember from Problem 62C, is interested in selling its subsidiary, Trucking Corporation (Trucking). As indicated in Problem 62C, Trucking has a substantial amount of accumulated earnings and profits. Your client, Joe Wheeler, has obtained an option from RCC to purchase for cash the stock of Trucking. Joe does not have enough available cash to exercise the option. Being an inventive fellow, however, he has come up with a couple of plans which may make possible the purchase of the Trucking stock. Despite being an inventive fellow, Joe is completely confused by the intricacies of the Internal Revenue Code and would like your advice, as an income tax expert, as to the tax consequences which may result from the carrying out of his various plans.

Joe's first proposal is to create Truck Servicing Corporation (TSC) and contribute to it, in exchange for its stock, one-half the cash needed to purchase the stock of Trucking. Family members and friends will lend TSC, in return for its bonds or notes which Joe will personally guarantee, the rest of the cash needed. Joe will assign the option to purchase the Trucking stock to TSC which will purchase the stock and after about two years merge "downstream" into Trucking. During the two years, TSC will operate the truck servicing division of Trucking. After the merger, Trucking, using its accumulated earnings, will pay off the obligations to the family members and friends which Joe had guaranteed.

As an alternative, Joe proposes that, rather than imposing on family members and friends, TSC borrow the other half of the purchase price of the stock of Trucking from a bank with Joe's personal guarantee and pledge to the bank as security for the loan all of the Trucking stock acquired. After TSC acquires the stock, the bank will lend Trucking the same amount which the bank had loaned TSC, which amount Trucking will then pay to TSC as a dividend. TSC will use the funds received as a dividend to repay the bank loan made to it. The corporations will file a consolidated income tax return for the year involved, seemingly eliminating any tax on the dividend. The next year, Trucking will be merged "upstream" into TSC, and the combined entity then will be merged into a newly organized corporation called Wheeler Trucking, Inc.

Assuming that for the last year RCC has been using a new law firm to represent it, what ethical considerations are involved in your representing Joe in this transaction? How should you resolve any concerns?

Note:

See Note on Interviewing and Client Counseling following Problem 1P at page 4.

PROBLEM 93C

One of the general partners in the tax department of the firm with which you are associated recently received a letter from a close personal friend, George Morris. The letter asks for some income tax advice. The general partner has given you the letter, set out below, and asked you to inform her in the next few days of the advice which should be given to Mr. Morris.

KITCHEN MAID APPLIANCE, INC.
723 Portage Road
Kalamazoo, MI   49002

December 15, Year*

Anabelle Storinski
Yampolsky, Eichorn, Seligman & Peters
2225 Main Street, Suite 400
Kalamazoo, MI   49001

Dear Ann:

For the last twenty years Kitchen Maid Appliance, Inc. (Kitchen Maid) has been in the business of developing and manufacturing small home appliances.   Unfortunately, Kitchen Maid has had little success in this venture and at present has $6,000,000 in net operating loss carryovers of which $4,000,000 are about to expire.   Kitchen Maid owns a plant in Kalamazoo, which it uses to manufacture fry pans and toasters under the brand name of several large retailers.   Although the plant is basically sound, most of the equipment in it is virtually obsolete.   The plant and equipment have a net fair market value of approximately $400,000.   Kitchen Maid's other assets consist of $100,000 in inventory and a patent which has a basis of $20,000 and is worth approximately $5,500,000.   The corporation has liabilities of $6,000,000 which are in the form of notes to me and several corporations which I control.

Kitchen Maid's principal asset, the patent, is the recent product of one of its employees, Ms. Nora Schmidt.   The patent covers a revolutionary device which can be incorporated in micro-wave ovens and which will permit the manufacture of toaster ovens operating as a micro-wave would for sale in department stores for under $100.

I would like to: (1) use the Kitchen Maid net operating loss carryovers; (2) have a corporate vehicle for promoting the Schmidt patent which is free of the unfortunate financial history of Kitchen Maid; and (3) retain the loyalty and interest of Ms. Schmidt in my business ventures.   I therefore propose that a new Michigan corporation be formed and given the name of Handy Maid Appliance, Inc.   I will retain from 50 to 85 percent of its stock, and Ms. Schmidt will be permitted to purchase the balance of the stock.   I anticipate that the corporation will be incorporated with 100 shares of stock for which the subscribers will pay one hundred dollars per share. I then will cause Kitchen Maid to sell the Schmidt patent to Handy Maid for a

* See explanatory footnote in Introduction, page vii, note 1.

Handy Maid note in the amount of $5,500,000. The note will be assignable, will bear interest at three percentage points in excess of the prime rate at the time the note is given, will be secured by the patent and will be payable in ten years. The value of $5,500,000 has been assigned to the patent based on the fact that Kitchen Maid has received several offers from unrelated third parties willing to pay between $5,000,000 and $6,000,000 for the patent.

I anticipate that Handy Maid will license several major appliance manufacturers to produce micro-wave toaster ovens under the patent. At the present time, I am not sure whether Kitchen Maid will continue in operation and be licensed to manufacture micro-wave toaster ovens or will be liquidated or sold to any available buyer. Whether Handy Maid will manufacture micro-wave toaster ovens cannot be determined until I resolve the fate of Kitchen Maid.

Ann, I am most anxious that you evaluate this proposal and tell me if it will result in the use of the net operating loss carryover of Kitchen Maid and whether Handy Maid will obtain a wasting asset with a depreciable basis of $5,500,000 and a life of 15 years (the remaining term of the patent). If you have any suggestions as to how I should structure this transaction to maximize any available tax benefits to me or my companies, I would be interested in hearing about them.

Sincerely yours

George

George Morris
President

Note:

See Note on Interviewing and Client Counseling following Problem 1P at page 4.

Part G

AFFILIATED CORPORATIONS

————

1. MULTIPLE CORPORATIONS

PROBLEM 94C

George Morris, who sought your advice in Problem 93C with respect to the formation of Handy Maid Appliances, Inc., has decided to go ahead with its formation with Ms. Schmidt owning at least 51% of the stock and Mr. Morris owning the balance of the stock so that the sale of the patent stands a good chance of not running afoul of the liquidation-reincorporation doctrine. Mr. Morris and Ms. Schmidt have entered into a shareholders' agreement which requires the election of each of them to the two-member board of directors of the corporation and provides that, if for any reason Ms. Schmidt ever leaves the employ of the corporation or desires to sell her stock, she will sell the stock to Mr. Morris for its then appraised value. In addition, in order to maintain Ms. Schmidt's loyalty, Mr. Morris has sold Ms. Schmidt a small, 10%, interest in Kitchen Maid which is also subject to a similar shareholders' agreement.

In order to take advantage of the lower corporate taxable income brackets, Mr. Morris is considering: (1) having Kitchen Maid continue in operation manufacturing micro-wave toaster ovens under a non-exclusive license which Handy Maid will grant to Kitchen Maid under the same terms which it intends to offer to major appliance manufacturers; and (2) causing Handy Maid to create a new wholly owned subsidiary, Handy Manufacturing, Inc. (Manufacturing), which will also manufacture microwave toaster ovens under a similar license.

George Vetter, the corporate partner who is handling Mr. Morris' affairs, would like your views on the impact of Sections 269, 482, 1561 and 1563 or any other general tax doctrines on the proposed sale to Handy Maid, the establishment of Manufacturing and the licenses to Kitchen Maid and Manufacturing.

PROBLEM 95C

As a new attorney on the staff of the Tax Legislative Counsel in the Treasury Department you received the following memorandum from Alma Carrillo, a senior staff member, who would like to discuss the matter described in the memo with you and a number of other attorneys at a staff conference. Prepare yourself to attend the conference and to be able to comment on the matters which are most likely to be discussed.

To: Tax Legislative Counsel Legal Staff

From: A.M. Carrillo

Re: General Re-evaluation of Section 482 Regulations

Date: April 12, Year*

As you are aware, the Treasury has been accorded by Congress virtual legislative authority in the development of regulations under Section 482. As part of our general oversight responsibilities in this area, the entire thrust of the Section 482 regulations is being reexamined. At a staff conference which will be held tomorrow in my office, and which you will be expected to attend, we will be comparing the approaches presently contained in Reg. Sec. 1.482-2(a) (loans) and Reg. Sec. 1.482-2(e) (sales of tangible property). Prepare yourself to attend and participate in the conference.

---

* See explanatory footnote in Introduction, page vii, note 1.

Note:

See Note on Legal Drafting following Problem 3P at page 15.

2. CONSOLIDATED RETURNS

PROBLEM 96C

In Problem 92C Joe Wheeler proposed using the accumulated earnings of Trucking Corporation to help finance Truck Servicing Corporation's purchase of the stock of Trucking Corporation. As you may remember, Truck Servicing Corporation borrowed from a bank some of the funds necessary to purchase the stock of Trucking Corporation. Then, after the purchase of the stock, Trucking Corporation, where all of the real assets would then be located, was to borrow from the bank the same amount which Truck Servicing Corporation had borrowed and distribute the proceeds to Truck Servicing Corporation as a dividend. Truck Servicing Corporation would then use the proceeds to pay its loan. Joe proposed having the corporations file a consolidated return to avoid Truck Servicing Corporation having to pay any tax on the dividend. Would Joe have gained any advantage by having Truck Servicing Corporation make the election provided in Section 243(b) rather than filing a consolidated return?

PROBLEM 97C

A. Acme Products, Inc. (Acme) and its 90% owned subsidiary Plastics Galore, Inc. (Plastics) file a consolidated tax return. Earlier this year, Plastics sold Acme the following: (1) ten acres of land it had purchased for $100,000 three years ago as a potential plant site; and (2) a patent developed seven years ago by Plastics and in which it had a basis of zero. Plastics received $90,000 for the plant site on which Acme intended to locate a warehouse and $200,000 for the patent which Acme intended to use in its business. In each case the presence of Plastics minority shareholders caused Plastics to employ several independent appraisers to fix the price. Advise Acme and Plastics of the proper tax treatment of these items on their consolidated return.

B. Atkins Industries, Inc. (Atkins) and its two wholly owned subsidiaries, Ceramic Products, Inc. (Ceramic) and Builder's Supply, Inc. (Builders), along with several other wholly owned Atkins subsidiaries, have been filing consolidated returns since January 1, Year*-3, when Atkins

* See explanatory footnote in Introduction, page vii, note 1.

acquired all the outstanding stock of Ceramic and Builders for $200,000 each. In Year-3, both corporations showed current undistributed earnings and profits of $100,000. In Year-2, Ceramic realized a net operating loss of $400,000 which Atkins used on the group's consolidated tax return to reduce its net taxable income. Builders, which operated at a profit, increased its undistributed earnings and profits by $400,000. In Year-1 Atkins sold all the Ceramic and Builders stock to Ira Houston for $200,000 and $500,000, respectively. Assume that these are all the financial activities which went on between the three corporations. Maria Locklear, the tax manager of Atkins, solicits your advice as to the proper tax treatment of the sales proceeds on Atkins' tax return.

C. Joplin Holding Co., Inc. and its five wholly owned subsidiaries file a consolidated return. Early this year Joplin acquired, in a tax-free reorganization described in Section 368(a)(1)(B) of the Code, all the stock of Barker Properties, Inc., a real estate developer with a net worth of $400,000. Joplin parted with $440,000 worth of Joplin stock to consummate the acquisition, paying the $40,000 premium since it hoped to be able to use $200,000 of net operating loss carry-forwards owned by Barker. After the acquisition the former Barker shareholders owned 42% of the stock of Joplin. Assuming that use of the losses is not barred by Section 269, explain to Joplin the problems it will encounter under the consolidated return regulations in using Barker's losses against the group's combined income.

AVAILABILITY, SURVIVAL AND TRANSFER OF CORPORATE TAX ATTRIBUTES

PROBLEM 98C

A. Siggy Sipwich developed a very successful business in cosmetics for men. After his early years of operating as a sole proprietorship, Siggy incorporated in the state of Illinois under the name Sipwich's Sophisticated Suave for Men, Inc. As the years went on, the demand for the products grew astronomically, and Siggy formed a number of corporations to take care of the distribution and sales of the products in various areas of the country. Currently Siggy owns not only all the stock of the Illinois corporation but also all the stock of a New York corporation called Sipwich's Sophisticated Suave for Men East, Inc., an Alabama corporation called Sipwich's Sophisticated Suave for Men South, Inc. and a Colorado corporation called Sipwich's Sophisticated Suave for Men West, Inc.

Last year Siggy, who turned 65, decided to take things a little easier and moved himself and the head office and manufacturing facilities of the cosmetic business to Whitened Sepulchre, Arizona. Following the advice of his then counsel, he had the Illinois corporation transfer all its assets, other than those related to sales and marketing, to a newly formed Arizona corporation, Sipwich's Sophisticated Suave for Men Sun Belt, Inc., in return for all the stock of the Arizona corporation. He then changed the name of the Illinois corporation to Sipwich's Sophisticated Suave for Men Central, Inc.

Siggy has now consulted you. He would like to eliminate the complexities of operating all the separate corporations described above. He proposes that an Arizona corporation to be called Sipwich's Sophisticated Suave for Men World Wide, Inc. (World Wide) be formed and, pursuant to Arizona corporate law, all the other corporations be consolidated into this corporation. Thereafter, the distribution and sales of the cosmetic products in other parts of the country will be carried on through divisions of World Wide.

Siggy asks your advice whether this consolidation can be accomplished tax-free while retaining the various "tax attributes" of each of the separate corporations. In addition, Siggy informs you that presently the

Alabama and Colorado corporations have unused net operating losses. He would like to carry forward these losses against the income which he is sure World Wide will produce in coming years.

B.   Two years after accomplishing the consolidation described in paragraph A above, Siggy returned to your office for some advice. It seems that despite Siggy's hard work, the disruption caused by the consolidation and a general downturn in the nation's economy have resulted in World Wide incurring a net operating loss for each of its first two years of operation. Siggy would like to know if, and to what extent, such operating losses can be carried back to the separate profitable years of the Illinois and New York corporations.

PROBLEM 99C

In Problem 92C you considered whether Truck Servicing Corporation (TSC) should make the election provided in Section 243(b) or file a consolidated return with its subsidiary, Trucking Corporation (Trucking), in order to avoid paying any income tax on the dividend which TSC received from Trucking. Armed with the knowledge you have recently acquired with respect to the limitations on the availability, survival and transfer of corporate tax attributes, review the situation giving rise to, and the transactions surrounding, the payment of the dividend from Trucking to TSC, as set forth in Problem 92C.

Now advise your client whether, in your opinion, making the election provided in Section 243(b) or filing a consolidated return presents an avenue less susceptible to successful attack by the Internal Revenue Service. In addition, you might, if feasible, suggest to your client changes in its proposal which would render the contemplated transaction less susceptible to challenge by the Internal Revenue Service.

PROBLEM 100C

Your client, Fiesta, Inc. (Fiesta), whose stock trades on the NASDAQ, owns and operates a number of dance halls and night clubs in eight east coast states. Fiesta operates its dance halls and night clubs in facilities which formerly housed governmental, industrial or commercial operations. Fiesta typically purchases failing or abandoned governmental, industrial and commercial ventures and creates an entertainment environment which features the unique characteristics of each location.   At present, Fiesta operates 32 facilities at sites which formerly housed enterprises such as jails, automobile dealerships, bottling plants, and railroad stations. Michelle Lang, Fiesta's vice-president for acquisitions and expansions, has contacted you about a possible acquisition and would like your advice with respect to some of the tax consequences of this acquisition.

Swan Soap, Inc. (Swan), a family owned manufacturer of soap products, has an aging physical plant and a long history of annual operating losses.   The 1,000 outstanding shares of Swan stock are held by the four Corrigan brothers who each own 250 shares. Ms. Lang believes that Swan's land, building and processing plant would provide Fiesta with a new, interesting backdrop for a night club which would be called "The Soap Factory." The balance sheet of Swan as at the end of the previous month is set forth below:

SWAN SOAP, INC.
Balance Sheet
(in 000's)

Assets

	Book or Adjusted Basis	Fair Market Value
Cash	$ 50	$ 50
Receivables	80	80
Building	1,400	1,800
Processing Plant	200	250
Land	1,100	1,800
Inventory	170	220
Goodwill	0	200
	$3,000	$4,400

Liabilities

	Book or Adjusted Basis	Fair Market Value
Payables	$ 80	$ 80
Operating Loan with Citicorp	220	220
Mortgage on Land and Building	1,100	1,100
Paid-in-Capital	1,600	1,600
Surplus		1,400
	$3,000	$4,400

The value assigned to the goodwill on the balance sheet reflects the use of Swan's assets for the purpose intended by Fiesta. Because of its lengthy history of generating losses, Swan has a net operating loss carry forward (NOL) of $2,000,000 and a deficit in accumulated earnings and profits of $1,800,000. If Fiesta acquires Swan it intends to collect Swan's receivables, sell off its remaining inventory and convert all other assets to use as a night club. Ms. Lang estimates that after purchasing Swan as outlined below, Fiesta will have to add $600,000 to the "quick assets" of Swan including $50,000 of cash, the $220,000 of inventory sales proceeds and the $80,000 of receivables to permit "The Soap Factory" to operate as intended.

Ms. Lang has informed you that the Corrigan brothers are willing to accept either cash or Fiesta stock in exchange for their interests in Swan. The acquisition, therefore, could be conducted as a taxable cash purchase or as a tax free reorganization. Since Ms. Lang anticipates that Fiesta will use some, or all, of Swan's NOL against its income, she wants Fiesta, after either a taxable or tax free reorganization, to be left in the position in which Swan will function as an operating division of Fiesta. For example, following a cash purchase of all of the Swan stock, Swan likely would merge into Fiesta and operate "The Soap Factory" as a division of Fiesta. In a tax free reorganization Swan might be merged into Fiesta in exchange for Fiesta stock.

Fiesta has had a long history of financial success and last year had net taxable income of $35 million. Ms. Lang informs you that Fiesta management projects that for the foreseeable future, earnings should grow at 8-10% per year. She has asked you to assist Fiesta management in developing a dollar offer (either in cash or stock) for the purchase of Swan stock. Fatima Bijar, a senior partner in the law firm with which you are associated, who is a member of your firm's acquisition team, has asked you to consider the following issues. First, is it possible for Fiesta to use Swan's NOL? Second, if it is possible for Fiesta to use Swan's NOL, what are the limitations on the use of the NOL and will there be any difference resulting from whether the acquisition is carried out as a cash purchase or as a tax free merger? Third, what will be the effect on the purchase price, of the fact that the Swan assets have a fair market value considerably in excess of their adjusted bases?

After obtaining your advice with respect to the above questions, and after considering the fair market value of Swan's assets as well as the disparity between the fair market value of the assets and their adjusted basis, and the amount of Swan's NOL and the limitations on the NOL's use by Fiesta, your firm's acquisition team determined that it would be fair to offer to pay the Corrigan brothers in either cash or stock no more than $3,200,000. Mrs. Bijar has now asked for your help with respect to the following matters. First, assuming an 8% long term tax exempt rate, what is the dollar amount of the NOL of Swan which Fiesta will be able to use each year? Second, could this amount be increased by the following strategy suggested by one of the members of the acquisition team? Fiesta would first contribute $3,200,000 to Swan in exchange for 1,000 newly issued shares of Swan common stock. Fiesta then would offer to acquire, in a merger in which Swan would be merged into Fiesta, all 2,000 shares of Swan stock then outstanding in exchange for $6,400,000 of Fiesta common stock. Mrs. Bijar said that one of the members of the acquisition team, based on his hazy recollection of his corporate tax class a number of years ago, said that he believed that this was a clever way of getting around the limitation on the use by Fiesta of Swan's NOL. Prepare yourself to assist Mrs. Bijar.

PROBLEM 101C

You have earned a reputation as one of the most adept and potentially one of the best associates your firm has had in many years. The talk around the office is that in December of this year you will be made a partner in the firm. As a result of your reputation, and possibly as a way of determining whether you are ready for partnership status, the partners have been asking you to take over increasingly complex matters. Just today your secretary handed you the following letter, together with a note from Homer Trees, the partner in charge of the corporate department of the firm. The note stated, "Please let me have your analysis of the income tax ramifications of the transactions proposed in the attached letter and any suggestions you have for improving the tax results. I have never been able to understand all of that carryover stuff; it strikes me as quite complex."

Maddox Industrial Enterprises, Inc.
1700 Livemont
Toledo, Ohio 43613

October 3, Year*

Homer Trees, Esq.
Raines, Trees & Forrest
1020 Harding Building
840 Broadway
Toledo, Ohio 43609

Dear Homer:

As you know, Maddox Industrial Enterprises, Inc. (Maddox) was formed by myself, my sister Georgia, Sonja Ling, Lorna Fuzak and William Schapiro about twenty years ago. Each of us purchased and still owns 2,000 shares of the authorized common stock of 20,000 shares. The other 10,000 shares have never been issued. For a number of years Maddox was very successful and achieved surprising growth for a closely held corporation. Presently Maddox has four operating divisions. The heavy equipment division manufactures and sells heavy industrial equipment such as hydraulic presses and lathes. The net value of this division is about $1,400,000. The tool and die division manufactures and sells specialized small tools and dies to industrial users. The net value of this division is about $400,000. The structural steel division fabricates structural steel to order for various users of structural steel. The net value of this division is about $800,000. Lastly, the industrial fastener division is a wholesaler of numerous kinds of industrial fasteners. The net value of this division is about $600,000. The values given above include the cash, accounts receivable, inventory, machinery and equipment, fixtures, buildings, goodwill and all liabilities allocated to each division. In addition, Maddox has about $800,000 in unallocated cash and certificates of deposit. The per share value of Maddox's outstanding stock is therefore about $400 per share. Maddox has about $1,400,000 in accumulated earnings and profits for income tax purposes, and we estimate that our current earnings and profits for this year will amount to about $20,000. Maddox is on the calendar year and uses the accrual method of accounting for income tax purposes. However, we frequently sell heavy equipment on, and account for such sales using, the installment method.

---

* See explanatory footnote in Introduction, page vii, note 1.

In the last few years the profitability of Maddox has decreased. There are a couple of reasons for the decrease in profitability. First, the tool and die and the industrial fastener divisions have been operating at a loss. We have examined the operations of those divisions and the markets they serve and are quite certain, taking into account our organization and capabilities, that there is little we can do to improve their profitability. Secondly, the heavy equipment and structural steel divisions, although still marginally profitable, are at a competitive disadvantage since, unlike most of our competitors, we do not have our own structural and mechanical engineering staff and have to subcontract such work. We believe that the profitability of the heavy equipment and structural steel divisions could be greatly improved by the addition of an engineering staff. This is why we have had some discussions with Graham Engineering, Inc. about combining our respective operations.

Graham Engineering, Inc. (Graham) was formed in Year-3 by ten engineers. It has authorized and outstanding 1,000 shares of stock. Each engineer owns 100 shares. Graham offers engineering consulting services in structural, mechanical and electronic engineering. We have used Graham's services at times in our heavy equipment and structural steel divisions and were impressed with its performance. Graham incurred net operating losses of $180,000 in its first year, $120,000 in its second year and $100,000 in its third year. This year it expects to lose about $20,000. Even though it has incurred the losses described above, as you can see, the amount of loss is decreasing, and both our and Graham's expectations are that it may eventually become very profitable if certain changes are made in its organization and most certainly if it operates as part of, or a division of, Maddox.

Six of the engineer-stockholders of Graham are electronic engineers, and the net value of the electronic engineering part of the corporation is about $80,000. Two of the engineer-stockholders are mechanical engineers, and the net value of the mechanical engineering part of the corporation is about $100,000. Two of the engineer-stockholders are structural engineers, and the net value of the structural engineering part of Graham is about $180,000. The net value of the parts of Graham stated above were determined in the same way as the net value of each of our divisions. Graham does not have any unallocated cash or investments. It has an accumulated earnings and profits deficit of $400,000 and expects a deficit this year in current earnings and profits of $20,000. Graham uses the cash method of accounting and the calendar year for income tax purposes.

The electronic engineering part of Graham's organization has suffered the largest losses and, as stated above, it is felt that the mechanical and structural engineering parts can be very profitable, especially when combined with Maddox either as a separate division providing services to our heavy equipment and structural steel divisions as well as third parties when time is available, or as part of our heavy equipment and structural steel divisions. If the latter alternative is chosen, the mechanical engineers in our heavy equipment division and the structural engineers in our structural steel division will provide consulting services to third parties through Maddox when time is available. We feel that, over the years, the engineering services may prove more profitable than both our heavy equipment and structural steel divisions.

We have discussed the facts and opinions stated above with the officers and stockholders of Graham, and they are in general agreement. They have also agreed that it is in everyone's best interest to combine, in somewhat altered form, the operations of Maddox and Graham. Toward this end we have tentatively agreed with the officers and stockholders of Graham that the following steps will be taken.

First, prior to the end of this year, Maddox will purchase for about $216,000 in cash the Graham stock held by the six electronic engineers. The purchase price will be about $360 per share. As a result, at the start of next year, Maddox will own 60% of the authorized and outstanding common stock of Graham. Next year, Graham will perform all of the structural and mechanical engineering work required by Maddox for a reasonable fee somewhat below the amount which would be paid if Graham had to bid for every separate item of work.

Second, during next year Maddox will sell to third parties the tool and die and industrial fastener divisions for their respective net fair market values, $400,000 and $600,000. This should produce a loss of about $200,000 since Maddox's basis in the tool and die division is $500,000 and its basis in the industrial fastener division is $700,000. Maddox will use $800,000 of the proceeds from the sales to redeem all of Sonja Ling's stock in Maddox. Sonja has been in charge of the tool and die division and has no interest in continuing as a stockholder of Maddox if the corporation is not engaged in the tool and die business. Also during next year, Graham will sell the electronic engineering part of its business for its fair market value, $80,000, possibly to the six former stockholders. This should produce a loss of about $40,000 since Graham's basis in the electronic engineering part of its business is $120,000.

Third, effective as of January 1, Year+2, Maddox and Graham will be merged, with Maddox being the surviving corporation. The four engineer-stockholders of Graham will receive 90 shares of Maddox for every 100 shares of Graham they own. During Year+2 we will decide whether to keep

Graham as a division of Maddox or integrate it as part of our heavy equipment and structural steel divisions.

Please let me know at your earliest convenience if you see any problems with the foregoing.

Sincerely yours,

Bill

William Maddox, President